The Gospel of Mark

PUBLISHED VOLUMES

Vol. 1: The Gospel of Mark, Daryl D. Schmidt

The Gospel of Mark

DARYL D. SCHMIDT

with Introduction, Notes, and Original Text
featuring the NEW Scholars Version Translation

POLEBRIDGE PRESS
Salem, Oregon

Cover: Portrait of Mark from a Gospel According to the Four Evangelists.

Library of Congress Cataloging-in-Publication Data
Bible. N.T. Mark English. Scholars. 1991.
    The Gospel of Mark with introduction, notes and original text /
by Daryl D. Schmidt.
      p.   cm. — (The Scholars Bible ; vol. 1)
    Includes bibliographical references and index.
    ISBN 0-944344-33-X : $21.95.—ISBN 0-944344-14-3 (pbk.) : $15.95
    I. Schmidt, Daryl Dean. II. Bible. N.T. Mark. Greek. 1991.
III. Title. IV. Series.
BS2583. 1991
226.3'05208–dc20   90-26436
                                                      CIP

Printed in the United States of America

Contents

The Scholars Version

General Editors

Robert W. Funk
Westar Institute

Julian V. Hills
Marquette University

Editors, Apocryphal Gospels

Ron Cameron
Wesleyan University

Karen L. King
Occidental College

Translation Panel

Edward F. Beutner
Santa Clara University

Lane C. McGaughy
Willamette University

J. Dominic Crossan
DePaul University

Marvin W. Meyer
Chapman College

Jon B. Daniels
Defiance College

Robert J. Miller
Midway College

Arthur J. Dewey
Xavier University

Stephen J. Patterson
Eden Theological Seminary

Robert T. Fortna
Vassar College

Daryl D. Schmidt
Texas Christian University

Roy W. Hoover
Whitman College

Bernard Brandon Scott
Phillips Graduate Seminary

Arland D. Jacobson
Concordia College

Philip Sellew
University of Minnesota

John S. Kloppenborg
University of Toronto

Chris Shea
Ball State University

Helmut Koester
Harvard University

Mahlon H. Smith
Rutgers University

Preface

The seeds for this book were planted twenty years ago when I began studying the synoptic gospels with Edward C. Hobbs at the Graduate Theological Union in Berkeley, CA. Since then many groups of students, mostly at Texas Christian University, have nurtured this way of presenting Mark through their thoughtful responses and questions.

The idea for the book itself grew out of discussions during the preparation of the Scholars Version translation of Mark. The process of completing a fresh translation stimulated many new insights about Mark's story and style of story-telling.

Polebridge Press sponsored this translation in an effort to provide the reading public with access to a translation that incorporates the best of current scholarly insights in a fresh English style. The SV translation is also meant to engage the reader in dialogue with the text. Reader comments are invited.

The actual shape of this book and many of its features owe much to the suggestions and contributions of the editor of this new series, Robert W. Funk. The staff of Polebridge Press, especially Char Matejovsky, were magnificent in their expeditious handling of the manuscript and giving final form to the book.

A special thanks goes to Ruth Wilkins Sullivan, Research Curator Emeritus, Kimbell Art Museum, Fort Worth, TX, for selecting and making available most of the photos that were used.

Finally, I am grateful for all the encouragement I received during the preparation of this book the past year from many friends in the Fort Worth area, including those in church adult education groups who so warmly responded to early drafts of the material.

Rosh Hashana 1991
Berkeley, CA

Abbreviations

Cabinet with the Books of the Four Evangelists. Detail from *St. Lawrence's Martyrdom.* Mosaic in the apse lunette, S. Vitale, Mausoleum of Galla Placidia, Ravenna, ca. 425–450. The gospels are in the order: Mark, Luke, Matthew, and John. This is a rare instance of an early Christian depiction suggesting priority for the gospel of Mark. Photograph: Ruth Sullivan.

INTRODUCTION

1. Mark's Gospel

The gospel of Mark is the shortest of the four New Testament gospels and, for most of its existence, the least studied. However, for over a century now Mark has been viewed by many New Testament scholars as the earliest surviving written gospel and the primary source for Matthew and Luke. This has made it the focal point of recent gospel studies.

1.1 A "Gospel"

The credit for calling stories like Mark a "gospel" belongs, in fact, to Mark. It is the only New Testament gospel that uses the word *euangelion* ("gospel," "good news") in its opening line. The term was popularized in the early church by Paul to refer to the good news he preached about God and Jesus the Anointed. Most of the time in Mark it refers to the content of Jesus' own preaching (1:14, 15; 8:35; 10:29; 13:10; 14:9). However, Mark uses the word in 1:1 in a new sense, as "good news" in story form, although it is not clear from Mark's story what it means to use "gospel" this way. Of the other "gospels" written in the first century, Luke and John do not use the word at all, and Matthew seldom uses it the same way Mark does. Nonetheless, by the middle of the second century these four stories of Jesus are collectively called "gospels."

It is also in the second century that the official label "gospel according to . . ." gets attached to each gospel. The stories themselves are actually anonymous. They do not give the reader any direct indication about authorship. However, by the early second century Christian tradition had attached an explicit name to each of the stories, and by the end of the century the tradition had fixed the same formula to each of the gospels.

Thus the story presented here has been known since early times as "The Gospel according to Mark." Tradition does not preserve for us how early such a designation may have been used, nor if it was first used for the gospel that first called itself by that name.

1.2 A "Synoptic" Gospel

The scholarly opinion that Mark was the first written gospel is based on a careful comparison of Mark with Matthew and Luke. These three share many common features, and are often studied together as the "synoptic" gospels (those with a similar view of Jesus). Matthew and Luke follow Mark's general outline and have many direct parallels with Mark's stories, often word-for-word, though individual stories are usually somewhat shortened. Most scholars are convinced that these three gospels are thus somehow dependent upon one another. Because most of Mark is similar to material in Matthew or Luke, often both, the most common explanation has been that Matthew and Luke each borrowed heavily from Mark and added other material to it. An alternative explanation, though not as widely accepted, is that Mark has combined the common stories of Matthew and Luke, which would make Mark the last of the synoptic gospels.

1.3 A "War-time" Gospel

As an anonymous gospel, Mark's narrative also does not indicate anything directly about the circumstances surrounding its composition. Scholarly opinions must be based on evidence internal to the narrative itself. The discussions below about composition, style and motifs will summarize some of this evidence. The overall tone of the narrative is its sense of urgency. The story begins suddenly and ends suddenly. Jesus' first words are "The time is up." Events succeed one another "right away," and Jesus never stays very long in one place. Those who want to follow must drop everything and be on their way.

The setting shifts from the opening phase of Jesus' career in Galilee to the traumatic ending in Jerusalem. The final events are preceded by Jesus' warning directly to the reader (13:14) to understand the "devastating desecration" that will take place in the midst of a time of war (13:7–8).

But you look out for yourselves! They will turn you over to councils, and beat you in synagogues, and haul you up before governors and kings, on my account, so you can make your case to them. (13:9)

And one brother will turn in another to be put to death, and a father his child, and children will turn against their parents and kill them. And you will be universally hated because of me. Those who hold out to the end will be saved! (13:12–13)

. . . then the people in Judea should head for the hills; no one on the roof should go downstairs; no one should enter the house to retrieve anything; and no one in the field should turn back to get a coat. It's too bad for pregnant women and for nursing mothers in those days! Pray that none of this happens in winter! For those days will see distress the likes of which has not occurred since God created the world until now, and will never occur again. And if the Lord had not cut short the days, no human being would have survived! (13:14–20)

The description in these warnings seems too realistic to be a hollow threat or mere speculation about "the last days." Rather, most scholars see it as the best indication of the circumstances of Mark's immediate situation—a time of war.

We know enough about the Roman-Judean War of 66–70 C.E. from the historian Josephus to be able to picture it as the context for at least some of Mark's readers. This description is so vivid that Mark must have been written while the war was still being fought, or even possibly as it was just beginning. Some scholars are convinced that the opening scene of this section fits better the hindsight of a post-war period. Jesus comments about the temple buildings: "You may be sure not one stone will be left on top of another! Every last one will certainly be knocked down!" (13:2). In Mark's narrative Jesus has already ended the functioning of the temple (11:16) and treated it like a fruitless fig tree (11:13–14, 20), to be replaced by "trust in God" (11:22) and his own teaching (12:35; 14:49). This is more likely a post-war perspective. The advice that "the people in Judea should head for the hills" (13:14) has been interpreted by some as locating Mark's origins among a group of Judean-Christian refugees who fled Jerusalem during the war and settled in the north towards Galilee, or beyond, perhaps in Pella in trans-Jordan. Jesus promised to lead them to Galilee (14:28), and in fact, did so (16:7), according to Mark.

The tradition of Christian authors from the second century and later is that Mark's source of information was Peter, and that Mark wrote in Italy after Peter's death in Rome. Those who want to interpret Mark in this context point to the era of persecution in Rome under Nero following the infamous fire of 64 C.E. as accounting for the betrayal of family members and the accusations before governors. This is probably the time when both Peter and Paul were martyred.

The two scenarios of Neronian persecution and ravages of war also overlap. Nero's suicide in 68 C.E. left the empire in civil war for more than a year until General Vespasian, proclaimed emperor in Alexandria, gained control of Rome. He had been in charge of the province of Judea during the first years of the war. As emperor he put his son Titus in charge of the troops that conquered Jerusalem in 70 C.E. Josephus describes the devastation as taking over a million lives, mostly of visitors in Jerusalem for the passover festival, and of nearly 100,000 prisoners-of-war. (These large numbers seem highly improbable.) The prisoners most fit were picked for Titus' triumphant march to Rome, along with the best treasures from the temple. The commemorative arch of Titus in Rome still depicts the scene

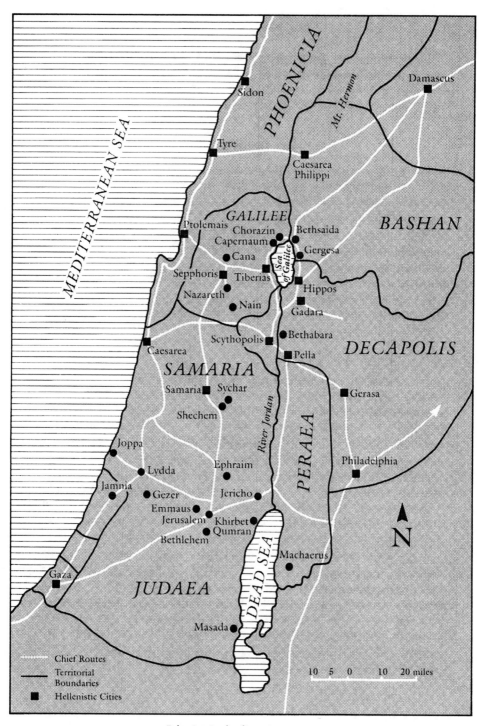

MEDITERRANEAN SEA

PHOENICIA

Mt. Hermon

Damascus

Sidon

Tyre

Caesarea Philippi

GALILEE

BASHAN

Ptolemais
Chorazin
Capernaum
Bethsaida
Cana
Gergesa
Sepphoris
Tiberias
Sea of Galilee
Nazareth
Hippos
Nain
Gadara

Scythopolis
Bethabara
DECAPOLIS
Caesarea
Pella

SAMARIA

River Jordan

Samaria
Sychar
Gerasa
Shechem

PERAEA

Joppa

Ephraim
Philadelphia
Lydda
Jamnia
Jericho
Gezer
Emmaus
Jerusalem
Khirbet
Qumran
Bethlehem

DEAD SEA

Machaerus

JUDAEA

Gaza

N

Masada

Chief Routes
Territorial Boundaries
Hellenistic Cities

10 5 0   10   20 miles

Palestine in the first century C.E.

of the seven-member gold lamp stand being carried in triumphal procession, just as Josephus described it. Thus the memory of the war was implanted in Rome forever. Mark's narrative seems to be aware of this war legacy, and so is best considered a war-time gospel.

2. Mark's Building Blocks

If Mark is indeed the first written gospel, we can only speculate about the kinds of sources that would have been available for its composition. Because it presents itself as "good news" in story form, it is likely that the oral traditions of early Christian communities were a significant force in shaping the story. Some scholars see the entire period preceding the composition of Mark as a time in the life of the church that depended on retelling traditional stories about Jesus. In such a setting Mark is viewed primarily as the one who first assembled units from early Christian stories.

It is more likely that some kinds of material about Jesus were already circulating in longer units before the story as we have it was first written down. Such collections probably included:

2.1. Testimonies from scripture

Mark begins with a quotation from "Isaiah," but it is more than that. The opening line, "Here is my messenger, whom I send on ahead of you," corresponds to Exod 23:20; the next line, "to prepare your way," is modified from Mal 3:1, "to prepare the way before me," and then comes the actual quotation from Isa 40:3. This combination of texts may have preceded Mark and been available in some kind of collection of such texts circulating among early Christians. Elsewhere, especially in chapters 10–12 (but also 4:12; 7:6-7, 10; 13:24-26; 14:27, 62; 15:34), Mark builds on other Old Testament texts. These generally follow the style of the Greek translation of the Old Testament used by early Christians, known as the Septuagint, the translation of the Seventy (LXX). In addition, there are many allusions to LXX texts, especially in the passion narrative (chapters 14–15). It seems likely that, from the earliest days of the church, Christians began defending their understanding of Jesus with arguments from scripture. Those who became "believers" looked back in hindsight at the things that happened to Jesus and realized that this was "as the scriptures predict" (14:21). With the conviction that these events were the scriptures "come true" (14:49), they naturally told their stories about Jesus in the familiar language of their religious tradition, the stories from the bible.

2.2 Controversy stories

Many of the incidents Mark tells about Jesus involve controversies Jesus had with the contemporary religious authorities. The first sequence of such

Mark's Building Blocks
Clusters and Sequences

1 Testimonies from scripture (§2.1)

Mark 1:2–3	Mark 10:6–8	Mark 14:27
Mark 4:12	Mark 11:17	Mark 14:62
Mark 7:6–7	Mark 12:29–31	Mark 15:34
Mark 7:10	Mark 13:24–26	

2 Controversy stories (§2.2)

Mark 2:1–3:6
Mark 11:15–12:40

3 Anecdotes (§2.5)

Mark 3:20–35

4 Parables (§2.3)

Mark 4:2–32

5 Miracles (§2.4)

Mark 4:35–42	Mark 6:47–52
Mark 5:1–20	Mark 8:22–26
Mark 5:21–24a, 35–43	Mark 7:24b–30
Mark 5:24b–34	Mark 7:31–37
Mark 6:35–44	Mark 8:1–10

6 One-liners (§2.6)

Mark 2:21–22	Mark 3:28–29	Mark 9:33–50
Mark 2:27–28	Mark 4:21–25	Mark 11:23–25
Mark 3:23c–26	Mark 7:14–23	Mark 12:38–40
Mark 3:27	Mark 8:34–9:1	

7 Discourse (§2.7)

Mark 13:3–37

8 Passion narrative (§2.8)

Mark 14:2–15:47

9 Other narrative sequences

One day at Capernaum, Mark 1:21–39
Death of John the Baptist, Mark 6:14–29

10 Insertions and framing devices (§3.3)

Mark 2:1–5b/5c–10b/10c–12	Mark 6:7–13/14–29/30–34
Mark 3:1–3/4–5c/5d–6	Mark 11:12–14/15–19/20–25
Mark 3:20–21/22–30/31–35	Mark 14:53–54/55–65/66–72

• Mark's story incorporates earlier narrative material. Some of it would have existed in sequences formed by others from traditional Christian sources, and some of it in clusters that the author had previously put together. The most likely clusters and sequences that can be identified in Mark are outlined above.

stories (2:1–3:6) occurs in the Galilee section, quickly culminating in a plot against Jesus' life. Another sequence (11:15–12:40) occurs in Jerusalem, although the opponents seem different (§4.6). If these were separate collections of stories prior to Mark, they may reflect different periods of growing harassment between Christians and their non-Christian neighbors. Christians likely would have retold such stories, either as encouragement to one another or as propaganda. The stories themselves may have originated as anecdotes about Jesus (§2.5).

2.3 Parables

Jesus was known as a teller of riddles/parables (Mark 3:23). Mark inserts a parable theory (4:10–12) into his one main parable (4:2–9) and its allegorical interpretation (4:13–20). Afterwards, Mark adds four isolated parabolic sayings and a concluding editorial comment (4:33–34). There is also a parable given on location in Jerusalem (12:1–12). It is surely part of Mark's irony (§3.5) that the only parable unmistakably successful was the one directed to the opponents (12:12).

Some of these parables may well have come from collections that were earlier than the first written gospel. This would be most likely for parables with common themes, such as the three "seed" parables in Mark 4. Parables were probably repeated among Christians in a number of different circumstances, which could have included the preaching and teaching of the church, but also anecdotal settings (§2.5) or even informal "parable-sharing."

However, Mark's theory of parable-as-riddle seems to have been developed by Mark to serve a particular purpose. This suggestion has stimulated much scholarly speculation about the original Markan audience and circumstances. For whom do the parables remain riddles, and what is the key to their understanding? Careful study of individual parables reveals how they contribute to larger themes in Mark, and so must be seen as given their final shape by the author. The two longest parables in Mark (4:3–8, 14–20; 12:1–11) are so carefully developed to suit allegorical interpretation that the allegorical features, if not the entire parables, may be Markan creations.

2.4 Miracles

Jesus was equally well remembered as a healer and miracle-worker. Stories about the "cures" that happened to people in Jesus' presence developed into a regular pattern. The stories focus on the condition of the afflicted person, the singular act that affected the cure, and a demonstration of the restored person's healthy state. This pattern can be seen in the early stories in Mark (1:29–31, 40–42), and spread throughout the other pre-Jerusalem materials. Apparently for some groups within the Jesus move-

ment the miracle-working tradition would have been their primary understanding of Jesus. It must be remembered that "healing stories" were also
associated with "medicine" in the ancient world, and as such were a
common phenomenon.

There may also have been early collections of miracle stories, such as a
source for the three miracles in Mark 5. It is also noteworthy that they are
preceded by a sea-crossing story (4:35–41) and followed eventually by a
feeding story (6:35–44). Mark is unique in presenting a repetition of this
cycle (6:47–52; 7:24–8:10). Scholarly opinion differs on whether there were
one or more such cycles circulating earlier than Mark, or if the author of
Mark is responsible for developing them. The shape of these collections
seems influenced by the exodus tradition, featuring sea-crossing and
feeding stories, and by the collection of Elijah and Elisha stories (1 Kings
17–19; 2 Kings 1–9). The function of such collections in Mark is unclear.
Do they promote Jesus as a miracle-worker, or does Mark rework the stories
to play that down in light of his concern for Jesus as the one who suffers and
dies? Or, To what extent does Mark treat miracles as "acted parables?"

2.5 Anecdotes

There are various brief stories about Jesus that feature him responding to
a typical situation with a memorable saying, or action. Scholars have tended
to focus on the longer "pronouncement stories" that feature a decisive
judgment from Jesus. In ancient Greek rhetoric a brief anecdote making a
point about a person is called a *chreia*. *Chreiai* were being collected long
before the time of the gospels, first about famous philosophers, but later as a
way of remembering other important people. The popularity of chreiai-
practice in schools suggests they influenced both the formation of such
stories about Jesus and their collection by his followers. These anecdotes
probably changed and grew in the retelling to meet changing circumstances, such as on the practice of fasting (Mark 2:18–22). Indeed, the
entire unit of controversy stories (Mark 2:1–3:6) appears to be derived from
chreiai, with the anecdote expanded into controversy and the punch line
featuring a memorable saying (or action in 3:1–6). Their narrative context
would be a Markan creation, designed to fit the needs of Mark's story.
Likewise, Mark 3:20–35 appears to be another unit that grew out of a small
group of related anecdotes, and most of chapters 10 and 12 are also
expanded anecdotal stories.

2.6 One-Liners

Anecdotes in Mark often have attached to them additional aphorisms,
one-liners without narrative setting. The fasting section just mentioned
adds two pithy sayings (2:21, 22), and the sabbath controversy in 2:23–28

concludes with two sayings (vv. 27, 28) that have a separate introduction, "and he continued," suggesting they were from an independent tradition. Mark's best known one-liner is "Whoever has two good ears should use them!" (4:9), which gets added elsewhere in some early manuscripts (7:16; §8.2).

2.7 Discourse

The longest connected speech in Mark is chapter 13. Scholarly opinion varies widely on the likely origin of this material. It could have been put together from early Christian material speculating about the nearness of the end of the world, or only slightly revised from similar Jewish material. Such "eschatological" ("end time") hope would have intensified during the war (§1.3). Mark includes such material (13:24–27), but puts it in the context of warning: "It is not yet the end" (13:7); and "Be on your guard" against counterfeit messiahs and phony prophets (13:22). Always "be on your guard! Stay alert! For you never know what time it is" (13:33). Mark further combines this material with advice for missionaries derived from the legacy of Christian martyrs (§1.3). Therefore, whatever the source(s) for this discourse, its present form appears to have been significantly edited by Mark.

2.8 Passion narrative

The basic sequence of events narrated in Mark 14–15 (final meal with companions, arrest involving Judas, Council appearance and Peter's denial, "trial" by Pilate, execution, and burial) is followed also by the usually independent gospel of John. For some scholars this is evidence of an earlier passion source. The dramatic end of Jesus' life in Jerusalem had been a challenge to Christian claims that Jesus was the Anointed, but Paul soon turned it into the cornerstone of Christian preaching. Both of these circumstances would have been motivation for the formation of tradition about these final events. Indeed, the passion narrative contains much apologetic material, both political (improving Pilate's role 15:14–15) and theological (scriptural proofs 14:27, 34, 49, 62; 15:24, 29, 33, 34). The continuity of Markan themes running through the passion suggests that the shape of the narrative as we now have it owes much to the editorial work of Mark.

2.9 Summary

Whatever the nature of the source material available to the author of Mark, the narrative unity of Mark's story suggests that the author be viewed, not just as a preserver of tradition, but also as a shaper of tradition, even as the originator of some tradition. Recent scholarship has focused on Mark as story, to be understood and appreciated much like a work of art. So there is less interest today in speculating about the historical author and the possible materials out of which the narrative was constructed. While the oral tradition most certainly provided Mark with access to various kinds of sayings, anecdotes and miracles stories, much scholarly attention has come to be focused rather on the structure of the narrative and the qualities of its literary and rhetorical features — all those devices that give an individual story its distinctive character.

3. Markan Style

The writing style of Mark was once thought of as inelegant and unsophisticated, credited to someone who was incapable of writing better literary Greek. Those same features are now identified as giving Mark its story-telling quality. The style suggests the vitality and immediacy of an oral setting. This is accomplished through a number of interrelated stylistic and rhetorical devices.

3.1 Orality

The pattern of sentences is quite simple, mostly short sentences connected by the common conjunction *kai* ("and"). One of Mark's most distinctive words (42 times) is *euthus* ("right away," "right then and there," "suddenly"), and two out of three times it comes right after *kai*. A third feature of this style is narrating past events with present tense verbs (over 150 times, almost half are "say"): "They come and ask him" (2:18); "And they wake him up and say to him" (4:38). Occasionally all three of these features are put together: "And right away the spirit drives him out into the wilderness" (1:12).

Another way Mark achieves the sense of orality is through the amount of direct speech that is part of the narrative. The only long discourse is chapter 13, and there are few summary sections with no speech content. Most of Mark consists of narrative units that present Jesus in direct dialogue with other characters in the story: "And they say to him, 'Look, your mother and your brothers and sisters are outside looking for you.' In response he says to them: 'My mother and brothers—who ever are they?'" (3:32). Mark seldom reports on a conversation second-hand: "And he gave them strict orders that no one should learn about this, and he told them to give her something to eat" (5:43).

3.2 Repetition

Mark employs devices at several levels of the narrative that reinforce previously narrated aspects of the story. At the vocabulary level, one of Mark's favorite words is *palin* ("again"). After establishing a basic pattern for Jesus' ministry in Mark 1:16–45, the narrative begins to repeat itself: "he went back to Capernaum" (2:1); "again he went out by the sea" (2:13); "then he went back to the synagogue" (3:1); "once again a crowd gathers" (3:20); "once again he started to teach" (4:1). Each of these introduces a second narrative setting built on a previous, and therefore familiar, incident. In this way Mark creates typical scenes for the reader.

Familiarity is also part of a larger pattern of doublets and duality, which often overlap. This occurs already at the vocabulary level: "early, while it was still very dark" (1:35); "now, in the present time" (10:30); "in the resurrection, after they rise" (12:23); "the chosen people whom he selected" (13:20). While these may appear to be mostly redundant, more careful consideration has led to the suggestion that Mark rather deliberately says many things twice, first more generally, then more specifically. We also find "Be quiet, shut up!" (4:39); "Don't be afraid, just have trust!" (5:36); "I do trust! Help my lack of trust!" (9:24); "It's all over! The time has come!" (14:41). These kinds of dual expressions add to the overall effectiveness of Mark's gospel as an oral text, meant to be read and heard aloud.

At the story level there are also doublets that share several similar features: two exorcisms (1:23–28; 5:1–8); two sea crossings (4:35–41; 6:45–52); two crowd feedings (6:34–44; 8:1–9). Likewise, these are not merely redundant; the second one has a different setting, and raises to another level an issue introduced the first time. The unique transitional story of the blind person needing to be touched "a second time" before "he saw everything clearly" (8:25) reinforces a Markan theme: What you see the first time is not all there is!

Mark also makes significant use of a three-fold pattern. Within individual stories there are often groups of three: Peter, James and John (5:37; 9:2; 14:33); two Marys and Salome (15:40; 16:1); the ranking priests and scholars and elders (11:27; 14:43, 53; 15:1); Jesus finds the three disciples sleeping three times (14:32–42, emphasized with "a third time" in v. 41); followed by Peter's triple denial (14:66–72, the second time using the earlier formula: "once again he denied it"). This three-fold pattern is also integrated into the structure of the whole narrative. The central section of the gospel (8:27–10:45) reintroduces the main theme of "the Anointed" and then repeats this sequence three times: Jesus talks about the coming suffering, the disciples fail to understand, so Jesus teaches them.

3.3 Framing Devices

The central section (8:27–10:45) is further set off in importance by the framework it is given. Both the story preceding it (8:22–26) and the story following it (10:46–52) are stories about the blind who again see, in stark contrast to the three-fold pattern of what lies between: the disciples' complete failure to perceive the thrust of Jesus' teaching. This theme, in turn, is highlighted in the previous section through the repetition of they "look with eyes wide open but never quite see" (4:12) and "though you have eyes, you still don't see" (8:18).

Mark also intertwines two stories by using one to frame the other, such as the healing stories of two females in chapter 5. The introduction of the plight of Jairus' daughter (5:21–24) provides the setting for telling the story of the woman with the bleeding problem (5:25–34). The narrative then returns to resolve the first story (5:35–43). The two females needing cures are related by their condition of "twelve years." A twelve year old girl (5:42) is ready to enter womanhood and begin menstruation, which will make her unclean in the Levitical code (Leviticus 15), while a woman with a "vaginal flow" for twelve years has been perpetually unclean by that same code. Both are cured by "trust" (5:34, 36).

The most intriguing framing story is the withered fig tree (11:12–14, 20–21). The narrative presents Jesus' harsh words to the tree for its lack of "fruit" while he is on his way to the temple area. The effect on the tree is noted the next morning, after Jesus had put an end to all temple activity (11:15–19). The leafy fig tree, withered "from its roots" and no longer capable of bearing fruit, provides a framework for interpreting Jesus' activity in the temple area as symbolic of the anticipated demise of the temple itself.

3.4 Prediction and Suspense

Mark begins his narrative with the prophetic text from "Isaiah," which is actually a combination of several texts (§2.1). Scripture is used as a foundation from which to launch this new narrative. The quoted text serves a predictive function both in setting forth the general theme, "the way of the Lord," and in getting the narrative underway by announcing the forthcoming voice "in the wilderness." John the Baptizer then appears "in the wilderness" to take on that announced role, but, in turn, himself announces his successor (1:7). Then Jesus appears on the scene. The dynamic of the narrative is thus established and the reader will want to follow how this logic works itself out in the story.

However, not every predictive announcement finds its completion within the limits of Mark's story itself. The most important instance of this is Mark's ending. Although Jesus has assured the disciples, "After I'm raised I'll go ahead of you to Galilee" (14:28), and the witnesses in the tomb at the end are given the charge to tell the disciples "he is going ahead of you to Galilee" (16:7), yet the story ends abruptly without the completion of this final charge.

3.5 Irony

Many aspects of Mark's narrative have an ironical tone to them. At the most explicit level, irony involves characters in the story saying (and doing) things that have a very different, often contrary, meaning from another perspective, usually that of the reader, who already knows the outcome of the narrative. The feeding stories present the disciples in such an ironic role. During the first feeding they innocently ask, "Are we to go out and buy half a year's wages worth of bread and donate it for their meal?!" (6:37). Even after Jesus shows them how to feed such a crowd in a desolate place, Mark reports that "they hadn't understood about the loaves" (6:52). The second feeding story then would seem to give them a second chance. However, Mark has them saying, "How can anyone feed these people bread out here in this desolate place?" (8:4). The reader surely remembers what the disciples do not.

Irony plays a significant role also in Mark's telling of the passion story. The opening scene (14:3–9) finally narrates how "the Anointed" gets anointed, but the setting is not a formal ceremony in the temple presided over by the high priest. Rather, it is in a leper's house in Bethany, and the anointer is a woman—both the kinds of people typically attracted to "the Anointed" earlier in the story (1:40; 5:27). And the anointing anticipates the Anointed's death rather than his reign.

There is surely irony involved when Pilate three times uses "the King of the Judeans" in reference to Jesus (15:2, 9, 12), as do the mockers (15:18), who also bring a royal garment and a mock crown (15:17). Finally, the inscription makes it official (15:26). Mark's Christian readers probably heard the irony in these "false witnesses" unwittingly affirming the church's faith. Other mockers add their three-fold voices: "Save yourself and come down from the cross!" (15:30); "he saved others, but he can't save himself!" (15:31); "'The Anointed', 'the King of Israel,' should come down from the cross here and now, so that we can see and trust for ourselves!" (15:32). The reader knows how the outcome of the story makes mockery of these taunts.

Some scholars suggest that Peter's words before his denial should be heard as irony: "If they condemn me to die with you, I will never disown you!" (14:31). While in the narrative Peter does indeed disown Jesus rather than go with him to his death, Mark's readers would be aware of the tradition of Peter's martyrdom. And some level of irony must be involved in the very nickname "Rock" (3:16). In Mark's story he turns out more like the "rocky" faith that has "no depth" (4:4), but is "short-lived" and "easily shaken" under pressure (4:16–17). Afterall, it is Peter who leads the disciples in rejecting Jesus' forecast that "You will all desert ⟨me⟩" (14:27). And soon "they all deserted him" (14:50).

Another ironical dimension to the whole story has to be the contrast between the content and the mode of telling. The content is bold in a big public way. Jesus is the Anointed, the King, the agent of "God's imperial rule." But the "good news" is a "secret" announced in "parables" (4:11, 30), which is not understood (4:13), even though privately explained (4:33–34). The ending is then the ultimate irony; the final command to proclaim is greeted by silence.

3.6 Explanatory asides

Mark's narrative is interspersed with a number of different editorial comments. Foreign terms are translated (5:41; 7:11, 34; 14:36; 15:34) and unfamiliar customs are explained (7:3–4). Once, the readers are even addressed explicitly (13:14). The most common kind of aside in Mark is introduced with the conjunction *gar*, traditionally translated "for" (for example, 2:15; 3:10, 30; 5:28, 42; 6:14, 31, 52; 9:6; 11:13, 18, 32; 16:4). Such asides usually provide editorial information to the reader regarding the significance of what has just been narrated. Some asides may have originated as marginal notes added after the final draft of Mark and included in the text by an early copyist. This would be most likely for the translation of foreign terms or customs. However, most of the asides are probably from the original author, rather than later additions. (The Scholars Version translation usually places these asides within parentheses.)

3.7 Other Rhetorical Features

The reader of the gospel will readily note other features that are typical of Mark's style:

1) Generalizations. Mark makes frequent use of "all," "each," "every," "whole," "entire," "much," "many:" "everyone from the Judean countryside and all the residents of Jerusalem" (1:5); "the whole city" (1:33); "he cured many people . . . and drove out many demons" (1:34); "it kept begging him over and over" (5:10).

2) Indefiniteness. Mark uses sentences with no specific subject: "They were astonished at his teaching" (1:22); "they would bring all the sick" (1:32); "they continued to come to him from everywhere" (1:45).

3) Unanswerable questions. Jesus often has the last word in the form of a rhetorical question, or two: "How are you going to understand other parables?" (4:13); "Why are you so cowardly? You still don't trust, do you?" (4:40); "You still aren't using your heads, are you? You still haven't got the point, have you? Are you just dense?" (8:17).

3.8 Summary

The current scholarly interest in ancient rhetoric has stimulated new interest in features of Markan style that contribute to the overall effectiveness of Mark's narrative as a persuasive text. Unlike the more literary gospels that follow Mark, Mark's narrative must be heard to be appreciated.

It is "good news" for those with "two good ears." Its deceptively simple style only suggests that it is in the literary style of popular culture, and not fine art. However, there is no scholarly consensus on what kind of popular literature this is. Some find the closest style in biographical writing; others now see it mostly as a rhetorical text; still others argue for the uniqueness of Mark's literary creation, either as a new kind of theological tract, or even as fiction.

4. Markan Motifs

The discussion of other aspects of Mark and Markan style has already presented some of the more distinctive Markan themes, for example, Mark as "good news" (§1.1). There are other major themes that scholars have identified as essential to understanding Mark's narrative.

4.1 The Way

The first theme announced in Mark's story is the theme of the prophetic quotations used as the springboard for the story: "Prepare your way!" and "Make ready the way of the Lord" (1:2, 3). Most interpretations of Mark see John as the preparer of "the way" for Jesus, who goes "on the road" as the central section of Mark begins (8:27). The movement throughout this section continues "on the road" (9:33, 34; 10:17) until the destination is Jerusalem (10:32), and finally the cross. The section ends with the framing story of Bartimaeus regaining his sight and "following him on the road" (10:52).

Both "way" and "road" translate Greek *hodos*, the metaphor often used in the biblical tradition for the journey motif. It describes the activity of God symbolized by the exodus, "Your way was through the sea, your paths through the great waters, yet your footprints were unseen" (Ps 77:19), but it also suggests the conduct of one's life, "Teach me your way, Lord, that I may walk in your truth" (Ps 86:11). The prophets developed further the image of "the way," from which Mark derives his beginning theme, "Make ready the way of the Lord" (Isa 40:3; §2.1). Mark's use of "on the road" at 8:27 and 10:52 is often seen as a direct echo to "the way," and indicates the beginning and end, and main theme, of the central section of Mark's gospel.

4.2 Symbolic Geography

If Mark is using "the way" in more than a literal sense, other vague spatial references also seem to have symbolic value. Mark's narrative begins with John "in the wilderness" (1:4), where Jesus also goes (1:12). Jesus starts his career "by the sea" (1:16), finding companions, and he begins the second phase by going "to the mountain" (3:13) to form a leadership group of twelve. What all these general designations have in common is their deep roots in Israel's past.

Mark's narrative takes place in the same highly symbolic geographical settings as the old narrative told in scripture about ancient Israel's formative period, the exodus. The importance of these exodus images can be seen in the language of Israel's worship in the Psalms. The exodus event began when the Lord rebuked the sea and led the people through (106:9), who then went to the mountain (73:54) where earlier God was revealed to Moses as "I am." The people wandered in the wilderness, hungry and thirsty, until God delivered them and guided them to a straight path (107:4–7). God gave them heavenly messengers charged to keep them in the ways of God (91:11). The people were fed bread in abundance (78:25), but they still tempted God because their hearts were hardened. They then spent forty years in the wilderness because they did not know the ways of God (95:8–10).

The language of the exodus was equally important to the prophets of the exile. Their vision for a new Israel called for a new exodus, where once again the Lord would lead them "on the way" through "the wilderness" to the promised land. Mark's opening quotation from "Isaiah" (§2.1) provides the link between the exodus tradition as a prophetic hope and Mark's narrative world. The biblical narrative of the exodus told in Exodus, Numbers and Deuteronomy describes those events with details that are often paralleled in Mark. Some of the important examples will be indicated in the translation notes.

4.3 God's Domain

Mark presents Jesus as beginning his career with the message: "The time is up: God's imperial rule is closing in" (1:15). This then becomes what Jesus seeks to impart to the disciples: "You have been given the secret of God's imperial rule" (4:11). God's rule usually had not been thought of as a secret. The exodus hymn celebrates that event as demonstrating that "the Lord rules for ever" (Exod 15:18), an affirmation also repeated in the Psalms (10:16; 145:13). Mark presents a "kingdom" that is not so obvious, and therefore, not just an extension of the common belief in God's eternal dominion.

Jesus talks about God's rule in somewhat different terms. He promises that some will see "God's imperial rule set in with power" (9:1), while others are told they must accept it like a child would (10:15). Sometimes the more fitting image is God's "domain," since people enter or are near to it (9:47; 10:23–24; 12:34). Finally, at his farewell Jesus looks forward to a feast in God's domain (14:25).

4.4 Riddles and Secrecy

The secret about God's imperial rule is told in riddle-like parables (4:11, 30, 34). Even though the riddles are privately explained, they do not cease being riddles. Likewise, even though "there is nothing hidden that won't be brought to light" (4:22), this "secret," like the riddles, is for those with "two good ears" (4:9, 23). This seems to be part of Mark's paradox, along with the blind who perceive what Jesus is about, and those who see everything, but cannot understand it. Similarly, those who know too much are silenced (1:25, 34, 44; 3:12). Even though this story is "good news," there are some things Jesus does not want talked about. So when he does explain, Mark emphasizes the privacy (4:34; 9:28). Jesus is also described elsewhere as doing things in private (7:33), away from the crowd (5:37), and wanting to be alone (7:2; 8:13), in an "isolated place" (1:35, 45), with his companions (6:32), or on "the mountain" (6:46; 9:2).

4.5 Obstinacy

Interwoven into several of these themes is the failure of Jesus' companions to comprehend. Parables remain riddles for "those outside," who "look with eyes wide open but never quite see," and "listen with ears attuned but never quite understand" (4:11-12). These are the images that Mark now develops. It is the blind who are able to see, rather than those with eyes wide open, and those with two good ears had better listen, because they never quite understand. Mark then singles out the disciples: "So how are you going to understand other parables?" (4:13). The first long section of Mark culminates with Jesus' strongest words to his companions, unanswerable questions ending with "Are you just dense?" (8:17), followed by the repetition of "Though you have eyes, you still don't see, and though you have ears, you still don't hear!" The accusation of being "dense" echoes in Greek an earlier editorial statement by Mark that the disciples were "obstinate" in not understanding about the loaves (6:52). Similar language is used elsewhere only of Jesus' opponents (3:5; 10:5). In Greek this condition is described as "hard-hearted," because the heart was the location for thinking, understanding and, therefore, decision-making. The most famous case of "hard-heartedness" in the biblical tradition is that of Pharaoh, which plays an important role in the exodus story (especially Exodus 7-9).

4.6 Opposition

Any narrative that includes the tragic death of the hero, must present opponents who contributed to, or were responsible for, the outcome. In Mark's narrative the inevitability of opposition is already indicated when the "preparer of the way" is himself "locked up" (1:14), without explanation. This becomes the context for "the successor" to begin his career, which is immediately contrasted with "the scholars" (1:22). After a brief sample of the kinds of activities that typified Jesus' ministry (1:23–45), opposition awaits the next time Jesus returns to the same location (2:1,6). Mark then presents a series of "controversy stories" (§2.2) that quickly culminate in a conspiracy against Jesus' life (3:6).

The initial opponents are "the scholars" (2:6), also called "the Pharisees' scholars" (2:16), or just "the Pharisees" (2:24; 3:6). In 3:6 they collaborate with "the Herodians," apparently a political faction that Mark associates with Herod Antipas, who has jurisdiction over Galilee. Later it will be scholars "from Jerusalem" (3:22) and then "the Pharisees and the scholars" (7:1, 5) as well as just the Pharisees (8:11; 10:2; 12:13). The latter time they are mentioned again with their political collaborators, since Mark seems to associate both groups primarily with Galilee.

While it is not clear how Mark relates the more general term "scholars" to "Pharisees," there is little doubt that he sees Jesus primarily in confrontation with religious authorities. However, when the narrative enters the main central section, the forecast of Jesus' demise no longer involves mention of the Pharisees. Now it is the collective membership of the Sanhedrin (SV: the Council), the religious establishment, "the elders and the ranking priests and the scholars" (8:31; 11:27; 14:43, 54; 15:1), who play the leading opposition role in Jerusalem. However, when Mark talks about direct involvement in Jesus' death, the elders are not mentioned (10:33; 11:18; 14:1; 15:31). In fact, it is the ranking priests alone who seem to take charge (14:10; 15:3,10), even in the unlikely role of inciting the crowd (15:10) and ridiculing Jesus on the cross (15:31).

The issues provoking the opposition are likewise religious issues: forgiving sins (2:7), "eating with sinners" (2:16), fasting (2:18), and especially, "doing what's not permitted on the sabbath day" (2:24; 3:4). The controversy over interpretation of what is "permitted" extends to other sensitive issues: divorce (6:18; 10:2) and taxes (12:14).

4.7 Fearful Followers

In the face of strong opposition, Jesus' closest companions turn out to be less than fearless followers. In addition to being described as obstinate (§4.5), they are also often filled with fear. The disciples are "cowardly" (4:40) and "distrustful" (9:19), and they act terrified (4:41; 6:50; 9:6), even "dreaded to ask" about what they failed to understand (9:32). Not only are his followers afraid (10:32), eventually even the opponents fear both Jesus (11:18) and the crowds that follow him (11:32; 12:12). Most strikingly, the story ends suddenly, because those who receive the news of the resurrection are terrified to the point of silence (16:8).

In contrast to fearful companions such as these, relatives who think he is crazy (3:21), and neighbors who resent him (6:3), it is an unlikely audience that responds favorably to Jesus. The leper falls on his knees before him (1:40), as do those possessed with unclean spirits (3:11; 5:6), a synagogue official (5:22), and anonymous others (5:33; 7:25; 10:17).

4.8 Trust

What distinguishes many of these individuals is their trust. "Trust" is the opposite of "fear" (5:36), and leads to cures (5:42). Both an anonymous healed woman and formerly blind Bartimaeus are commended, "Your trust has cured you" (5:34; 10:52). The most instructive story about trust involves the distraught father of an epileptic (9:17–27), who approaches Jesus because the disciples are incapable of producing a cure. Jesus' first response is to call them a "distrustful lot" (v. 19). The father asks Jesus for help, "if you can do anything," to which Jesus replies, "All things are possible for the one who trusts." The father immediately confesses, "I do trust! Help my lack of trust!" (vv. 22–24), and Jesus performs an exorcism.

Furthermore, this story is set in the central section of Mark, which begins with someone blind who comes to see "everything clearly" (8:25), in contrast to those with eyes who cannot see (8:18), and so are worse off than the one-eyed (9:47). This sections ends with Bartimaeus receiving sight through "trust" (10:52), while the disciples, with their eyes open, have already demonstrated their lack of trust (4:40). It is then the same four disciples who first followed who are warned not to trust any other messiah (13:3, 21).

Trusting God (11:22) is the recommended response to accepting God's rule. Those who trust the good news will turn their lives around (1:15) and thus make all things possible (9:23; 11:23–24). This message of renewal was in continuity with John's preaching (1:4). But those who did not trust John (11:31) are the same ones who mockingly dare Jesus, "Come down from the cross here and now, so that we can see and trust for ourselves!" (15:32). The first irony here is that only moments later the centurion indeed "saw" that Jesus "really was God's son!" (15:39), thereby adding even greater irony to the claim that "seeing is believing." Earlier Jesus had described believing as unflinching conviction: "Trust that what [you] say will happen" (11:23).

4.9 Jesus the Teaching Miracle Worker

The major motifs in Mark involve the narrative's main character. Jesus' primary activity is called teaching (1:21–22) and, unlike the scholars, he gives "a new kind of teaching" (1:27). His teaching permeates all sections of the narrative, and is used by Mark to summarize his activity (6:6; 10:1), including his last days in the temple area (14:49).

Likewise, "teacher" is the most widely used form of address for Jesus in Mark, both by his companions (4:38; 9:38; 10:35; 13:1) and by his opponents (12:14, 19, 32). Jesus even uses it about himself (14:14). The Jewish title, "Rabbi," which became customary for teachers, is used by both Peter (9:5; 11:21) and Judas (14:45), and the more intimate "Rabbouni" is used by Bartimaeus (10:51).

Although Jesus begins his teaching in the synagogue (1:21), the last time he goes there the result is resentment and distrust (6:3, 6) and he never returns. Instead his classroom becomes the seashore (6:34), as it had been earlier (4:1), then the road to Jerusalem (10:1), and finally the temple area (14:49). Mark's picture thus moves from the typical synagogue master to the itinerant populist of hellenistic philosophy to the founder of a new school that replaces the temple.

Despite the importance of the "teaching" theme, Mark seldom presents collections of Jesus' teaching (exceptions: 4:2–32; 13:3–37). More typically, Mark tells anecdotes that contain a memorable saying by Jesus. A number of these sayings are introduced with the formula: "I swear to you," followed by an expression of strong conviction, often regarding things that have not yet happened (9:1,41; 10:15; 13:30; 14:25).

Another Markan theme in Jesus' teaching is the use of "the son of Adam," a term that is never explained in the narrative. It is first introduced in the controversy stories of chapter 2. In response to the challenge, "Who can forgive sins except the one God?" (2:7), Mark explains, "the son of Adam has authority to forgive sins" (2:10). Likewise, when challenged about what is permitted on the sabbath day, Jesus declares, "the son of Adam lords it even over the sabbath day" (2:28). Jesus does not use the expression again until he first forecasts that in Jerusalem "the son of Adam must suffer a great deal" (8:31). Most of the remaining uses are similar to this (9:9, 12, 31; 10:33, 45; 14:21, 41). There is yet a third "son of Adam" theme, which talks about a future "coming" (8:38) that will be visible (13:26; 14:62).

Jesus' approach to teaching is summarized by Mark in his parable theory (§2.3): "to those outside everything is presented in parables" (4:11), but then Jesus "would spell everything out in private to his own disciples" (4:34). Parabolic acts are included as well as words. The secret of God's imperial rule is evident as much in Jesus' "mighty deeds" as it is in various sayings. In fact, the initial response, "A new kind of teaching backed by authority!" is given after the first *miracle* (1:27), an exorcism that must be seen as a parabolic "teaching" about God's rule. The later dispute over exorcism (3:22) provokes Jesus to respond "in riddles" (3:23). And Jesus gets the same kind of "amazement" after "his words" (10:24) as after an exorcism (1:27). In fact, his companions address him also as "teacher" when they want him to do something (4:38; 9:38; 10:35). One of the ironic elements in Mark's story is that Jesus can open the eyes and ears of blind and deaf strangers, but as for his own companions, "though you have eyes, you still don't see, and though you have ears, you still don't hear!" (8:18).

4.10 Jesus' Lifestyle

Among the important issues that recur in the flow of Mark's narrative are food and table fellowship with common folk. The opening round of controversy stories (2:1–3:6) features three issues: table fellowship with "sinners" (2:15–17), fasting (2:18–22) and picking grain on the sabbath day (2:23–28). Later a lengthy discussion takes place over the relation of "clean" to food and eating (7:1–23). Jesus twice feeds large groups in an isolated place (6:35; 8:4), but the disciples fail to understand (6:52), and the first half of the narrative ends with a showdown over bread (8:14–21). The bread at the last supper is then the third time the disciples have experienced this sequence,"he took a loaf, gave a blessing, broke it into pieces and offered it to them" (14:22) Despite their full participation and best intentions (14:29–31), they are not prepared to endure what this commitment demands.

Another noteworthy dimension of Mark's Jesus is his rebuking. "Rebuke" is used in biblical stories to demonstrate control and chastisement. The Psalms celebrate the Lord's rebuke of the nations (9:5) and the proud (119:21). But especially the Lord rebuked the sea at the exodus crossing (106:9), the same way the Lord controlled the waters at creation (18:15; 104:6–7). So in Mark Jesus acts like the Lord in controlling the wind at the exodus-like crossing of the sea (4:39). This is also the language used for Jesus controlling the unclean spirits (1:25; 9:25), where it may have become a technical term for exorcists. A related context is "warning" those who would expose him, both unclean spirits (3:12) and disciples (8:30). The disciples, in turn, "scold" the crowd (10:13) and the crowd chastizes Bartimaeus (10:48). The other rebuking context is the confrontation between Jesus and Peter (8:32,33). Peter admonishes Jesus for talking about suffering, and in response Jesus reprimands Peter.

Mark also uses another harsh word, *embrimaomai*, which originally meant to "snort at" in anger, but is usually taken to mean "scold" or "censure" in Mark. In 1:43 it expresses Jesus' reaction to curing a leper, which may suggest it is a term associated with a kind of exorcism. The other use is in 14:5 for the disciples reaction to the anointing woman, another indication of their failure to comprehend a situation where the topic is Jesus' death.

4.11 Passion Apologetic

A number of the themes already considered in Mark's narrative have a role in preparing the reader for Jesus' passion (chapters 14–15). One of the linguistic motifs that Mark uses for much of the passion is the verb *paradidomi*, "turn someone in" or "turn someone over to someone." This verb is first used to narrate the arrest of John: "John was locked up" (1:14). It is then the ominous label given to Judas, when he is first introduced as the one who "turned him in" (3:19). The forecasts of death in Jerusalem use the same language: "The son of Adam is being turned over to his enemies" (9:31); "the son of Adam will be turned over to the ranking priests and the scholars, and they will sentence him to death, and turn him over to foreigners" (10:33).

The passive form of these constructions may suggest more than merely the betrayer who turns him in. In the biblical language of Isaiah 53, an innocent one suffers because "the Lord gave him up for our sins" (v. 6), so he "was delivered to death," "delivered because of our offenses" (v. 12). In the Greek translation all three statements use the same verb that Mark now uses for Jesus. Elsewhere the prophets report the Lord's judgment, "I will deliver you into the hands of strangers" (Ezek 11:9). This prophetic language seems to have been important in the defense given by early Christians against those who challenged the notion of a crucified Messiah. Using such language in relation to Jesus' crucifixion suggests it was necessary so that scripture would come true.

The passion account in Mark gets underway when Judas goes "to turn him over to [the ranking priests]" (14:10). This becomes the preoccupation of the next part of the story (14:11, 18, 21, 41, 42, 44). The chain then continues as the Council turns Jesus over to Pilate (15:1, 10), who "turned him over to be crucified" (15:15). And the sequence does not end there. Jesus' words about what his companions can expect promise them that they too must be prepared for similar treatment: "They will turn you over to councils," "lock you up," and "one brother will turn in another" (13:9–12).

4.12 Summary

These themes have been selected as particularly crucial for appreciating Mark's narrative, and as representative of significant scholarly discussion about Mark's story. However, they are meant to be suggestive of many other aspects of this intriguing story that will catch the attention of the careful reader.

5. Scholars Version

5.1 Translation Guidelines

The Scholars Version (SV) is a new translation of the Bible. The first phase is a translation of all known gospels. As the name suggests, Scholars Version will include all gospel materials that provide significant information about Jesus of Nazareth and Christian origins.

The major goal of this translation is to find fresh language that will make biblical narratives and discourse come to life for the modern reader. A more explicit goal is to render the stories and dialogue in a style similar to that of the original language, while also incorporating the best scholarly insights about the content of the text. For SV Mark this means an oral style that captures Mark's lively and colloquial Greek in spoken American English. Mark's style is evident in this passage almost certainly composed by him:

> They forgot to bring any bread and had nothing with them in the boat except one loaf. Then he started giving them directives: "Look," he says, "watch out for the leaven of the Pharisees and the leaven of Herod!"
>
> They began looking quizzically at one another because they didn't have any bread. And because he was aware of this, he says to them: "Why are you puzzling about your lack of bread? You still aren't using your heads, are you? You still haven't got the point, have you? Are you just dense? Though you have eyes, you still don't see, and though you have ears, you still don't hear! Don't you even remember how many baskets full of scraps you picked up when I broke up the five loaves for the five thousand?"
>
> "Twelve," they reply to him.
>
> "When I broke up the seven loaves for the four thousand, how many big baskets full of scraps did you pick up?"
>
> And they say, "Seven."
>
> And he repeats: "You still don't understand, do you?" (8:14–21)

Traditional church-sponsored translations render such passages in a style suitable for use in public worship. Since a liturgical context demands more formal language, a uniform literary style, often alien to the original text, is imposed across diverse kinds of biblical material. The Scholars Version, in contrast, attempts to reproduce Markan style so that the modern reader will have a reading or listening experience similar to that of the original listeners.

In their quest for fresh language the SV translators persistently sought to avoid traditional biblical terms and expressions—words that have lost their impact through overuse. For example, the first words attributed to Jesus in Mark are translated in the Revised Standard Version as: "The time is fulfilled, and the kingdom of God is at hand; repent and believe in the Gospel" (1:14). Contrast the Scholars Version: "The time is up: God's imperial rule is closing in. Change your ways, and put your trust in the good news!"

The key terms *repent* and *believe* have remained unchanged from the first great English translation of Tyndale in 1526 through the New Revised Standard Version of 1990. In the meantime, these English terms have taken on specific meanings of their own, which have moved them farther and farther away from the sense of the underlying Greek. *Believe* is now used mostly in the mental sense, "accept as true," and only secondarily is it "have confidence in, trust." The second, and not the first, sense is the primary meaning of the Greek verb *pisteuo* and other related words, such as the noun *pistis*, usually translated "faith." But the common understanding of *believe* has overpowered the basic sense of *faith*, so that both have come to signify mental activity: accept a statement as true. As a result, in traditional English versions Jesus' message comes out, "Accept the words I say as true," when Jesus is actually calling on his hearers to put their trust in the good news. And when the distraught father tells Jesus, in traditional language, "I believe, help my unbelief" (9:24), it sounds like he is trying to convince himself to "accept as true" something that is not. Actually, he is exclaiming, "I do trust! Help my lack of trust!" That plaintive cry is something quite different than the frequent, often bitter, debates between Christians over which group fully accepts certain words and phrases as true, when the real issue has been trust and confidence.

Trust is not exactly the same, however, as *confidence*. In healing stories, translating "have confidence" would be appropriate. The person healed does place confidence in the healer. However, the opposite, "lack of confidence," is not at all the same as "lack of trust." The father's plea was not "Help my lack of confidence!" (9:24). That kind of confidence today means self-reliance, the very opposite of trust.

The other traditional key term in Jesus' message, *repent*, is used today primarily to express an attitude, "feel regret for wrongdoing." Its older sense, "show resolve to change" or "desire to turn from sin," is almost completely lacking. However, in Greek the sense of *change* dominates. The verb *metanoeo* used here (1:15), and the noun *metanoia* describing John's baptism (1:4), both suggest "change one's way of thinking" as the basis for turning one's life around. SV captures this in John's call for "a change of heart" (1:4). Later the disciples announce that "people should turn their lives around" (6:12). When Jesus then says, "Change your ways, and put your trust in the good news!" (1:15), this challenge provides the momentum for the rest of the story. Those who trust in the good news are the ones prepared to change their ways. Mark's story is about people who encounter the "good news" and are challenged to turn their lives around.

Some traditional biblical terms, such as *baptize* (Greek *baptizo*), have few good options in English. Sometimes the word means simply "wash" or "bathe" (Mark 7:4). However, that seems too mundane for most uses in the gospels. John's symbolic act at the Jordan River was probably an "immersion," but that does not describe all acts of "baptism." To choose a more specific term would take sides in the long debate over types of ritual washing. The emphasis is on the ritual itself, "baptize," not on the amount of water used or how it is done. Likewise, the object of baptism remains "forgiveness of sin" in SV. *Sin* is still used today to mean "morally wrong," and *forgive* retains its association with moral offenses. The more general terms "wrongdoing" and "pardon" are not adequate substitutes. For example, "Pardon me" is used today mostly as a polite social nicety, no different than "Excuse me." So words like "baptize," "sin" and "forgive" continue to be used in SV, when they still communicate in English what the Greek suggests.

The translators also have avoided traditional idioms such as "lo" and "behold." These quaint terms are no longer part of spoken English. When the gospels use *idou*, derived from the verb "see," this exclamation tells the listener, "pay attention to what follows." SV Mark uses appropriate attention-getting devices: "*Here* is my messenger" (1:2); "*Look*, your mother and your brothers are outside" (3:32); "*Look at us*, we left everything to follow you!" (10:28). Mark makes similar use of the related word *ide*: "*You see* what a long list of charges they bring against you!" (15:4); "*Listen*, he's calling Elijah" (15:35).

Many modern readers unfamiliar with the gospels would naturally hear "Jesus Christ" in Mark's opening line as a proper name: Jesus, a member of the Christ family. To avoid this misunderstanding, the SV translators leave the Greek *christos* as an adjective and render it "the Anointed." Mark's opening, "the good news of Jesus the Anointed," now conveys to the reader that this story tells the good news that it is Jesus who is the Anointed. And Peter's words, "You are the Anointed!" (8:29), are more readily recognized as a high point in the story.

The reader also needs to understand that the name "Peter" begins as a nickname. The SV captures this when *Petros* is first introduced: "And to Simon he gave the nickname Rock" (3:16). From then on it functions as Simon's given name, so it is rendered "Peter," except the final time he is mentioned in the story. After he and the other specially selected disciples have abandoned Jesus (14:50), they are given another chance to become followers. The young messenger in the tomb instructs the women, "Go and tell his disciples, including 'Rock,' he is going ahead of you to Galilee!" (16:7). But before the message gets to Peter, the story suddenly ends: "And they didn't breathe a word of it to anyone" (16:8). By using "Rock" for *Petros* this last time, the SV translators remind the reader that Peter's name began as an affirming nickname. However, Mark's ending now makes "Rock" sound ironical (§3.5).

Effective translators realize that translating is an act of interpretation. They take the meaning of a text as they encounter it in the original language and put it into an equivalent vernacular of another language. The resulting translation provides a new occasion for readers to be in dialogue with the meaning of the text. A translation is successful when it so engages the readers that they feel in direct contact with the text's meaning. On the other hand, a translation that strives to imitate the Greek too carefully is better suited for those who already know Greek! And for those, *The Gospel of Mark* provides the Greek text alongside the translation. The SV translation is designed to function in its more legitimate capacity as a vehicle for giving full expression to Mark's story.

The Judeans

The religious tradition known today as Judaism—the religion practiced by Jews—has a long history, which may be divided into three major periods:

The religion of the first temple (ca. 950–586 B.C.E.)

The religion of the second temple (ca. 520 B.C.E.–70 C.E.)

The religion of rabbis and synagogue (ca. 90 C.E. and continuing)

By convention, scholars refer to the religion of the first temple as Israelite religion. The first temple was constructed in Jerusalem by King Solomon in the mid-tenth century B.C.E. and became the center of Israelite national life. The first temple was destroyed by the Babylonians, who completed their conquest of Judah—the southern kingdom—in 586 B.C.E.

The temple was reconstructed about seventy years later, around 520 B.C.E., under the leadership of Zerubbabel, the local governor commissioned by the Persians. The second temple was renovated and extended by Herod the Great (37 B.C.E.–4 C.E.). It was the second temple in its new splendor that Jesus and his contemporaries visited when they came to Jerusalem.

In determining what to call the religion of the second temple, it is necessary to recall some important earlier history.

The people of Israel had become a nation by the tenth century under Kings Saul, David, and Solomon. When Solomon died, the nation divided into a northern and a southern kingdom; the northern kingdom alone was known as Israel, the southern as Judah. The northern kingdom ceased to exist when its capital, Samaria, fell after a long siege by the Assyrians in 721 B.C.E. Citizens of the northern kingdom were deported by the score, and the northern monarchy never recovered.

The restoration that began around 520 B.C.E. was focused in Judah and Jerusalem. The central part of the northern kingdom, meanwhile, had become peopled by Samaritans, who were of mixed ethnic background, and who worshiped in their temple on Mt. Gerizim. They preserved their own version of the Torah (the five books ascribed to Moses) and claimed the legacy of northern Israelite religion as their own. The southern legacy passed exclusively into the hands of citizens of Judah, who came to be known as Judeans and their territory as Judea.

The religion of the second temple should be termed Judean religion, just as the people who practiced this religion (even outside Judea) were known as Judeans. The religion of the second temple centered in the sacrificial cult connected with Jerusalem and dominated by a priestly caste. That would make it possible to refer to the religion of the third major period as Judaism, the religion practiced by Jews, whose religious leaders are rabbis and whose worship is centered in the synagogue rather than the temple. In current terminology, scholars find it necessary to add the qualifier "rabbinic" to Judaism to distinguish the third period from the religion of the second temple.

The Scholars Version, accordingly, has adopted the following terminology for the three phases of the religion practiced by the Israelites, the Judeans, and the Jews:

(1) Israel, Israelites and Israelite religion: first temple
(2) Judea, Judeans and Judean religion: second temple
(3) Jews and Judaism: religion of the rabbis, talmud, and synagogue

In the Scholars Version, the placard placed on the cross reads: "King of the Judeans," and those stereotyped opponents of Jesus in the Gospel of John are regularly "Judeans." This terminological adjustment has been a long time in coming. The failure to observe crucial transitions in the history of Judaism has contributed to the tragic history of antisemitism among Christians, which the new terminology will help put to an end. Further, it will set the historical record straight.

5.2 The SV Style

The Scholars Version seeks to use vernacular American English in a style that sounds like the way we actually use it. When SV translates a text that is highly oral in style, it uses the natural contractions of spoken English, rather than the formality of a written style:

> When they had found him they say to him, "They're all looking for you."
> But he replies: "Let's go somewhere else, to the neighboring villages, so I can speak there too, since that's what I came for." (1:37–38)

The SV translation also uses inclusive language wherever the text warrants it. Traditional translations make extensive use of "man" and "men" for the general Greek word *anthropos* ("person"). Even if "man" was once used generically, for many people it no longer functions that way, and must be replaced by other words that are inclusive. In SV *anthropos* is translated in ways that fit its various contexts: "Become my followers and I'll have you fishing for *people*" (1:17). "It's not what goes into a *person* from the outside that can defile" (7:15). "For *mortals* it's impossible, but not for God" (10:27).

The most troublesome lack of inclusive language in English is its dependence on the personal pronoun "he." The translator is confronted with this issue especially in Greek constructions of "whoever," "the one who," "anyone who," "if anyone," followed by a personal pronoun. This well-known passage from the Revised Standard Version is a typical example:

> If any man would come after me, let him deny himself and take up his cross and follow me. For whoever would save his life will lose it; and whoever loses his life for my sake and the gospel's will save it. For what does it profit a man, to gain the whole world and forfeit his life? For what can a man give in return for his life? (8:34–37)

Among the natural ways to avoid these problems are to use plural constructions or ones that do not require gendered pronouns:

> Those who want to come after me should deny themselves, pick up their cross, and follow me! Remember, those who try to save their own life are going to lose it, but those who lose their life for the sake of the good news are going to save it. After all, what good does it do a person to acquire the whole world and pay for it with life? Or, what would a person give in exchange for life?

This passage also illustrates the inadequacy of the traditional "let him" to translate third person commands. Not only is the masculine pronoun troublesome in a truly inclusive context, but "let" does not well convey the sense of giving a command. In SV these constructions have been rendered with an auxiliary verb to express the attitude of obligation or necessity: "Anyone here with two good ears had better listen!" (4:9). The traditional translation introduces two pronouns where Greek has none: "He who has ears to hear, let him hear."

Another stylistic feature of SV is to avoid the repetition of the same ordinary verbs that tend to be used over and over again. English utilizes a more extensive vocabulary in selecting verbs that are specially appropriate to the context. In traditional translations, Jesus "goes" somewhere, or "sees" someone, or "says" something, and then soon does it again. When calling the first disciples Jesus "saw Simon and Andrew" and then a little further "he saw James." (1:16, 19 RSV). The SV translators chose the sequence: "he saw Simon and Andrew" and then "he caught sight of James."

In a narrative sequence variation in the choice of verbs can make the story come to life again:

Revised Standard Version	Scholars Version	
He asked his disciples	He started questioning	
And they told him	In response they said	
And he asked them	But he continued to press them	
Peter answered	Peter responds	(Mark 8:27–29)

And Peter took him,	And Peter took him aside	
and began to rebuke him.	and began to lecture him.	
But turning	But he turned,	
and seeing his disciples,	noticed his disciples,	
he rebuked Peter,	and reprimanded Peter	
and said,	verbally:	(8:32–33)

The last sequence also illustrates the way traditional translations imitate the Greek style of using participles ("-ing" words in English) preceding the main verb in the sentence: "turning and seeing his disciples, he rebuked Peter." The SV translators prefer the more natural style of verbs in sequence: "he turned, noticed his disciples, and reprimanded Peter."

The sayings of Jesus that challenge translators the most include the ones that seem to present Jesus making predictions: "Truly, I say to you, this generation will not pass away before all these things take place" (13:30 RSV). The "truly (*amen*) I say to you" is a formula indicating that the speaker is preparing to utter an oath. SV uses expressions in English that make more explicit the quality of oath in this sayings: "I swear to you" and "So help me!" For a more formal oath, the introduction is rendered: "I swear to God." Such an oath is found once in Mark: "I swear to God, no sign will be given this generation" (8:12). The actual Greek construction involves part of a conditional sentence, similar to saying in English: "So help me God, if any sign will be given this generation!"

A number of the sayings introduced by "I swear to you" do not actually use a verb in the future tense at all. In "this generation will not pass away," the "will not" is not future in Greek. The verb form is rather subjunctive, with two negatives preceding. The sense of a subjunctive is usually "should" or "would" in an expression of conviction about what someone wants to, or expects to, happen. While this relates to future events, the emphasis is on the speaker's strength of conviction, not on the predictive nature of what is said. The SV translators capture this difference by using "certainly won't" for the subjunctive with the double negative, and "will" for the actual future: "I swear to you, this generation certainly won't pass into oblivion before all these things take place! The earth will pass into oblivion and so will the sky, but my words will never be obliterated!" (13:30–31). This style of speech is very reminiscent of the Greek translation (LXX) of the Old Testament prophets. Thus the text of Isa 6:9, which influenced Mark 4:12, could be translated "They may look with eyes wide open, but they certainly won't see, and they may listen with attentive ears, but they certainly won't understand."

6. SV Mark

The SV style lends itself especially well to capturing the orality of Mark. Dialogue is presented in a vernacular style that includes contractions and idioms of spoken English (§5.2). The narrative emphasizes the action in the story by frequently placing verbs one after another. Additional Markan features include: sequences of simple sentences connected by *and*, interruptions of the narrative for explanatory comments, and a large number of verbs in the present and imperfect tenses.

6.1 Sentence Connectors

Although the Greek language has a relatively large number of conjunctions suitable both for compound sentences and connections between sentences, Mark's style depends on the frequent use of *and* (*kai*) between sentences (§3.1). In SV Mark the translators have handled *kai* in a variety of ways. The effect this has on the flow of the narrative can be seen by comparing the opening of the following consecutive verses (Mark 1:16–24) in the RSV with SV:

RSV	**SV**
And passing along	As he was walking along
And Jesus said	and Jesus said
And immediately	And right then and there
And going on	When he had gone
And immediately	Right then and there
And they went	Then they come
And they were astonished	They were astonished
And immediately	Now right there
And he cried out	which shouted

Sometimes *and* is quite appropriate, but more often another connecting word is better suited, such as *now, then,* and elsewhere, *but, so,* or *yet.* In some instances it is best not to impose a conjunction in English at all, almost like the "ah" between sentences often heard in spoken English, but a style that would not be translated.

Mixed in with Mark's rather fast-paced narrative are a number of asides to the reader for explanatory comments (§3.6). One device in Greek that indicates these is the conjunction *gar* ("for"). The SV translators use several devices to help the reader recognize these narrative inserts. When Jesus sees Simon and Andrew casting their nets, Mark explains "—since they were fishermen—" (1:16). When Jesus has the disciples get a boat ready for him to avoid a mob, Mark adds "(After all, he healed so many, that all who had diseases were pushing forward to touch him.)" (3:10). When he then goes home and his relatives come to get him, another aside tells the reader: "(you see, they thought he was out of his mind)" (3:21). The aside is usually indicated both by punctuation, parentheses or dashes, and by the introductory words: *since, after all, you see,* and elsewhere, *remember, in fact,* and *incidentally.*

6.2 Verbs

A characteristic feature of Mark's narrative is the frequent use of present tense verbs for telling past events. SV has retained this character of Mark by preserving the present tense as an effective device for making the past activity of the narrative more immediate to the reader. Mark prefers this style especially in the opening of individual units: "Then they come to Capernaum" (1:21); "Then a leper comes up to him" (1:40); "They come to Bethsaida, and they bring him a blind person, and plead with him to touch him" (8:22). Most translations rely on proper literary style and render these as past tenses, as do Matthew and Luke. This obliterates one of the obvious oral features of Mark, even though that style is similar to the spoken idiom of American English.

When Mark's narrative is told in past time, it makes extensive use of verbs in the imperfect tense, rather than the simple past. In English this distinction is traditionally made by using constructions such as "was telling" for the imperfect, rather than "told." The imperfect form is also used to indicate habitual past activity, "used to tell."

More recent study of narrative technique suggests that one of the common functions of the imperfect in a narrative is to suggest that the scene being described happened more than once, even frequently or regularly, but the narrative is providing only one typical, or composite, example. The context and the nature of the activity may imply, "this is the first such instance," or "this is one of many such instances," or "this continued for some time," or "something like this happened on other occasions," or even "this (almost) always happened on these kinds of occasions." In SV these different effects are accomplished through a variety of translation techniques.

The choice of vocabulary can suggest the on-going nature of the activity. In the opening narrative scene describing the response to John, crowds from everywhere "streamed out to him and were baptized" (1:5). And during Jesus' forty days in the wilderness, "the heavenly messengers looked after him" (1:13). Both "streamed out" and "looked after" are used to translate imperfect tense verbs, which suggest activities that took place over a period of time, or were not limited to a single event.

More often, verbs in the imperfect are translated to indicate that the scene is something that "would" typically happen: "they were astonished at his teaching, since he *would* teach them on his own authority" (1:22). This style is utilized especially in summary passages:

> In the evening, at sundown, they *would* bring all the sick and demon-possessed to him. And the whole city *would* crowd around the door. On such occasions he cured many people afflicted with various diseases and drove out many demons. He *would* never let the demons speak, because they realized who he was. (1:32–34)

Mark's introductions to Jesus' sayings have this same quality: "He *would* then teach them many things in parables" (4:2); "those close to him . . .

would ask him about the parables. And he *would* say" (4:10–11, 21, 26, 30); or "he *went on to* say" (4:24).

The imperfect can also suggest that what is being described became typical from then on. When Jesus first went to the synagogue in Capernaum he "*started* teaching" (1:21). And then he "stole away to an isolated place, where he *started* praying" (1:35) When Mark wants to emphasize that the scene is clearly the beginning of a type of activity, the verb *archomai* ("begin to" or "start") is used: "After he went out he *started* telling everyone" (1:45). However, sometimes this construction seems parallel to the imperfect. Mark introduces the parable section with this verb, "Once again he *started* to teach beside the sea. An enormous crowd gathers...." (4:1). This is quite reminiscent of the imperfect in 2:13: "Again he went out by the sea. And, with a huge crowd gathered around him, he *started* teaching." The construction in 4:1 with *archomai* is also parallel to the imperfect in 4:2, already noted, "he *would* teach." Thus, the use of *archomai*, rather than being redundant, as has often been said, reinforces the effect of the imperfect as an important feature of Mark's narrative style. SV is distinctive in capturing this aspect of Mark in its treatment of the imperfect verbs.

6.3 God's Basileia (domain, rule, government)

Among the phrases most crucial to Mark's narrative, none is more central, yet hotly debated, than Jesus' use of "the *basileia* of God." This expression encompasses the activity of God as sovereign ruler, the sphere over which God rules, and the nature of the "rulership" that characterizes all of that. It involves various aspects of "empire," "sovereignty," "rule," "reign," "domain," and "kingship."

There was already by the first century a long history of Jewish discussion about the relationship of God's ultimate authority to human structures of government. Moreover, Mark's audience might well have heard this term in the context of the on-going discussion in the hellenistic world about the nature of true "emperorship." (For example, in the early second century C.E. Dio Chrysostom wrote four treatises on *basileia*, which had been a popular philosophical topic for several centuries.) Thus by the time of Mark's gospel "the *basileia* of God" was a term that had come to represent a whole set of expectations, which were not the same for everyone who used the term.

The challenge for translators is to find a way to capture these various dimensions in a set of related expressions in English capable of functioning at several levels. The use of "kingdom" for *basileia* in the gospels goes back to the first English translation of Wycliffe in the fourteenth century. This spatial image was then powerfully reinforced in the Authorized Version under King James. Some modern translations have tried to recover the more dynamic, non-spatial, dimensions of *basileia* by using "rule" or "reign." The SV translators recognize that *basileia* must be translated differently according to its narrative context. When the image is a realm to enter or belong to, "God's domain" is used: "It is better for you to enter God's domain one-eyed than to be thrown into Gehenna with both eyes" (9:47); "You are far from God's domain" (12:34). When the focus is the exercise of God's sovereignty, "God's imperial rule" was chosen: "God's imperial rule is closing in" (1:15); "Some of those standing here won't ever taste death before they see God's imperial rule set in with power!" (9:1). When *basileia* is not related to "God," other translations are "government" (3:24), "kingdom" (11:10), and "empire" (13:8).

6.4 Titles for Jesus

Equally crucial for understanding Mark's narrative is Jesus' use of the Greek phrase *ho huios tou anthropou*, traditionally translated "the Son of Man." At one level the phrase symbolizes humankind, so it could be simply "person" or collective "humanity," or a way of referring to oneself. It could also be a title, "The Human One," or "Son of Adam," which would reflect the Hebrew, "ben Adam." The latter understanding seems especially appropriate, though not necessarily as an actual title, for such gospel contexts as the parallel use with *anthropos* by itself: "The sabbath day was created for Adam and Eve, not Adam and Eve for the sabbath day. So, the son of Adam lords it even over the sabbath day" (2:28). "Adam" and "son of Adam" make clear the Jewish origin of the imagery: "What are human beings (*adam*) that you are mindful of them, mortals (*ben adam*) that you care for them" (Ps 8:4 NRSV). So, also, Ezekiel is regularly addressed as *ben adam* ("O son of man" RSV; "O Mortal" NRSV).

The same expression is used for the description of a human-like figure in Dan 7:13–14:

> I saw one like a human being coming with the clouds of heaven. And he came to the Ancient One and was presented before him. To him was given dominion and glory and kingship, that all peoples, nations, and languages should serve him. His dominion is an everlasting dominion that shall not pass away, and his kingship is one that shall never be destroyed.

In the Greek translation (LXX) the "human being" is *huios anthropou* ("a son of man") and "kingship" is *basileia*. This image from Daniel has surely influenced Mark: "they will see the son of Adam coming on the clouds with great power and splendor" (13:26); "you will see the son of Adam sitting at the right hand of Power and coming with the clouds of the sky!" (14:62). The human figure in Daniel originally represented "the holy ones of the Most High" (Dan 7:18), martyrs who would receive an everlasting *basileia*.

By the time this image was used by Jesus, and Mark, it had come to symbolize an individual figure who would bring the hoped-for restoration of God's imperial rule on earth.

The challenge facing any translation is to convey this powerful image with an English expression that also relates to its fundamental sense as a "human figure." No one term is equally well suited for both tasks, but the SV translators have chosen a distinctive phrase, "son of Adam," that reflects its biblical roots in the creation story, and at the same time can function more narrowly to symbolize the figure described by Daniel, and used by Mark.

The use of "Lord" (*kyrios*) in relation to Jesus is another term that functions at several levels. *Kyrios* by itself is the way Greek translators (LXX) rendered the Hebrew *adonai*, the substitute for the unspeakable name of God, *Yahweh*. Most translations render this as "the LORD." Mark begins by quoting such a passage: "A voice of someone shouting in the wilderness: 'Make ready the way of the Lord, make his paths straight'" (1:3 from Isa 40:3). The image in Isaiah is of Yahweh, the God of the exodus, again leading the chosen people through the wilderness to the promised land. When Mark presents John as the preparer of the way for Jesus, this suggests Jesus is, or will become, "the way of the Lord."

Alongside this very specialized use, Mark also has the more general Greek use of "lord" as referring to someone with social position, a "master" or "patron." The healing story in the Greek Decapolis is an appropriate setting for this usage: "Go home to your people and tell them what your *patron* has done for you—how he has shown mercy to you" (5:19). Mark again makes the reader think of Jesus as "patron" or "lord" (*kyrios*), when he narrates in the next verse that the man started proclaiming "what *Jesus* had done for him."

Mark later presents Jesus as playing these two usages against one another to challenge the traditional interpretation that the Anointed must be a descendant of David. Jesus' rejoinder is to quote the opening of Psalm 110 as David himself speaking: "The Lord [Yahweh] said to my lord [master or patron], 'Sit here at my right.'" Jesus then observes, "David himself calls him [the Anointed] 'lord,' so how can he be his son?" (Mark 12:35–37). The reader is clearly expected to understand the significance of the two different meanings of "Lord/lord" in Greek.

The ambiguity of these two uses is most evident when the polite address, "Sir," is used. The Greek *kyrie*, vocative form of *kyrios*, is the respectful way to address one's "master" or "patron," or anyone of greater social status. When the pagan woman calls Jesus *kyrie* (7:28), the reader hears it ironically. She is only showing respect, by saying "Sir." However, the narrative began by suggesting to the reader that "the way of the Lord" (1:3) was being prepared for Jesus, and then Jesus had acted as "lord" (*kyrios*) of the sabbath day (2:28), and finally, the pagan man had reported what Jesus had done for him as his "patron" (*kyrios*, 5:19–20). To hear Jesus now called *kyrie* brings to the reader's ear echoes of the earlier uses of "Lord/lord."

6.5 Parables and Riddles

Mark's Jesus is a teller of "parables" (§2.3), but they often seem to function more as "riddles" (§4.4). The SV translators make this distinction because the Greek *parabole* is broader than the English "parable." The basic sense of "parable" as "comparison" or "analogy" derives from Greek rhetoric and is used at least once by Mark: "Take a cue from the fig tree" (13:28). More often the term refers to a kind of simple story told to make a point about something else, for which "parable" is still an appropriate translation: "He would teach them many things in parables" (4:2). However, in some Markan contexts a *parabole* is more like a Jewish proverb, which is closer to a *riddle*: "I will incline my ear to a proverb [*parabole*]; I will solve my riddle to the music of the harp" (Ps 49:4). Here a "riddle" is something with hidden meaning that needs explaining. Mark uses it also in this sense: "He would speak to them in riddles," followed by a puzzling saying about Satan (3:23). And after an enigmatic saying about what defiles a person, "his disciples started questioning him about the riddle" (7:17).

If "parables" can be "riddles" for Mark, then the reader needs to hear ambiguity in this saying of Jesus: "You have been given the secret of God's imperial rule; but those outside have everything presented in parables, so that 'They may look with eyes wide open but never quite see, and may listen with ears attuned but never quite understand, otherwise they might turn around and find forgiveness'!" (4:11–12). That this "parable" is indeed a puzzle to be solved is confirmed when Jesus says to the disciples, "You don't get this parable, so how are you going to understand other parables?" (4:13).

7. Text and Translation Notes

Both the Greek text and SV translation of Mark are accompanied by a set of notes designed to help the reader more fully explore the meaning of Mark's narrative. The notes both remind the reader of pertinent discussions in the introduction and add other information related to particular items in the story or to literary traits of Mark's narrative style.

Some of the notes call attention to distinctive features of the SV translation. The translators have carefully chosen individual words, expressions, and grammatical devices to convey to the reader specific aspects of the Greek text, without mimicking the Greek itself. Only a small selection of items receive comment, including some where traditional translations have been particularly misleading. Important examples of these have already been discussed (§§5–6).

Translation notes are also provided for some items that would have been familiar to the original listeners and readers, but are likely to be obscure to American readers. One such category is cultural or historical matters: the custom of "reclining at table" (2:15), and who the "Herodians" might have been (3:6). Likewise, geographical designations have been explained. Mark also presupposes an audience that is quite familiar with scripture. Occasionally there is an explicit mention: "what David did" (2:25); but more common are the many allusions to Old Testament stories in the words and images of Mark's narrative. The more important of these have been called to the reader's attention.

Along with the translation notes there are also notes on the Greek text. Sometimes the Greek is ambiguous and could be read more than one way: for example, whether 1:1 is a title or the beginning of a sentence. Since ancient Greek was written without punctuation marks, it is not always clear where every sentence ends or whether some sentences are statements, questions or commands (1:27). There are also uncertainties about the Greek text itself. The notes call attention to the more significant and interesting differences among the major early Greek manuscripts of Mark. The following discussion of the Greek text provides a brief introduction to the nature of the manuscript evidence.

8. The Greek Text

The Scholars Version translation is based on a new edition of the Greek text that represents a scholarly "first edition" of Mark's gospel. Such a text has to be reconstructed from the surviving manuscripts of the NT.

8.1 Manuscripts (MSS)

The earliest complete MSS are those on parchment from the fourth and fifth centuries, copies made after the last official persecution against Christianity ended early in the fourth century. The only earlier MSS are on papyrus and fewer than 100 of those have survived, often in very fragmentary condition.

The earliest papyrus to contain portions of all the gospels is designated 𝔓45, from the third century. The fragments from Mark include parts of chapters 4–9 and 11–12. The next oldest fragment of Mark is 𝔓88, from the fourth century, the only papyrus manuscript containing only Mark. The one surviving sheet is two joined pages with most of chapter 2 (see photos). Since these two papyri provide only a glimpse of the early text of Mark, to reconstruct the complete text it is necessary to rely on four or five well-preserved fourth and fifth-century parchment manuscripts

Consideration also is given to some later copies that appear to preserve older readings. Since the date of a manuscript does not tells us how carefully it was prepared nor about the quality of the copy from which it was made, some of the later MSS can still be valuable witnesses to the legacy of the original Greek text.

In addition to the Greek MSS themselves, the early versions of the New Testament in other ancient languages, such as Old Latin, Syriac, Coptic, and Armenian, are also important witnesses to the early tradition of the text. Likewise, quotations of the gospel in the writings of early church authors provide valuable secondary evidence for the Greek texts then in use.

8.2 Variant Readings

After identifying which of the distinctive readings in each of the early MSS might be authentic, the major challenge in the process of reconstructing the text is to separate out those readings that most likely were the result of scribes (copiers) making inadvertent errors, "correcting" perceived errors in the text, "improving" the style of the text, "harmonizing" it to the more familiar texts of Matthew and Luke, or keeping it up-to-date with the theological developments of the Christian community. Occasionally, the evidence is so divided that a reasonable choice cannot be made, so the uncertain text is printed in brackets, for example [and sisters] in Mark 3:32.

Both the beginning and ending of Mark provide uncertainties that must be faced by editors of the Greek text. Mark 1:1 in SV reads "The good news of Jesus the Anointed begins," whereas most MSS add "son of God" after "Anointed." SV follows the shorter text preserved in two of the early parchment MSS and cited in some of the early Christian authors. As a title "Son of God" could have been added in later copies when Christians used that term more frequently as an expression of their christology. An equally important consideration is what fits the style and structure of Mark, and "Son of God" is not the most prominent title in Mark's story.

The ending of Mark is especially distinctive. The two earliest parchment MSS end abruptly at 16:8 with a conjunction in Greek, as do some copies in Latin, Syriac, Armenian, and Georgian, as well as quotations in some of the early Christian authors. Further evidence that this is the original ending is seen in the several combinations of longer endings (mostly featuring 16:9–20) found in the other MSS and early versions. While previous scholars speculated that the last page of Mark may have been lost accidentally, recent studies on the narrative style and structure of Mark have argued that 16:8 is a very fitting ending for Mark's kind of story. (Five other verses found in some MSS have also been judged to be later additions, since they are identical to material elsewhere in Mark or in Matthew or Luke: 7:16; 9:44, 46; 11:26; 15:28.)

SV in Mark 1:41 reads "Jesus was indignant," which is found in one of the early parchment MSS, in some copies of the Old Latin, and in an early Christian commentary. In contrast, the rest of the surviving tradition reads

clearly a softening of the more striking portrayal found in Mark. While these are the more interesting manuscript variations in Mark, the notes also cite other instances where the text remains quite uncertain.

9. To The Reader

This volume has been designed to provide the reader with direct access to the linguistic world of Mark's gospel. The introduction discusses the style in which the gospel is written and the major motifs that give it shape. A newly edited Greek text presents a scholarly reconstruction of the "first edition" of the gospel. The translation is from the new Scholars Version (SV).

The introduction often takes the reader inside the translation process to explore the considerations that make both Mark and SV distinct. In only a few instances, however, have complete lists of examples been given. The general aim of the introduction is rather to be suggestive of what the reader can look for in Mark.

Many current insights into understanding Mark have come from attention to the narrative world of Mark's story. Any reader who enters that narrative world can appreciate its author as a story teller who captures the vividness of the story's oral roots in a distinctive narrative style. The reader will be able to add to the observations provided here about the style and motifs of Mark, and will want to challenge some of them.

The introduction was written for a general audience and, therefore, without footnotes. However, it is hoped that the brief summaries of the scholarly discussion on these topics will stimulate the reader's interest for more detailed presentations. A "Bookshelf of Basic Works" is provided in the back to indicate both the sources for many of the comments in the introduction and notes, as well as some of the best recent scholarship on Mark, especially that written for a wider audience.

𝔓⁸⁸, one of the oldest fragments of the Gospel of Mark, contains Mark 2:2–26 and dates to the fourth century c.e. It came to light only recently in the library of the Catholic University, Milan, Italy. Where and when it

The
Gospel
of Mark

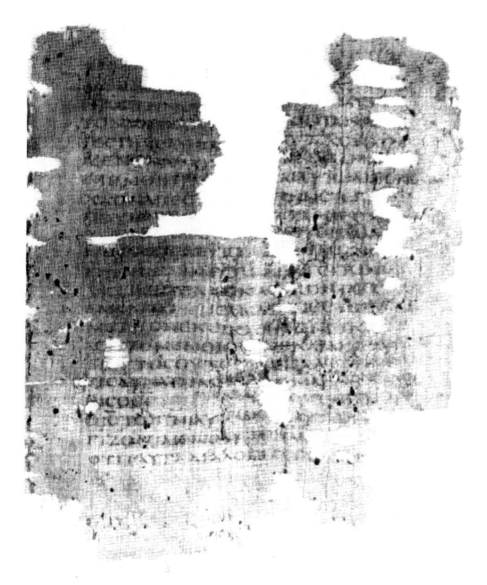

was first discovered are unknown. Shown here are the two outside
pages containing Mark 2:20–26 (facing) and Mark 2:2–8 (above). Photograph courtesy of Catholic University of the Sacred Heart, Milan, Italy.

A voice in
the wilderness

1 Ἀρχὴ τοῦ εὐαγγελίου Ἰησοῦ Χριστοῦ, ² καθὼς γέγραπται
ἐν τῷ Ἡσαΐᾳ τῷ προφήτῃ,

Ἰδοὺ ἀποστέλλω τὸν ἄγγελόν μου
πρὸ προσώπου σου,
ὃς κατασκευάσει τὴν ὁδόν σου·
³ φωνὴ βοῶντος ἐν τῇ ἐρήμῳ,
Ἑτοιμάσατε τὴν ὁδὸν κυρίου,
εὐθείας ποιεῖτε τὰς τρίβους αὐτοῦ.

⁴ ἐγένετο Ἰωάννης ὁ βαπτίζων ἐν τῇ ἐρήμῳ κηρύσσων
βάπτισμα μετανοίας εἰς ἄφεσιν ἁμαρτιῶν. ⁵ καὶ ἐξεπορεύετο
πρὸς αὐτὸν πᾶσα ἡ Ἰουδαία χώρα καὶ οἱ Ἱεροσολυμῖται πάντες,

---

1. *Anointed:* many MSS add *the son of God* (§8.2).   **2.** *Isaiah the prophet:*
some MSS read *the prophets.*   **4.** Some MSS begin, *John was baptizing in*
the wilderness and calling.

• **1:1–13.** Mark introduces his gospel about Jesus by presenting John as the forerunner who introduces Jesus to Mark's readers. Stories of John and Jesus are briefly interwoven until the time of John ends and the time of Jesus begins (v. 14).

• **1:1.** Verse 1 is read in continuity with v. 2, rather than separately as a title for the whole book (or a heading for the opening section): *Here begins the good news of Jesus the Anointed. The good news:* the meaning of *euangelion* as used by early Christians. Mark was apparently the first Christian author to use it to refer to a story about Jesus. The translation "gospel" is more appropriate for its later use when it became the standard term for the Christian message and for narrative accounts of the life, death, and resurrection of Jesus.

The Anointed: makes clear that *christos* is here a title, not a family name. It properly translates the meaning of the Greek adjective, which in the Greek Old Testament (LXX) translated the Hebrew adjective *mashiach*, which means *anointed* (1 Sam 2:10, 35; Pss 2:2; 20:6; Dan 9:25). Although the Hebrew term became the title *Messiah* for Judean Christians (as in John 1:41; 4:25), it would have been among Christians from pagan backgrounds that *Christ* became used as a proper name, unassociated with its root meaning. Most surviving copies of Mark add the additional title *Son of God*, which is missing in several important MSS and in quotations cited in a

number of early Christian authors. Since this became a popular Christian confession of faith attached to *Christ* (such as in John 11:27; 20:31), it was naturally added here when Mark 1:1 was treated as a title for the book.

Anointing was the common symbolic act in ancient Israel for designating sacred places (the "tabernacle" Exod 40:9), and for conferring authority on individuals. The priests traced their authority to the "ordination" of Aaron: "take the anointing oil and pour it on his head" (Exod 29:7). This ritual was especially associated with the ancient monarchy, which was initiated when "Samuel took a vial of oil and poured it on [Saul's] head" (1 Sam 10:1), conferring the authority and protection of Yahweh. The prototype for this act became king David, who was first designated to be the next king of Israel, and given "the spirit of the Lord," when Samuel anointed him while Saul was still king (1 Sam 16:13). David only became king (ca. 1000 B.C.E.) after the people anointed him (2 Sam 2:4; 5:3). When the line of Davidic kings ended with the exile to Babylon (587 B.C.E.), prophets speculated about another ruler "like David" coming to deliver the Israelites from foreign domination, but the Davidic monarchy was never restored. During Roman control in the first century B.C.E. and first century C.E., a number of popular "messiah" figures arose who sought to restore Judean independence. Galilee was

1 The good news of Jesus the Anointed begins ²with something Isaiah the prophet wrote:

A voice in the wilderness

Here is my messenger,
whom I send on ahead of you
to prepare your way!
³A voice of someone shouting in the wilderness:
'Make ready the way of the Lord,
make his paths straight.'

⁴So, John the Baptizer appeared in the wilderness calling for baptism and a change of heart that lead to forgiveness of sins. ⁵And everyone from the Judean countryside and all the resi-

---

particularly noted as a place for such "messianic pretenders," especially after the death of Herod the Great in 4 B.C.E., about the time Jesus was born.

- **1:2–3.** Only v. 3 actually quotes Isaiah. The text, Isa 40:3, is from the opening section of the secondary portion of Isaiah (chs. 40–55), derived from an unknown exilic prophet (587–538 B.C.E.), who was looking forward to returning to Jerusalem. Verse 2 combines Exod 23:20 ("I am going to send a messenger ahead of you") with Mal 3:1 ("I am sending my messenger to prepare the way for me). Verses 2 and 3 are tied together by the common device of a catch-word, here *the way*, an important biblical journey motif, which Mark develops further as Jesus makes his way to Jerusalem (discussed in §4.1). Compilations of such biblical texts were probably circulating among early Christians as evidence of how to interpret Jesus as the Anointed (for the use of scripture as "testimonies" see §2.1).

- **1:3–4.** *The wilderness*: (Greek *eremos*) builds on the exodus image of the uninhabited barren plains of the Sinai peninsula where the ancient Israelites spent a generation in transition between deliverance from bondage in Egypt and arrival in the promised land of Canaan. It is nostalgically remembered as the locale of the mountain where the covenant relationship was formed with Yahweh, as well as where the people rebelled and tempted Yahweh (Ps 95:8–9; the stories are narrated in Numbers 11; 14). Thus it also symbolized their need to turn ("change their ways") back to trusting Yahweh for deliverance. Isaiah 40 (Mark 1:3) views the exile as preparation for a new

exodus, including another wilderness experience leading to divine deliverance. In later periods "the wilderness" was a place for protest groups, such as those who withdrew to the barren countryside near the Dead Sea to found the community at Qumran, and revolutionaries and bandits who plotted conspiracies against the Roman army stationed in Judea. Mark now associates this tradition with the barren hill country along the Jordan valley where John is leading a renewal movement (for Mark's use of symbolic geography see §4.2).

- **1:4.** *The baptizer*: Mark uses the noun *baptist* elsewhere (6:25; 8:28), but here the verb form is used. *Baptism and a change of heart*: the logical relationship between these two terms, traditionally rendered by *of*, is expressed here by *and*, in the sense "together with." It cannot be discerned from the Greek whether baptism "represents" or "confirms" or "requires" a change of heart. *A change of heart*: the Greek (and the equivalent Hebrew) inherently suggests a complete change of direction, in a biblical context, "back to Yahweh," which the traditional *repent* no longer conveys (for the senses of the Greek term and possible translations see §5.1). *That lead to*: or *that result in*. *Forgiveness of sins*: sin was traditionally thought of as rebellion against God, and sins were violations of God's will, as expressed in the Mosaic law. In response to the acknowledgement of sin (v. 5), God released the sinner from the burden of past sins ("I said, 'I will confess my transgressions to the Lord,' and you forgave the guilt of my sin," Ps 32:5). John's preaching is presented elsewhere as demanding con-

καὶ ἐβαπτίζοντο ὑπ' αὐτοῦ ἐν τῷ Ἰορδάνῃ ποταμῷ ἐξομολογούμενοι τὰς ἁμαρτίας αὐτῶν. ⁶ καὶ ἦν ὁ Ἰωάννης ἐνδεδυμένος τρίχας καμήλου [καὶ ζώνην δερματίνην περὶ τὴν ὀσφὺν αὐτοῦ], καὶ ἐσθίων ἀκρίδας καὶ μέλι ἄγριον. ⁷ καὶ ἐκήρυσσεν λέγων,

Ἔρχεται ὁ ἰσχυρότερός μου ὀπίσω μου, οὗ οὐκ εἰμὶ ἱκανὸς κύψας λῦσαι τὸν ἱμάντα τῶν ὑποδημάτων αὐτοῦ· ⁸ ἐγὼ ἐβάπτισα ὑμᾶς ὕδατι, αὐτὸς δὲ βαπτίσει ὑμᾶς ἐν πνεύματι ἁγίῳ.

⁹ Καὶ ἐγένετο ἐν ἐκείναις ταῖς ἡμέραις ἦλθεν Ἰησοῦς ἀπὸ Ναζαρὲτ τῆς Γαλιλαίας καὶ ἐβαπτίσθη εἰς τὸν Ἰορδάνην ὑπὸ Ἰωάννου. ¹⁰ καὶ εὐθὺς ἀναβαίνων ἐκ τοῦ ὕδατος εἶδεν σχιζομένους τοὺς οὐρανοὺς καὶ τὸ πνεῦμα ὡς περιστερὰν καταβαῖνον εἰς αὐτόν· ¹¹ καὶ φωνὴ ἐγένετο ἐκ τῶν οὐρανῶν, Σὺ εἶ ὁ υἱός μου ὁ ἀγαπητός, ἐν σοὶ εὐδόκησα.

¹² Καὶ εὐθὺς τὸ πνεῦμα αὐτὸν ἐκβάλλει εἰς τὴν ἔρημον. ¹³ καὶ ἦν ἐν τῇ ἐρήμῳ τεσσαράκοντα ἡμέρας πειραζόμενος ὑπὸ τοῦ Σατανᾶ, καὶ ἦν μετὰ τῶν θηρίων, καὶ οἱ ἄγγελοι διηκόνουν αὐτῷ.

---

6. The words in brackets are omitted in some MSS.   **11.** Some MSS begin without any verb; others read *A voice from the skies was heard.*   **13.** *Forty days:* some MSS add *and forty nights*, as found in Matt 4:2, similar to Moses in Exod 34:28.

---

duct "fit for a change of heart" (Matt 3:8; Luke 3:8).

- **1:5.** *The Jordan river:* John's activity is traditionally located at a site six miles north of the Dead Sea, northeast of Jericho.
- **1:6.** The words in brackets are borrowed from the description of Elijah (2 Kgs 1:8), who is associated with the coming judgment of the "day of the Lord" (Mal 4:5). The scribal addition, which harmonizes Mark with Matt 3:4, makes it clear that John is being depicted as an Elijah figure, a fitting predecessor for a messiah.
- **1:7.** *Someone . . . will succeed me:* in the double sense of both "to come next" and "to replace." In Mark this completes the promise that a messenger is being sent *ahead of you* (v. 2). To *untie* and remove someone's sandals is a function slaves perform for their masters.
- **1:8.** Jesus does not actually baptize anyone in this gospel. Only John 3:22 and 4:1 suggest that Jesus continued the practice of John's water baptism, but then John 4:2 immediately withdraws the suggestion. Baptism "with holy spirit," instead of "with water," is elsewhere called baptism "with

holy spirit *and fire*" (Matt 3:11; Luke 3:16). Fire was a common image for the coming judgment ("like a refiner's fire," Mal 3:2, that "shall burn them up" like stubble, Mal 4:1). Then the chaff will be separated from the grain and will be burned (Matt 3:12; Luke 3:17). Spirit (= breath) was sometimes associated with the fire of judgment (Isa 30:27–28). However, baptized "with holy spirit," apart from "fire," is more likely used by Mark as a positive image. In the Christian understanding of baptism (Acts 1:5; 2:38), the holy spirit is received at baptism, fulfilling the promise of Joel 2:28–29 (as cited in Acts 2:17, in those days "I will pour out my spirit upon everyone"). For Mark, the holy spirit helps the Christian endure persecution (13:11).

- **1:9.** Mark narrates without comment Jesus' baptism by John. The other gospel writers seem troubled by its connection with the "forgiveness of sins" (v. 4), which Christians came to believe Jesus did not need, so they added an explanation (Matt 3:14–15), mentioned it only in passing (Luke 3:21), or dropped it completely (John 1:29–34). *During that same period:* Mark's imitation

dents of Jerusalem streamed out to him and were baptized by him in the Jordan river, admitting their sins. ⁶And John was dressed in camel hair [and wore a leather belt around his waist] and lived on locusts and raw honey. ⁷And he began his proclamation by saying:

"Someone more powerful than I will succeed me, whose sandal straps I am not fit to bend down and untie. ⁸I have been baptizing you with water, but he will baptize you with holy spirit."

⁹During that same period Jesus came from Nazareth in Galilee and was baptized in the Jordan by John. ¹⁰And just as he got up out of the water, he saw the skies torn open and the spirit coming down toward him like a dove. ¹¹There was also a voice from the skies: "You are my favored son—I fully approve of you."

¹²And right away the spirit drives him out into the wilderness, ¹³where he remained for forty days, being put to the test by Satan. While he was living there among the wild animals, the heavenly messengers looked after him.

---

of the narrative style of the Old Testament, more idiomatic than the archaic *it came to pass*, alerts the reader to Mark's "biblical" sounding introduction for Jesus. *Nazareth in Galilee*: a rather insignificant village in the central hill country of Galilee, apparently Jesus' "hometown" (6:1). Whether this word is related to *Nazarene* (v. 24) is unclear. *Galilee*: the northern-most region of what had been ancient Israel, in the area the Greeks called "Palestine" (after the ancient Philistines). It extended about 25 miles west of the "Sea of Galilee" and the Jordan River. Its former reputation was as a land of foreigners (Isa 9:1), since it fell into foreign control a century and a half earlier than Jerusalem did (722 B.C.E.). It was not part of Judea again until it was forcibly annexed at the end of the second century B.C.E. during reconquest of former Israelite territory by the priestly Hasmonean monarchy in Jerusalem, who imposed their religious practices on the Galileans (Josephus, *Antiquities of the Jews* 13:319).

• **1:10.** *The skies torn open*: much more vivid than the traditional picture of the heavens opening, an apocalyptic image that precedes divine revelation (Ezek 1:1; Rev 19:11). In ancient mythology "sky" is the name of the "dome" (Gen 1:6 NRSV) separating water above from water below. A similar image is used in Isa 63:12, *He forced*

the waters apart, after which *the spirit came down* to guide them (Isa 63:14 LXX). The *dove*: a traditional biblical symbol associated with the spirit of God, which hovered over the waters at creation (Gen 1:2).

• **1:11.** The words from the skies are familiar from scripture: *You are my son* are words from God that the king repeats at his coronation (Ps 2:7); *favored* [or *beloved*] *son* is what God calls Isaac when Abraham is asked to offer him in sacrifice (Gen 22:2 LXX); *my beloved son* is used by God in Jer 38:20 LXX where Hebrew (31:20) has *my dear* [or *precious*] *son*; *fully approve* is similar to God's words about "Israel, my chosen one," whom *my soul accepted* (Isa 42:1 LXX).

• **1:12.** *Drives him out*: the first of many times that Mark narrates past events in the present tense, which gives the reader a sense of immediacy (§6.2). *The wilderness*: apparently meaning the same area near the Jordan valley where John was located (vv. 3–4), though the wilderness is also a symbolic location for confronting evil spirits.

• **1:13.** *Forty days*: a traditional period of fasting derived from both Moses (Exod 34:28) and Elijah (1 Kgs 19:8), though Mark lacks the fasting motif (found in Matt 4:2; Luke 4:2). Forty days also corresponds to the forty years of the exodus (Num 14:34). *Put to the test*: rather than *tempted*,

A voice
in Galilee

¹⁴ Μετὰ δὲ τὸ παραδοθῆναι τὸν Ἰωάννην ἦλθεν ὁ Ἰησοῦς εἰς τὴν Γαλιλαίαν κηρύσσων τὸ εὐαγγέλιον τοῦ θεοῦ ¹⁵ καὶ λέγων ὅτι

Πεπλήρωται ὁ καιρὸς καὶ ἤγγικεν ἡ βασιλεία τοῦ θεοῦ· μετανοεῖτε καὶ πιστεύετε ἐν τῷ εὐαγγελίῳ.

¹⁶ Καὶ παράγων παρὰ τὴν θάλασσαν τῆς Γαλιλαίας εἶδεν Σίμωνα καὶ Ἀνδρέαν τὸν ἀδελφὸν Σίμωνος ἀμφιβάλλοντας ἐν τῇ θαλάσσῃ· ἦσαν γὰρ ἁλιεῖς. ¹⁷ καὶ εἶπεν αὐτοῖς ὁ Ἰησοῦς, Δεῦτε ὀπίσω μου, καὶ ποιήσω ὑμᾶς γενέσθαι ἁλιεῖς ἀνθρώπων. ¹⁸ Καὶ εὐθὺς ἀφέντες τὰ δίκτυα ἠκολούθησαν αὐτῷ.

¹⁹ Καὶ προβὰς ὀλίγον εἶδεν Ἰάκωβον τὸν τοῦ Ζεβεδαίου καὶ Ἰωάννην τὸν ἀδελφὸν αὐτοῦ, καὶ αὐτοὺς ἐν τῷ πλοίῳ καταρτίζοντας τὰ δίκτυα, ²⁰ καὶ εὐθὺς ἐκάλεσεν αὐτούς. καὶ ἀφέντες τὸν πατέρα αὐτῶν Ζεβεδαῖον ἐν τῷ πλοίῳ μετὰ τῶν μισθωτῶν ἀπῆλθον ὀπίσω αὐτοῦ.

A day's work

²¹ Καὶ εἰσπορεύονται εἰς Καφαρναούμ. καὶ εὐθὺς τοῖς σάββασιν εἰσελθὼν εἰς τὴν συναγωγὴν ἐδίδασκεν. ²² καὶ

---

14. Some MSS change the ending to *the good news of God's imperial rule.*
21. Several MSS, and Syriac and Coptic, omit *went*, Greek *eiselthon*, so *he right away started teaching in the synagogue.*

---

enticed to sin. In the exodus tradition, Israel's forty years in the wilderness is a time of testing (Deut 8:2). *Satan:* derived from the Hebrew word *satan*, for *adversary* or *accuser*, that which interferes with the will of God. *Satan* is first personified in Job 1–2 as the accuser among God's council of advisers, then later is depicted as the leader of evil forces, served by demons and "unclean spirits" and opposed by angels. *Wild animals:* traditional inhabitants, along with evil spirits, of the wilderness. *Heavenly messengers:* guard those who trust Yahweh and protect them from dangerous animals (Ps 91:11, 13).

The dominance of "biblical" language in this opening section conveys the importance of the scriptures (the "Old Testament") to Mark's readers. Mark assumes familiarity with the symbolic imagery and geographical settings from the story of Israel's salvation.

• **1:14–15.** The body of Mark's story opens with the transition from John to Jesus and Mark's summary of the central message of his gospel.

• **1:14.** *Locked up:* John's fate has suddenly changed, without explanation. This ominous note prepares the reader for John's death (6:14–29), which also anticipates the

fate of John's "successor," who himself gets *turned in* (for Mark's use of this language see §4.11).

• **1:15.** *The time is up:* the moment people had been waiting for had finally arrived. *God's imperial rule is closing in:* the awaited impending crisis is now here, "God is taking over!" *God's imperial rule:* translates "God's *basileia*," or "the *basileia* of God," as the dynamic effect of God ruling as emperor. (For the full range of translation considerations see §6.3). Mark borrowed this image from Jesus' parabolic use of it (4:11), in order to encompass the "good news" about Jesus—what Jesus said was around the corner had already been happening in the activity of Jesus. (The members of the Jesus Seminar, as reported in *Red Letter Mark*, consider all of v. 15 to be so formulated by Mark.)

Change your ways: Jesus' message is presented in terms of John's *change of heart* (v. 4). *Trust in the good news:* announces Mark's theme of "trust" (§4.8) with an unusual construction that has as the object of "trust" a message, rather than a person (similar to Ps 106:12, "They trusted his words.")

• **1:16–20.** Mark begins rather abruptly with two "call stories." In each a pair of brothers

¹⁴After John was locked up, Jesus came to Galilee pro-
claiming God's good news. ¹⁵His message went:

*A voice
in Galilee*

"The time is up: God's imperial rule is closing in. Change
your ways, and put your trust in the good news!"

¹⁶As he was walking along by the Sea of Galilee, he spotted
Simon and Andrew, Simon's brother, casting ⟨their nets⟩ into
the sea—since they were fishermen—¹⁷and Jesus said to them:
"Become my followers and I'll have you fishing for people!"

¹⁸And right then and there they abandoned their nets and fol-
lowed him.

¹⁹When he had gone a little farther, he caught sight of James,
son of Zebedee, and his brother John mending their nets in the
boat. ²⁰Right then and there he called out to them as well, and
they left their father Zebedee behind in the boat with the hired
hands and accompanied him.

²¹Then they come to Capernaum, and on the sabbath day he
went right to the synagogue and started teaching. ²²They were

A day's work

---

is called to follow Jesus. The pairings seem
traditional; Simon will become Peter
("Rock," 3:16), the spokesperson for the
group (8:29), while Andrew has no independent role in the story at all and is
mentioned only in connection with the
other three (1:29; 3:18; 13:3). James and
John are featured in only one story by
themselves (10:35-41), and John is alone
only once (9:38). They are more prominent
as forming a trio with Peter (5:37; 9:2;
14:33). Mark later uses the "call story"
format for Levi (2:14), although he does not
become one of the inner group of followers.
These stories reflect the idealized picture
early Christians had of making a sudden
decision to follow "the way of the Lord."
- **1:16.** *Sea of Galilee*: a name used only in
the New Testament, more commonly called
Lake Genneseret (Luke 5:1; Mark 6:53 has
the town "Genneseret") or the *Sea of
Tiberias* (John 6:1), after the capital city on
its west coast. This lake was important both
for fishing and for transportation. Fishermen cast weighted nets from near shore, or
used dragnets from a boat. Hereafter, Mark
refers to this lake mostly as *the sea*, which,
like *the wilderness* (vv. 2-3), is another one
of the symbolic locations associated with
the exodus (also *the mountain*, 3:13). The
events narrated at these locations take on
additional significance when interpreted in
light of the exodus tradition. "The sea"
represents the exodus crossing, where the
Israelites escaped from Egypt across "the

Sea of Reeds," by popular tradition "the
Red Sea," when Israel's God "rebuked the
sea" (Ps 106:10, echoes in Mark 4:39) and
brought deliverance.
- **1:17.** *Become my followers*: imitates the
language used by the prophet Elisha, Elijah's successor, in 2 Kgs 6:19. The Elijah-
Elisha cycle of stories (1 Kings 17–2 Kings
13) apparently influenced how Mark understood the relation of John and Jesus: it was
at the Jordan (v. 5) that Elijah designated
Elisha as his successor, after which the
spirit comes upon Elisha (2 Kgs 2:1-18)
and he is able to perform miracles (2 Kgs
2:19-7:20). *I'll have you fishing for people*:
an image used by the prophets to suggest
how God would go after people who were
avoiding God (Jer 16:16; Hab 1:14).
- **1:21-39.** Mark presents a series of incidents
tied together to make a typical day in the
activity of Jesus.
- **1:21.** *Capernaum*: a busy fishing village on
the north shore of the Sea of Galilee about
2 ½ miles from the Jordan River, the
border between the territories of Herod
Antipas and Philip, two sons of Herod the
Great, whom the Romans allowed to serve
as "tetrarchs" over portions of the former
"Kingdom of Herod."

Sabbath day and *synagogue* locate the
first activity of Jesus amidst the main
symbols of religious life apart from the
temple in Jerusalem. For the Judeans who
returned from exile (after the sixth century
B.C.E.), the rebuilt temple was the center of

ἐξεπλήσσοντο ἐπὶ τῇ διδαχῇ αὐτοῦ, ἦν γὰρ διδάσκων αὐτοὺς ὡς ἐξουσίαν ἔχων καὶ οὐχ ὡς οἱ γραμματεῖς.

²³ Καὶ εὐθὺς ἦν ἐν τῇ συναγωγῇ αὐτῶν ἄνθρωπος ἐν πνεύματι ἀκαθάρτῳ, καὶ ἀνέκραξεν ²⁴ λέγων, Τί ἡμῖν καὶ σοί, Ἰησοῦ Ναζαρηνέ; ἦλθες ἀπολέσαι ἡμᾶς; οἶδά σε τίς εἶ, ὁ ἅγιος τοῦ θεοῦ.

²⁵ Καὶ ἐπετίμησεν αὐτῷ [ὁ Ἰησοῦς] λέγων, Φιμώθητι καὶ ἔξελθε ἐξ αὐτοῦ.

²⁶ Καὶ σπαράξαν αὐτὸν τὸ πνεῦμα τὸ ἀκάθαρτον καὶ φωνῆσαν φωνῇ μεγάλῃ ἐξῆλθεν ἐξ αὐτοῦ. ²⁷ καὶ ἐθαμβήθησαν ἅπαντες, ὥστε συζητεῖν αὐτοὺς λέγοντας, Τί ἐστιν τοῦτο; διδαχὴ καινὴ κατ᾽ ἐξουσίαν· καὶ τοῖς πνεύμασι τοῖς ἀκαθάρτοις ἐπιτάσσει, καὶ ὑπακούουσιν αὐτῷ.

²⁸ Καὶ ἐξῆλθεν ἡ ἀκοὴ αὐτοῦ εὐθὺς πανταχοῦ εἰς ὅλην τὴν περίχωρον τῆς Γαλιλαίας.

²⁹ Καὶ εὐθὺς ἐκ τῆς συναγωγῆς ἐξελθόντες ἦλθον εἰς τὴν οἰκίαν Σίμωνος καὶ Ἀνδρέου μετὰ Ἰακώβου καὶ Ἰωάννου. ³⁰ ἡ δὲ πενθερὰ Σίμωνος κατέκειτο πυρέσσουσα, καὶ εὐθὺς λέγουσιν αὐτῷ περὶ αὐτῆς. ³¹ καὶ προσελθὼν ἤγειρεν αὐτὴν κρατήσας τῆς χειρός· καὶ ἀφῆκεν αὐτὴν ὁ πυρετός, καὶ διηκόνει αὐτοῖς.

³² Ὀψίας δὲ γενομένης, ὅτε ἔδυ ὁ ἥλιος, ἔφερον πρὸς αὐτὸν πάντας τοὺς κακῶς ἔχοντας καὶ τοὺς δαιμονιζομένους· ³³ καὶ ἦν ὅλη ἡ πόλις ἐπισυνηγμένη πρὸς τὴν θύραν. ³⁴ καὶ ἐθεράπευσεν πολλοὺς κακῶς ἔχοντας ποικίλαις νόσοις, καὶ δαιμόνια πολλὰ ἐξέβαλεν, καὶ οὐκ ἤφιεν λαλεῖν τὰ δαιμόνια, ὅτι ᾔδεισαν αὐτόν.

---

25. Several MSS do not have *Jesus*, which is closer to Mark's style of unspecified subjects. **27.** *A new teaching:* some MSS read *What is this new teaching?* **29.** A number of MSS have a singular subject, *He left the synagogue.*

---

religious life. The daily sacrifices offered by the priests and supported by a tax on the male population also made the temple the central economic institution in Judea, since it required both a livestock market and a treasury to collect the temple tax, which usually had to be converted from other currency. The majority of Judeans, however, remained in the diaspora ("dispersion") outside of Judea. While they aspired to make the annual passover pilgrimage to Jerusalem, their religious and social activity centered around the synagogue. A *synagogue* is initially an "assembly," not a building. It developed into a community center where Jews gathered for prayer, for study and teaching of Scripture, and for community meals. The *sabbath* is the seventh day, Saturday, the last day of the week, which begins at sundown Friday.

The ancient tradition of work restrictions on the sabbath day provided needed rest for both humans and work animals. The sabbath day also became a festival day, with special religious significance.

• **1:22.** *His own authority:* the nature and source of Jesus' authority is a central issue in Mark (1:27; 2:10; 11:28, 29, 33). *Scholars:* regarded as authorities because of their learned ability to interpret scripture and their status as arbiters who settle legal disputes. Mark's contrast between them and Jesus may suggest Jesus' more independent prophetic authority (aligned with John's in 11:28–33), his more powerful teaching style that leads directly to action (v. 27), or his refusal to base his teachings only on sacred texts.

• **1:23.** *Possessed by an unclean spirit:* an ancient way of personifying the forces of

astonished at his teaching, since he would teach them on his own authority, unlike the scholars.

²³Now right there in their synagogue was a person possessed by an unclean spirit, which shouted, ²⁴"Jesus! What do you want with us, you Nazarene? Have you come to get rid of us? I know you, who you are: God's holy man!"

²⁵But [Jesus] yelled at it, "Shut up and get out of him!"

²⁶Then the unclean spirit threw the man into convulsions, and letting out a loud shriek it came out of him. ²⁷And they were all so amazed that they asked themselves, "What's this? A new kind of teaching backed by authority! He gives orders even to unclean spirits and they obey him!"

²⁸So his fame spread rapidly everywhere throughout Galilee and even beyond.

²⁹They left the synagogue right away and entered the house of Simon and Andrew along with James and John. ³⁰Simon's mother-in-law was in bed with a fever, and they told him about her right away. ³¹He went up to her, took hold of her hand, raised her up, and the fever disappeared. Then she started looking after them.

³²In the evening, at sundown, they would bring all the sick and demon-possessed to him. ³³And the whole city would crowd around the door. ³⁴On such occasions he cured many people afflicted with various diseases and drove out many demons. He would never let the demons speak, because they realized who he was.

---

evil in the world that work against God. These demons (v. 32) were viewed as the cause of blindness, mental illness, and disease. As part of the forces of "Satan" (v. 13), they are immediately threatened by the presence of Jesus, who has received a divine spirit (v. 10) and acts as agent of God's imperial rule (v. 15).

• **1:24.** *You Nazarene*: a form of address, found mostly in Mark (10:47; 14:67; 16:6), which could mean *one from Nazareth* (1:9), or could reinforce *God's holy man* to mean a "Nazirite" like Samson (Judg 13:7; 16:17). *Get rid of us*: in the strong sense *ruin/ destroy*.

• **1:25.** *Yelled at*: expresses the intensity of the encounter, missed in the traditional *rebuked*. Mark uses combative language for exorcisms (v. 34), so also the stern *Shut up*, which occurs again at 4:39. Here it is part

of the secrecy motif (§4.4).

• **1:27.** *A new kind of teaching backed by authority!* The division between this sentence and the next is uncertain; it could be *A new kind of teaching! With authority he gives orders.* However, Mark's context (v. 22) associates "authority" directly with Jesus' teaching.

• **1:32–34.** Summary passages in Mark (also v. 28) typify the activity of Jesus. A distinctive Markan feature used for this effect is imperfect tense verbs, which the translators capture by using "would" in English (§6.2). *Demons*: include the "unclean spirits" who "possess" people (v. 23). When Jesus, and later his companions (3:15), "drive out" demons, a battle between opposing forces is taking place.

• **1:32.** *At sundown*: indicates the end of the sabbath day, which began Friday at sun-

³⁵ Καὶ πρωὶ ἔννυχα λίαν ἀναστὰς ἐξῆλθεν καὶ ἀπῆλθεν εἰς ἔρημον τόπον κἀκεῖ προσηύχετο. ³⁶ καὶ κατεδίωξεν αὐτὸν Σίμων καὶ οἱ μετ' αὐτοῦ, ³⁷ καὶ εὗρον αὐτὸν καὶ λέγουσιν αὐτῷ ὅτι Πάντες ζητοῦσίν σε.

³⁸ Καὶ λέγει αὐτοῖς, Ἄγωμεν ἀλλαχοῦ εἰς τὰς ἐχομένας κωμοπόλεις, ἵνα καὶ ἐκεῖ κηρύξω· εἰς τοῦτο γὰρ ἐξῆλθον. ³⁹ καὶ ἦλθεν κηρύσσων εἰς τὰς συναγωγὰς αὐτῶν εἰς ὅλην τὴν Γαλιλαίαν καὶ τὰ δαιμόνια ἐκβάλλων.

Jesus cures a leper

⁴⁰ Καὶ ἔρχεται πρὸς αὐτὸν λεπρὸς παρακαλῶν αὐτὸν καὶ γονυπετῶν καὶ λέγων αὐτῷ ὅτι Ἐὰν θέλῃς δύνασαί με καθαρίσαι.

⁴¹ Καὶ ὀργισθεὶς ἐκτείνας τὴν χεῖρα αὐτοῦ ἥψατο καὶ λέγει αὐτῷ, Θέλω, καθαρίσθητι· ⁴² Καὶ εὐθὺς ἀπῆλθεν ἀπ' αὐτοῦ ἡ λέπρα, καὶ ἐκαθαρίσθη. ⁴³ καὶ ἐμβριμησάμενος αὐτῷ εὐθὺς ἐξέβαλεν αὐτόν, ⁴⁴ καὶ λέγει αὐτῷ, Ὅρα μηδενὶ μηδὲν εἴπῃς, ἀλλὰ ὕπαγε σεαυτὸν δεῖξον τῷ ἱερεῖ καὶ προσένεγκε περὶ τοῦ καθαρισμοῦ σου ἃ προσέταξεν Μωϋσῆς, εἰς μαρτύριον αὐτοῖς.

⁴⁵ Ὁ δὲ ἐξελθὼν ἤρξατο κηρύσσειν πολλὰ καὶ διαφημίζειν τὸν λόγον, ὥστε μηκέτι αὐτὸν δύνασθαι φανερῶς εἰς πόλιν εἰσελθεῖν, ἀλλ' ἔξω ἐπ' ἐρήμοις τόποις ἦν· καὶ ἤρχοντο πρὸς αὐτὸν πάντοθεν.

---

40. *Falls down on his knees:* omitted in several early MSS.   **41.** *Jesus was indignant:* most MSS read *Jesus has compassion* (§8.2).

---

down (v. 21).

›1:35. Jesus returns to a wilderness-like setting (1:3, 4, 12, 13), as he responds to apparent success with a desire to be alone (§4.4).

›1:37. *They're all looking for you:* an ongoing quest that never succeeds in Mark, either by his family (3:32), or by his opponents (11:18; 12:12; 14:1), or even after he has gone (16:6).

›1:39. *So he went all around Galilee:* After narrating one full day of Jesus' activities, Mark concludes with a summary statement, typically vague and over-generalized.

›1:40–45. This story lacks any geographical or temporal relationship to either the preceding or following sequences. Thus it

seems Mark is using it as a transition between the two. A leprosy cure is more than a typical healing story, and the involvement of the religious authorities hints at the controversies in the next section.

• 1:40. *A leper:* a person with one of several skin diseases, of unknown original, thought to be contagious. The strict biblical regulations (Leviticus 13–14) were not intended to cure it, but to control its ritual "uncleanness." Such persons were required to live outside the community and to announce to anyone who approached that they were "unclean" (Lev 13:45–46), so for a leper to approach Jesus defies the prescribed social customs.

• 1:41. *Touched him:* in the levitical code on

³⁵And rising early, while it was still very dark, he went outside and stole away to an isolated place, where he started praying. ³⁶Then Simon and those with him hunted him down. ³⁷When they had found him they say to him, "They're all looking for you."

³⁸But he replies: "Let's go somewhere else, to the neighboring villages, so I can speak there too, since that's what I came for."

³⁹So he went all around Galilee speaking in their synagogues and driving out demons.

⁴⁰Then a leper comes up to him, pleads with him, falls down on his knees, and says to him, "If you want to, you can make me clean."

Jesus cures a leper

⁴¹Although Jesus was indignant, he stretched out his hand, touched him, and says to him, "Okay—you're clean!"

⁴²And right away the leprosy disappeared, and he was made clean. ⁴³And Jesus snapped at him, and dismissed him curtly ⁴⁴with this warning: "See that you don't tell anyone anything, but go, have a priest examine ⟨your skin⟩. Then offer for your cleansing what Moses commanded, as evidence ⟨of your cure⟩."

⁴⁵But after he went out, he started telling everyone and spreading the story, so that Jesus could no longer enter a city openly, but had to stay out in the countryside. Yet they continued to come to him from everywhere.

---

uncleanness (Lev 5:2–3) anyone who "touches" an unclean person becomes "defiled." Jesus thus overcomes the religious taboo by directly breaking it. *Okay—you're clean!* captures the tension of the scene as Jesus assents to the leper's imposition, *If you want to.*

• **1:42.** The matter-of-fact ending, *He was made clean,* like the imperative, *you're clean!* is the same as in the story of Elisha cleansing Naaman's leprosy (2 Kgs 5:14), adding to the similarity between Jesus and Elisha (v. 17).

• **1:43.** *Jesus snapped at him:* renders a very harsh Greek verb that probably reflects exorcism language (v. 25; §4.10).

• **1:44.** *What Moses commanded:* the Torah

prescribes the sacrifice that the priest is to command for the ritual "cleansing" of leprosy (Lev 14:2–32). *Evidence ⟨of your cure⟩:* the sacrifice commanded in Leviticus is not claimed to be related to a cure, so it is unclear how Mark means this. The Greek has the pronoun "to/for them," which the translators take to mean "the priests," with Jesus seeming to endorse compliance with the Torah. This same expression is used before a hostile audience in 6:11 (also 13:9), which SV renders *evidence against them.* Although this context also could be read as hostile (vv. 41, 43), it is difficult to know what *against them* would mean here.

2 Καὶ εἰσελθὼν πάλιν εἰς Καφαρναοὺμ δι' ἡμερῶν ἠκούσθη ὅτι ἐν οἴκῳ ἐστίν. ²καὶ συνήχθησαν πολλοὶ ὥστε μηκέτι χωρεῖν μηδὲ τὰ πρὸς τὴν θύραν, καὶ ἐλάλει αὐτοῖς τὸν λόγον. ³καὶ ἔρχονται φέροντες πρὸς αὐτὸν παραλυτικὸν αἰρόμενον ὑπὸ τεσσάρων. ⁴καὶ μὴ δυνάμενοι προσενέγκαι αὐτῷ διὰ τὸν ὄχλον ἀπεστέγασαν τὴν στέγην ὅπου ἦν, καὶ ἐξορύξαντες χαλῶσι τὸν κράβαττον ὅπου ὁ παραλυτικὸς κατέκειτο. ⁵καὶ ἰδὼν ὁ Ἰησοῦς τὴν πίστιν αὐτῶν λέγει τῷ παραλυτικῷ, Τέκνον, ἀφίενταί σου αἱ ἁμαρτίαι.

⁶Ἦσαν δέ τινες τῶν γραμματέων ἐκεῖ καθήμενοι καὶ διαλογιζόμενοι ἐν ταῖς καρδίαις αὐτῶν, ⁷Τί οὗτος οὕτως λαλεῖ; βλασφημεῖ· τίς δύναται ἀφιέναι ἁμαρτίας εἰ μὴ εἷς ὁ θεός;

⁸Καὶ εὐθὺς ἐπιγνοὺς ὁ Ἰησοῦς τῷ πνεύματι αὐτοῦ ὅτι οὕτως διαλογίζονται ἐν ἑαυτοῖς λέγει αὐτοῖς, Τί ταῦτα διαλογίζεσθε ἐν ταῖς καρδίαις ὑμῶν; ⁹τί ἐστιν εὐκοπώτερον, εἰπεῖν τῷ παραλυτικῷ, Ἀφίενταί σου αἱ ἁμαρτίαι, ἢ εἰπεῖν, Ἔγειρε καὶ ἆρον τὸν κράβαττόν σου καὶ περιπάτει; ¹⁰ἵνα δὲ εἰδῆτε ὅτι ἐξουσίαν ἔχει ὁ υἱὸς τοῦ ἀνθρώπου ἀφιέναι ἁμαρτίας [ἐπὶ τῆς γῆς] λέγει τῷ παραλυτικῷ, ¹¹Σοὶ λέγω, ἔγειρε ἆρον τὸν κράβαττόν σου καὶ ὕπαγε εἰς τὸν οἶκόν σου.

¹²Καὶ ἠγέρθη καὶ εὐθὺς ἄρας τὸν κράβαττον ἐξῆλθεν ἔμπροσθεν πάντων, ὥστε ἐξίστασθαι πάντας καὶ δοξάζειν τὸν θεὸν λέγοντας ὅτι Οὕτως οὐδέποτε εἴδομεν.

¹³Καὶ ἐξῆλθεν πάλιν παρὰ τὴν θάλασσαν· καὶ πᾶς ὁ ὄχλος ἤρχετο πρὸς αὐτόν, καὶ ἐδίδασκεν αὐτούς.

---

5. *Your sins are forgiven:* follows the two earliest parchment MSS; most others read *Your sins have been forgiven* (Luke 5:20).   10. *On earth:* three different locations in Greek in different MSS. The position here is supported by the only surviving papyrus copy of this text (§8.1), which also agrees with Matt 9:6; Luke 5:24. The other positions could be read as *earthly sins.* The original reading may be preserved in the few MSS that do not have the phrase at all.

• **2:1-3:6.** Mark now presents a series of stories set in the same locations established in ch. 1 as Jesus' familiar territory, but the second time around each one involves controversy. Collections of controversy stories may have been circulated prior to the writing of Mark's gospel (§2.2).
• **2:1.** Jesus returns to Capernaum, where he began his activities (1:21). *At home:* even though Nazareth (1:9) is apparently Jesus' hometown, Capernaum now becomes "home." Mark does not indicate whose house this actually is.
• **2:4.** *They removed the roof* by *digging it out:* most homes were single room dwellings

with walls of mud brick or limestone and outside stairs to the flat roof, which was resurfaced each year with branches, straw and packed clay.
• **2:5.** Their assertiveness in getting access to Jesus is used by Mark as an indication of their *trust,* one of Mark's dominant themes (§4.8). *He says to the paralytic:* the repetition of these words at the end of v. 10 suggests that the healing story naturally continues with v. 11. Mark, or possibly an earlier collector of controversy stories, has inserted the intervening verses with the controversy dialogue. *Your sins are forgiven:* this language is similar to that associated

2 Some days later he went back to Capernaum and was rumored to be at home. ²And many people crowded around so there was no longer any room, even outside the door. Then he started speaking to them. ³Some people then show up with a paralytic being carried by four of them. ⁴And when they were not able to get near him on account of the crowd, they removed the roof above him. After digging it out, they lowered the mat on which the paralytic was lying. ⁵When Jesus noticed their trust, he says to the paralytic, "Child, your sins are forgiven."

⁶Some of the scholars were sitting there and silently wondering: ⁷"Why does that fellow say such things? He's blaspheming! Who can forgive sins except the one God?"

⁸And right away, because Jesus sensed in his spirit that they were raising questions like this among themselves, he says to them: "Why do you entertain questions about these things? ⁹Which is easier, to say to the paralytic, 'Your sins are forgiven,' or to say, 'Get up, pick up your mat and walk'?" ¹⁰But so that you may realize that [on earth] the son of Adam has authority to forgive sins, he says to the paralytic, ¹¹"You there, get up, pick up your mat and go home!"

¹²And he got up, picked his mat right up, and walked out as everyone looked on. So they all became ecstatic, extolled God, and exclaimed, "We've never seen the likes of this!"

¹³Again he went out by the sea. And, with a huge crowd gathered around him, he started teaching.

*Jesus cures
a paralytic*

*Levi becomes
a follower*

---

with John's baptism (v. 4); the passive verb form implies "by God." The setting here, however, is very different. Someone with a disease would have been viewed in the ancient world as suffering the consequences of sin (the everyday view is expressed by Jesus' disciples in John 9:2); full repentance would have been necessary before someone could pray for their forgiveness and then for healing. One could not forgive the sins of others. In contrast, Jesus is presented as pronouncing God's forgiveness with no indication of any preceding "religious" activity by the paralytic.

• **2:6.** *Scholars*: trained in the practices of interpreting the Mosaic law (1:22). They were highly respected for preserving authentic Judean traditions, and thus they serve well as the stereotyped initial opponents of Jesus' activity (§4.6).

• **2:7.** *Blaspheming*: any activity disrespectful of God, either through irreverence, such as desecrating God's name, or by claiming for oneself a prerogative reserved for God. It

was the most serious religious offense in Judaism, punishable by death (14:64). Christians, in turn, charged that the ultimate, unforgivable (3:29) blasphemy was committed by those who did not recognize their claim that Jesus was God's Anointed (15:29). Thus in Mark's perspective, to accuse Jesus of blasphemy is itself an act of blasphemy.

• **2:10.** Since the end of the verse, *he says to the paralytic*, cannot be words of Jesus, it seems best to understand the entire verse as editorial comment inserted into the first controversy story to make clear what the central issue is. Mark introduces for the first time the term *the son of Adam* to explain to the readers that Jesus' ability to cure people validates his "earthly" *authority to forgive sins*, which continues to be practiced by the Christian community. The contrast of *the son of Adam* with God (v. 7) makes the claim that "any person," any descendant of Adam (and Eve), has such authority. A similar claim is made in v. 28 regarding

**Jesus dines
with sinners**

**Fasting
& feasting**

¹⁴Καὶ παράγων εἶδεν Λευὶν τὸν τοῦ ᾿Αλφαίου καθήμενον ἐπὶ
τὸ τελώνιον, καὶ λέγει αὐτῷ, ᾿Ακολούθει μοι.
Καὶ ἀναστὰς ἠκολούθησεν αὐτῷ.
¹⁵Καὶ γίνεται κατακεῖσθαι αὐτὸν ἐν τῇ οἰκίᾳ αὐτοῦ, καὶ
πολλοὶ τελῶναι καὶ ἁμαρτωλοὶ συνανέκειντο τῷ ᾿Ιησοῦ καὶ τοῖς
μαθηταῖς αὐτοῦ· ἦσαν γὰρ πολλοί. καὶ ἠκολούθουν αὐτῷ ¹⁶καὶ οἱ
γραμματεῖς τῶν Φαρισαίων, καὶ ἰδόντες ὅτι ἐσθίει μετὰ τῶν
ἁμαρτωλῶν καὶ τελωνῶν ἔλεγον τοῖς μαθηταῖς αὐτοῦ, ῞Οτι μετὰ
τῶν τελωνῶν καὶ ἁμαρτωλῶν ἐσθίει;
¹⁷Καὶ ἀκούσας ὁ ᾿Ιησοῦς λέγει αὐτοῖς [ὅτι] Οὐ χρείαν ἔχουσιν
οἱ ἰσχύοντες ἰατροῦ ἀλλ᾿ οἱ κακῶς ἔχοντες· οὐκ ἦλθον καλέσαι
δικαίους ἀλλὰ ἁμαρτωλούς.
¹⁸Καὶ ἦσαν οἱ μαθηταὶ ᾿Ιωάννου καὶ οἱ Φαρισαῖοι
νηστεύοντες. καὶ ἔρχονται καὶ λέγουσιν αὐτῷ, Διὰ τί οἱ μαθηταὶ
᾿Ιωάννου καὶ οἱ μαθηταὶ τῶν Φαρισαίων νηστεύουσιν, οἱ δὲ σοὶ
μαθηταὶ οὐ νηστεύουσιν;

---

14. *Levi, son of Alphaeus:* some MSS read *James, son of Alphaeus*, so that
he corresponds to one of the twelve (3:18). Otherwise Levi appears to be
an extra, uncounted disciple, a problem solved in Matthew (9:9) by
calling him "Matthew."   **16.** *The Pharisees' scholars:* some MSS read *the
scholars and the Pharisees. Eating* (the second time): some MSS have *eating
and drinking*, as does Luke 5:30.   **17.** Greek *hoti*, "that," preceding
direct discourse, is usually optional, so MSS often omit it, but the one
surviving papyrus copy and several other MSS have it here.

activity on the sabbath day. (See the note
and appended discussion there for further
significance of *the son of Adam.)*
• **2:14.** *Levi:* called in the same manner as
the first disciples (1:16–20), but not in the
list of twelve, though there is a "son of
Alphaeus," named James (3:16–19). The
name "Levi" may have symbolic value as
the patriarch of the Old Testament tribe
that is not counted among the twelve (Num
1:49), because they are designated as care-
takers of the tent of the covenant, and later
of the temple. The status of Levites as
"almost priests" makes this *Levi* quite ironical as a famous "sinner." *Toll booth:* a
customs station where duties were collected
on all goods and produce that were trans-
ported through each political jurisdiction,
in addition to the direct taxes already
assessed on all agricultural products both by
the secular government and by the temple
authorities in Jerusalem. Capernaum, a border town on the lake (1:21), was also a
harbor from which to travel to other loca-

tions around the lake, making it an important customs station for that area. The
customs collectors had a low reputation
among pious Judeans because they were
associated with the "foreign" Herodian and
Roman governments and were prosperous
only if they regularly overcharged (such as
Zaccheus may have done according to Luke
19:2, 8).
• **2:15.** *Recline at table:* the customary eating
posture in the ancient world, especially for
a group "dinner party." Low couches with
pillows were along the walls, with a table in
the center of the room. Guests ate reclining
and resting on one elbow. *Sinners:* those
who did not observe the daily religious
practices required by the Pharisees. This
would include especially the lower classes
and those in occupations, such as *toll
collectors*, that put them in regular contact
with pagans. *Jesus' disciples:* Mark is unclear at this stage what distinguishes *disciples* from the *many* who *were all following
him*, since disciples are those who "follow

¹⁴As he was walking along, he caught sight of Levi, the son of Alphaeus, sitting at the toll booth, and he says to him, "Follow me!"

And Levi got up and followed him.

¹⁵Then Jesus happens to recline at table in ⟨Levi's⟩ house, along with many toll collectors and sinners and Jesus' disciples. (Remember, there were many of these people and they were all following him.) ¹⁶And whenever the Pharisees' scholars saw him eating with sinners and toll collectors, they would question his disciples: "What's he doing eating with toll collectors and sinners?"

¹⁷When Jesus overhears, he says to them: "Since when do the able-bodied need a doctor? It's the sick who do. I did not come to enlist religious folks but sinners!"

¹⁸John's disciples and the Pharisees were in the habit of fasting, and they come and ask him, "Why do the disciples of John fast, and the disciples of the Pharisees, but your disciples don't?"

Jesus dines with sinners

Fasting & feasting

---

him" (1:18; 2:14). While the general sense of *disciple* is "student" or "learner," and Jesus will teach them in parables, sometimes followed by explanations (4:2, 34), only later does Mark have Jesus spell out that the full requirements for following him are preparation for martyrdom (8:34–37). *Remember* introduces a "narrative aside," a parenthetical comment that interrupts the narrative, usually placed in parentheses in SV. Mark commonly uses this device to explain something the reader may need to know to understand the narrative (§3.6; §6.1).

• **2:16.** *The Pharisees' scholars*: an unusual way to relate these two groups, who appear together again only in Mark 7:5, but more frequently in Matthew and Luke. Scholars were a class of scripture authorities (1:22; 2:6); Pharisees appear to have been a relatively small, but influential, group committed to full observance of Judean food customs and Sabbath practices in a manner that most Judeans expected only of priests, and that lower classes could not easily afford. Mark pictures only some Pharisees as being trained scholars; some may have come from priestly families, but they are mostly associated with local synagogues. *Eating with sinners and toll collectors*: group table fellowship (v. 15) was common within many social groups, including professional guilds such as scholars, and maybe even toll

collectors. But the Pharisees had made it an important part of Judean self-identity. In contrast, Jesus developed a reputation for a lifestyle that transcended social barriers (§4.10).

• **2:17.** It was a common proverb in the ancient world that doctors are for the sick. Several versions have been preserved in which it is used as a rejoinder to one's critics. (When Pausanias, exiled king of Sparta, commended the Spartans and was asked why he had left Sparta, he is said to have replied that physicians preferred to "spend their time not among the healthy, but where the sick are.") *Religious folks*: people who are considered "upright" and "decent" by the religious establishment. In the context of the preceding proverb, contrasting them with *sinners* sounds ironically obvious: those who are doing all the "right" things surely do not need to be enlisted. It brings to mind a modern church proverb: There's no need preaching to the choir.

• **2:18.** *Fasting*: to abstain from food. The Hebrew Bible required fasting by everyone only on the annual day of repentance, Yom Kippur (Lev 16:29–31). However, Pharisees practiced fasting twice a week (Luke 18:12), on Mondays and Thursdays (Did 8:1). Since John's disciples are only mentioned again when they bury John (6:29), their fasting could be in relation to mourning his death, but that is not indicated here. *The disciples*

¹⁹Καὶ εἶπεν αὐτοῖς [ὁ Ἰησοῦς], Μὴ δύνανται οἱ υἱοὶ τοῦ νυμφῶνος ἐν ᾧ ὁ νυμφίος μετ᾽ αὐτῶν ἐστιν νηστεύειν; ὅσον χρόνον ἔχουσιν τὸν νυμφίον μετ᾽ αὐτῶν οὐ δύνανται νηστεύειν· ²⁰ἐλεύσονται δὲ ἡμέραι ὅταν ἀπαρθῇ ἀπ᾽ αὐτῶν ὁ νυμφίος, καὶ τότε νηστεύσουσιν ἐν ἐκείνῃ τῇ ἡμέρᾳ.

²¹Οὐδεὶς ἐπίβλημα ῥάκους ἀγνάφου ἐπιράπτει ἐπὶ ἱμάτιον παλαιόν· εἰ δὲ μή, αἴρει τὸ πλήρωμα ἀπ᾽ αὐτοῦ τὸ καινὸν τοῦ παλαιοῦ, καὶ χεῖρον σχίσμα γίνεται.

²²Καὶ οὐδεὶς βάλλει οἶνον νέον εἰς ἀσκοὺς παλαιούς· εἰ δὲ μή, ῥήξει ὁ οἶνος τοὺς ἀσκούς, καὶ ὁ οἶνος ἀπόλλυται καὶ οἱ ἀσκοί· ἀλλὰ οἶνον νέον εἰς ἀσκοὺς καινούς.

Adam & Eve over the sabbath

²³Καὶ ἐγένετο αὐτὸν ἐν τοῖς σάββασιν παραπορεύεσθαι διὰ τῶν σπορίμων, καὶ οἱ μαθηταὶ αὐτοῦ ἤρξαντο ὁδὸν ποιεῖν τίλλοντες τοὺς στάχυας. ²⁴καὶ οἱ Φαρισαῖοι ἔλεγον αὐτῷ, Ἴδε τί ποιοῦσιν τοῖς σάββασιν ὃ οὐκ ἔξεστιν;

²⁵Καὶ λέγει αὐτοῖς, Οὐδέποτε ἀνέγνωτε τί ἐποίησεν Δαυίδ, ὅτε χρείαν ἔσχεν καὶ ἐπείνασεν αὐτὸς καὶ οἱ μετ᾽ αὐτοῦ; ²⁶πῶς εἰσῆλθεν εἰς τὸν οἶκον τοῦ θεοῦ ἐπὶ Ἀβιαθὰρ ἀρχιερέως καὶ τοὺς ἄρτους τῆς προθέσεως ἔφαγεν, οὓς οὐκ ἔξεστιν φαγεῖν εἰ μὴ τοὺς ἱερεῖς, καὶ ἔδωκεν καὶ τοῖς σὺν αὐτῷ οὖσιν;

²⁷Καὶ ἔλεγεν αὐτοῖς,

---

19. In some MSS the subject is unspecified, as at 1:25. Some of these MSS and others also omit the second saying, *So long as the groom is around . . .*, which is unique to Mark.   **22.** The last saying *Instead, young wine is for new wineskins* is omitted in a few MSS.

---

of the Pharisees is quite puzzling, since they are not mentioned elsewhere, and only some Pharisees are scholars (v. 16), who might be training "students." Otherwise, those who follow the ways of Pharisees would simply be "Pharisees." The forced parallel between *disciples* of John, Jesus and Pharisees may indicate that this dispute was current not in Jesus' day, but in the next generation between those who became Christians and those who adhered to the practices of either John the Baptist or the Pharisees.

• **2:19.** A wedding celebration began when the bride and groom culminated a year-long betrothal with a ceremony of the bride formally entering the groom's home. Several days of feasting usually followed. The wedding feast was also used parabolically by Jesus as an image associated with God's imperial rule (Matt 22:1; 25:1; Luke 14:8).

• **2:20.** By the end of the first century some Christians did adopt regular fast days, on Wednesdays and Fridays, in contrast to the Pharisees' Mondays and Thursdays (Did 8:1). This indicates how quickly the more radical aspects of Jesus' lifestyle (v. 16) were domesticated.

• **2:21-22.** These two sayings have only a general thematic relation to this context, in that appropriate dress and the wine supply would be typical concerns of any groom's guests. By appending sayings on the incompatibility of the new with the old, Mark again associates "new" with Jesus' teaching (as in 1:27), this time attaching "old" to the concerns of the adversaries. Both sayings also share the image of the inevitable threat of the new to the old.

Patching worn garments must have been a common practice. Garments were usually woven from wool or linen, or sewn together

¹⁹And [Jesus] said to them: "The groom's friends can't fast while the groom is present, can they? So long as the groom is around, you can't expect them to fast. ²⁰But the days will come when the groom is taken away from them, and then they will fast, on that day.

²¹"Nobody sews a piece of unshrunk cloth on an old garment, otherwise the new, unshrunk patch pulls away from the old and creates a worse tear.

²²"And nobody pours young wine into old wineskins, otherwise the wine will burst the skins, and destroy both the wine and the skins. Instead, young wine is for new wineskins."

²³It so happened that he was walking along through the grainfields on the sabbath day, and his disciples began to strip heads of grain as they walked along. ²⁴And the Pharisees started to argue with him: "See here, why are they doing what's not permitted on the sabbath day?"

²⁵And he says to them: "Haven't you ever read what David did when he found it necessary, when both he and his companions were hungry? ²⁶He went into the house of God, when Abiathar was high priest, and ate the consecrated bread, and even gave some to his men to eat. No one is permitted to eat this bread, except the priests!"

²⁷And he continued:

Adam & Eve
over the sabbath

---

from smaller pieces of cloth. Either type of garment would have to be patched with "pre-shrunk" cloth.

Winemaking was one of the most ancient and famous trades of Palestine. The juice collected from treading grapes in a large vat began to ferment naturally when the yeast on the grapeskins came in contact with the juice, converting its sugar content into alcohol and carbon dioxide gas. The fermentation process was not yet completed when the young wine was placed in containers for storage, either jars or skins made from whole goat hides. The gas produced from young wine still fermenting made even flexible new wineskins "ready to burst" (Job 32:19).

• 2:24. *What's not permitted*: the Pharisees were careful to avoid any work on the sabbath day (v. 16) and "harvesting" was one of the categories of forbidden work.

• 2:25–26. *Read what David did*: a story based on 1 Sam 21:1-6, between the time when David had been "anointed" as the next king, and when he was actually enthroned. While fleeing to escape King Saul's threat to his life, he sought bread

from the priest, who had only *consecrated bread*, restricted to use by the priests. Although David ate the bread, he is not condemned in the story for violating these restrictions. The Pharisees' interpretation is thus more strict than scripture itself.

Mark's retelling of the story is only partly accurate. He correctly notes the priestly use of consecrated bread. Every sabbath day the priest was required to place twelve loaves on the table in the tabernacle as an offering to God from the people. When fresh loaves were presented the following week, the previous loaves were for the use of the priests (Lev 24:5-9). However, the priest in the story was not *Abiathar*, but his father Ahimelech. When Saul learned of the priest's favor to David, he ordered all the priests in that place slain. Only Abiathar escaped. He joined David's entourage in hiding, and was later made high priest when David became king. Mark's factual error suggests this may have been a familiar story told from memory about "David's high priest, Abiathar."

• 2:27–28. The introductory words, *He continued*, suggest that the following sayings

Τὸ σάββατον διὰ τὸν ἄνθρωπον ἐγένετο
καὶ οὐχ ὁ ἄνθρωπος διὰ τὸ σάββατον·
²⁸ ὥστε κύριός ἐστιν ὁ υἱὸς τοῦ ἀνθρώπου καὶ τοῦ σαββάτου.

were originally independent from the preceding story (§2.6). *Adam and Eve* and *son of Adam*: the translators have preserved the parallel structure of these two sayings in Mark and their tie to the creation story. Since the sabbath (= seventh) day of course came after the creation of humankind ("Adam and Eve"), humanity (descendants of Adam and Eve) have priority over sabbath regulations. *Lords it over* describes the authority exercised by one who is *lord* or *master* over something (§6.4). In Mark this prerogative derives from creation and thus applies to everyone. However, *son of Adam*

Son of Adam

The traditional translation, "the Son of Man," is apt to be misleading. In ordinary English, "man" refers primarily to males of the species. But the Greek word (*anthropos*) means "human," as distinct from beast or god. It is a generic term that can apply to any member of the human species. *Anthropology* is thus the study of the behavior of all humans, male and female.

In the Hebrew Bible, the phrase, Son of Adam, is used in three different senses.

1. *Son of Adam: Insignificant Earthling*

The phrase is employed to refer to the human species as insignificant creatures in the presence of God:

> How can a human be right before God?
> Look, even the moon is not bright,
>   and the stars are not pure in his sight;
> How much less a human, who is a maggot,
>   and a *son of Adam*, who is a worm!   Job 25:4–6

2. *Sons of Adam: A Little Lower than God*

The phrase was also used to identify human beings as next to God in the order of creation:

> When I look at the heavens, the work of your fingers,
>   the moon and the stars that you set in place;
> what are humans that you should regard them,
>   and *sons of Adam* that you attend them?
> You made them a little lower than God
>   and crowned them with glory and honor;
> you gave them rule over the works of your hands
>   and put all things under their feet.   Ps 8:3–6

The sabbath day was created for Adam and Eve,
not Adam and Eve for the sabbath day.
²⁸So, the son of Adam lords it even over the sabbath day.

---

soon came to be interpreted as a special claim Jesus made for himself (see appended note below on "The Son of Adam"), as can be seen already in Matt 12:8 and Luke 6:5, where it is used without the saying about the sabbath day made for Adam and Eve. (In contrast to the secular proverb in v. 17, this one does not repeat conventional wisdom. The same Pausanias, in the previous saying, voices the opposite claim made here: ancient laws cannot be changed, because the laws must "lord it over" humans, not humans over the laws.)

3. Son of Adam: the Apocalyptic Figure

The Jewish scriptures portray the human being as the agent to exercise control over every living creature (Gen 1:28). This ideal decisively shaped Jewish visions of the end of history:

As I looked on, in a night vision,
I saw one like a *son of Adam* coming with heaven's clouds.
He came to the Ancient of Days and was presented to him.
Dominion and glory and rule were given to him.
His dominion is an everlasting dominion that will not pass away,
and his rule is one that will never be destroyed.   Dan 7:13–14

The phrase "son of Adam" is employed in three different senses in the gospels: (a) To refer to the heavenly figure who is to come; (b) To refer to one who is to suffer, die, and rise; (c) To refer to human beings.

(a) References to the figure who is to come in the future on clouds of glory to judge the world are found in Mark 8:38, 13:26, and 14:62 and parallels. This usage is derived from Daniel 7 (sense 3 above). On the lips of Jesus these references to the apocalyptic figure of the future are not self-references but allusions to a third person.

(b) References to the figure who is to suffer, die, and rise are scattered through the gospels. They refer to unique events in the story of Jesus' suffering and death, so that "son of Adam" seems to be only a roundabout way of saying "I."

(c) Two sayings highlight the authority of the "son of Adam" on earth, in one instance, to forgive sin (Mark 2:10), in a second, to "lord it" over the sabbath (Mark 2:28). These sayings appear to conform to the first two senses drawn from the Hebrew Bible mentioned earlier.

The confusion in how this phrase is to be understood owes to the fact that the Christian community tended to understand the phrase messianically or apocalyptically. The original senses derived from the Hebrew Bible were lost or suppressed.

Man with a crippled hand

3 Καὶ εἰσῆλθεν πάλιν εἰς τὴν συναγωγήν. καὶ ἦν ἐκεῖ ἄνθρωπος ἐξηραμμένην ἔχων τὴν χεῖρα· ²καὶ παρετήρουν αὐτὸν εἰ τοῖς σάββασιν θεραπεύσει αὐτόν, ἵνα κατηγορήσωσιν αὐτοῦ. ³καὶ λέγει τῷ ἀνθρώπῳ τῷ τὴν χεῖρα ἔχοντι ξηράν, Ἔγειρε εἰς τὸ μέσον. ⁴καὶ λέγει αὐτοῖς, Ἔξεστιν τοῖς σάββασιν ἀγαθὸν ποιῆσαι ἢ κακοποιῆσαι, ψυχὴν σῶσαι ἢ ἀποκτεῖναι; Οἱ δὲ ἐσιώπων. ⁵καὶ περιβλεψάμενος αὐτοὺς μετ' ὀργῆς, συλλυπούμενος ἐπὶ τῇ πωρώσει τῆς καρδίας αὐτῶν, λέγει τῷ ἀνθρώπῳ, Ἔκτεινον τὴν χεῖρα. Καὶ ἐξέτεινεν, καὶ ἀπεκατεστάθη ἡ χεὶρ αὐτοῦ. ⁶καὶ ἐξελθόντες οἱ Φαρισαῖοι εὐθὺς μετὰ τῶν Ἡρῳδιανῶν συμβούλιον ἐδίδουν κατ' αὐτοῦ ὅπως αὐτὸν ἀπολέσωσιν.

By the sea

⁷Καὶ ὁ Ἰησοῦς μετὰ τῶν μαθητῶν αὐτοῦ ἀνεχώρησεν πρὸς τὴν θάλασσαν· καὶ πολὺ πλῆθος ἀπὸ τῆς Γαλιλαίας ἠκολούθησεν· καὶ ἀπὸ τῆς Ἰουδαίας ⁸καὶ ἀπὸ Ἱεροσολύμων καὶ ἀπὸ τῆς Ἰδουμαίας καὶ πέραν τοῦ Ἰορδάνου καὶ περὶ Τύρον καὶ Σιδῶνα, πλῆθος πολύ, ἀκούοντες ὅσα ἐποίει ἦλθον πρὸς αὐτόν. ⁹καὶ εἶπεν τοῖς μαθηταῖς αὐτοῦ ἵνα πλοιάριον προσκαρτερῇ αὐτῷ διὰ τὸν ὄχλον ἵνα μὴ θλίβωσιν αὐτόν· ¹⁰πολλοὺς γὰρ ἐθεράπευσεν, ὥστε ἐπιπίπτειν αὐτῷ ἵνα αὐτοῦ ἅψωνται ὅσοι εἶχον μάστιγας. ¹¹καὶ τὰ πνεύματα τὰ ἀκάθαρτα, ὅταν αὐτὸν ἐθεώρουν, προσέπιπτον αὐτῷ καὶ ἔκραζον λέγοντες ὅτι Σὺ εἶ ὁ υἱὸς τοῦ θεοῦ. ¹²Καὶ πολλὰ ἐπετίμα αὐτοῖς ἵνα μὴ αὐτὸν φανερὸν ποιήσωσιν.

7-8. The transition between these two verses is ambiguous, because *a huge crowd* is mentioned twice. Various MSS smooth this out by omitting *followed*, or making it plural, or omitting the second *huge crowd*.

• **3:1-6.** This set of controversy stories culminates with an anecdote featuring a decisive action by Jesus: he heals on the sabbath day. His action prompts his opponents to hatch a plot against his life. The reader of Mark now for the first time catches sight of the tragic outcome of story.

• **3:4.** Jesus is presented as taking the Pharisees concern for "what's not permitted" on the sabbath day (2:24) and turning it into an all-encompassing ethical question.

• **3:5.** *Anger*: even stronger than the emotion, "indignant," attributed to Jesus in the final anecdote of the previous section (1:41). Mark's willingness to have Jesus express such emotions is without parallel in the other gospels. *Obstinacy*: the most serious kind of contrariness, a disposition to act against the will of God (§4.5). That Mark

uses such a severe label for the Pharisees (2:16) may suggest more the degree of antipathy between Mark's community and the non-Christian authorities than between Jesus and the Pharisees.

• **3:6.** *Herodians*: apparently political supporters, or administrative staff, of King Herod's son Antipas (6:14), who had jurisdiction over Galilee (mentioned again in 12:13). They are unlikely to have been particularly concerned with religious matters. Since the Pharisees typically avoided associating with such groups that did not maintain the Pharisees' distinction between things "clean" and "unclean," these two groups would have been most unlikely as co-conspirators.

• **3:7-12.** This is the longest summary passage constructed by Mark (for a shorter one,

3 Then he went back to the synagogue, and a fellow with a crippled hand was there. ²So they kept an eye on him, to see whether he would heal the fellow on the sabbath day, so they could denounce him. ³And he says to the fellow with the crippled hand, "Get up here in front of everybody." ⁴Then he asks them, "On the sabbath day is it permitted to do good or to do evil, to save life or to destroy it?"

But they maintained their silence. ⁵And looking right at them with anger, exasperated at their obstinacy, he says to the fellow, "Hold out your hand!"

He held it out and his hand was restored. ⁶Then the Pharisees went right out with the Herodians and hatched a plot against him, to get rid of him.

⁷Then Jesus withdrew with his disciples to the sea, and a huge crowd from Galilee followed. When they heard what he was doing, a huge crowd from Judea, ⁸and from Jerusalem and Idumea and across the Jordan, and from around Tyre and Sidon, collected around him. ⁹And he told his disciples to have a small boat ready for him on account of the crowd, so they would not mob him. (¹⁰After all, he had healed so many, that all who had diseases were pushing forward to touch him.) ¹¹The unclean spirits also, whenever they faced him, would fall down before him and shout out, "You son of God, you!"

¹²But he always warned them not to tell who he was.

Man with a crippled hand

By the sea

---

see 1:32–34). It exhibits many of the typical features of Mark's narrative style (§3): exaggeration, repetition, parenthetical asides (2:15), and the motif of secrecy. It serves as the transition between the first two major sections of the narrative, 1:16–3:7, which began with the selection of the first disciples, and 3:13–6:6, which begins with the formation of "a group of twelve," from among the disciples.

• **3:7–8:** Mark presents a significantly larger geographical area than the story has mentioned thus far. The summary in 1:39 had Jesus going "all around Galilee." Suddenly there are crowds coming, not just from the center of religious activity, *Judea and Jerusalem*, where John had attracted his following (1:5), but from outlying areas. *Idumea:* only here in the New Testament, the Greek name for ancient Edom, the area to the southeast of Judea below the Dead Sea. During the exile its inhabitants moved into vacated parts of southern Judea; so "Idumea" came to refer to the area imme-

diately south of Judea, within twenty miles of Jerusalem (1 Macc 4:29). During the Maccabean conquests, late second century B.C.E., of the areas that had once been part of ancient Israel, Idumea was taken over by Judea, and Judean religious practices were imposed on the Idumeans. While they were thus properly "Jewish," they were viewed with some disdain, similar to the Samaritans, by the religious authorities in Jerusalem. The most famous, or infamous, Idumean was Herod the Great. *Across the Jordan:* the area east across the Jordan had also been among the conquests of the Maccabees (1 Macc 11:60). Its Greek name was "Perea" from the Greek word for "across" (*peran*). In the Roman administrative arrangement, Perea was linked with Galilee, under the jurisdiction of Herod Antipas (6:14). *Around Tyre and Sidon:* the area northwest of upper Galilee associated with the ancient Phoenician cities along the Mediterranean coast was predominantly pagan (7:24–26), though it would have had

The twelve

¹³Καὶ ἀναβαίνει εἰς τὸ ὄρος καὶ προσκαλεῖται οὓς ἤθελεν αὐτός, καὶ ἀπῆλθον πρὸς αὐτόν. ¹⁴καὶ ἐποίησεν δώδεκα, ἵνα ὦσιν μετ᾽ αὐτοῦ καὶ ἵνα ἀποστέλλῃ αὐτοὺς κηρύσσειν ¹⁵καὶ ἔχειν ἐξουσίαν ἐκβάλλειν τὰ δαιμόνια· ¹⁶Καὶ ἐπέθηκεν ὄνομα τῷ Σίμωνι Πέτρον, ¹⁷καὶ Ἰάκωβον τὸν τοῦ Ζεβεδαίου καὶ Ἰωάννην τὸν ἀδελφὸν τοῦ Ἰακώβου, καὶ ἐπέθηκεν αὐτοῖς ὀνόματα Βοανηργές, ὅ ἐστιν Υἱοὶ Βροντῆς· ¹⁸καὶ Ἀνδρέαν καὶ Φίλιππον καὶ Βαρθολομαῖον καὶ Μαθθαῖον καὶ Θωμᾶν καὶ Ἰάκωβον τὸν τοῦ Ἀλφαίου καὶ Θαδδαῖον καὶ Σίμωνα τὸν Καναναῖον ¹⁹καὶ Ἰούδαν Ἰσκαριώθ, ὃς καὶ παρέδωκεν αὐτόν.

Beelzebul controversy

²⁰Καὶ ἔρχεται εἰς οἶκον· καὶ συνέρχεται πάλιν ὄχλος, ὥστε μὴ δύνασθαι αὐτοὺς μηδὲ ἄρτον φαγεῖν. ²¹καὶ ἀκούσαντες οἱ παρ᾽ αὐτοῦ ἐξῆλθον κρατῆσαι αὐτόν, ἔλεγον γὰρ ὅτι ἐξέστη. ²²καὶ οἱ γραμματεῖς οἱ ἀπὸ Ἱεροσολύμων καταβάντες ἔλεγον ὅτι Βεελζεβοὺλ ἔχει, καὶ ὅτι ἐν τῷ ἄρχοντι τῶν δαιμονίων ἐκβάλλει τὰ δαιμόνια.

---

14. *Twelve:* some MSS add *whom he called apostles* similar to Luke 6:13.
16. Several early MSS begin by repeating, *So he formed a group of twelve* from v. 14. **22.** *Beelzebul* is spelled *Beelzebub* in some Latin and Syriac MSS, apparently influenced by the name of an ancient Philistine god, "Baal [lord] of the house [temple]," whom the Israelites mockingly referred to as Baal-zebub, "Lord of the flies" (2 Kgs 1:2).

---

a sizable Judean population also. Noticeable by its absence in Mark is any mention of Samaria, the area between Galilee and Judea, another Maccabean conquest added to Judea. The Roman governor of Judea had control also over Samaria, which may explain Mark's failure to mention it separately.

• **3:13–35.** Mark refocuses attention on the disciples and adds anecdotes that contrast this self-designated group with Jesus' relatives (v. 21) and immediate family (v. 31).

• **3:13.** *The mountain:* in the biblical exodus tradition the setting where Moses led the Israelites to form a covenant with Yahweh, whom he had encountered there. "The mountain" thus symbolized where the community formed its commitment to God.

• **3:14–15.** *Twelve:* later becomes *the twelve* in Mark, an important symbolic number in the formation of ancient Israel; the "twelve tribes" derived from the "twelve sons" of Jacob. Mark thus pictures Jesus as forming a "new Israel," and he describes them as

authorized *to speak* and *to drive out demons*, the same activities Jesus was practicing (1:39). The one important category of Jesus' activity not passed on to the disciples is that of teaching (1:21, 22, 27; 2:13), except when the disciples function as *apostles* (6:30).

• **3:16.** The three who form the "inner circle" are given nicknames. *Rock:* translates Greek *petros*, hereafter *Peter*, except for its last appearance (16:7), when ironic *Rock* is appropriate. Using *Rock* here suggests that Mark saw irony in this as a nickname for the future deserter (§3.5, §5.1). This highlighted role for Peter sparked an early Christian tradition that Peter was Mark's source for this material, since Mark was not himself a disciple of Jesus. However, because the portrayal of Peter ends up rather negative in Mark, most modern scholars doubt the historicity of this tradition.

• **3:17.** *Boanerges:* likely derived from Aramaic, Jesus' native language (see 5:41), but the derivation is uncertain. Mark's interpre-

¹³Then he goes up on the mountain and summons those he wanted, and they came to him. ¹⁴He formed a group of twelve to be his companions, and to be sent out to speak, ¹⁵and to have authority to drive out demons.

The twelve

¹⁶ And to Simon he gave the nickname Rock, ¹⁷and to James, the son of Zebedee, and to John, his brother, he also gave a nickname, Boanerges, which means "Thunder Brothers"; ¹⁸and Andrew and Philip and Bartholomew and Matthew and Thomas and James, the son of Alphaeus; and Thaddeus and Simon the Zealot; ¹⁹and Judas Iscariot, who, in the end, turned him in.

²⁰Then he goes home, and once again a crowd gathers, so they could not even grab a bite to eat. ²¹When his relatives heard about it, they came to get him. (You see, they thought he was out of his mind.) ²²And the scholars who had come down from Jerusalem would say, "He is under the control of Beelzebul" and "He drives out demons in the name of the head demon!"

Beelzebul controversy

---

tation, *Thunder Brothers*, implies *hot-tempered*.

• **3:18–19.** The seven names between Andrew and Judas appear nowhere else in Mark's story. One, Thaddaeus, appears only on Matthew's list (Matt 10:3), but is replaced in Luke-Acts by a second Judas, son of James (Luke 6:16; Acts 1:13). The gospel of John has no list of twelve names at all. The phenomenon of having twelve names was thus more important than the twelve individuals themselves. *James, the son of Alphaeus* is apparently unrelated to *Levi, the son of Alphaeus* (2:14). Only Mark identified Levi this way. *Simon the Zealot*: the nickname is derived from Aramaic *qan'an*, "zealous." Luke uses the Greek term for "Zealot" (Luke 6:15; Acts 1:13). "Zealot" was the name given to those who strongly opposed the presence of Roman troops in Judea, and eventually provoked the 66–70 C.E. war.

• **3:19.** *Iscariot*: if derived from Hebrew, may mean "man from Kerioth," a town in Judea; though some MSS have *Scariot*, which could be taken from *sicarius*, a Latin word for "dagger," implying "assassin." This latter speculation implies political motives for Judas' role in the arrest of Jesus (14:43–46). *Turned him in*: since Jesus' ministry began after John had been *locked up* (1:14), a similar fate, announced for the first time at 3:6, is now anticipated for Jesus (§4.11).

• **3:20.** *Goes home*: could be *enters a house*, but the context is similar to "home" at 2:1; 9:28.

• **3:21.** *They came to get him*: suggests "unfriendly" intent that later becomes more hostile (12:12; 14:1, 44, 46). *They thought*: the indefinite *they* does not make clear whether it is *his relatives* or just some people.

• **3:22.** *He is under the control of Beelzebul*: describes someone "possessed" who needs exorcism from "unclean spirits" (3:30; 5:15; 7:25). The charge against Jesus: he is *practicing magic*, an accusation found in later rabbinic literature. In the riddle that follows Mark may be preserving an old play on the meaning of the Aramaic name, "Beel-zebul," about "Baal" [Satan] and his "house," if "dwelling" is taken as one possible meaning of *zebul*. The name could also be a later, more insulting label, utilizing a homonym *zebul*, "Lord [baal] of dung," which became one of many names used for the forces of evil, under the control of *the head demon*, Satan (1:34). The popular "Lord of the Flies" derives from the variant spelling in the Latin vulgate translation, *Beelzebub*, the name of an ancient Philistine god (2 Kgs 1:2–6), which the LXX renders "Baal Fly." Both *zebul* ("dung") and *zebub* ("fly") are probably Israelite spoofs of the original name, which is no longer preserved.

²³ Καὶ προσκαλεσάμενος αὐτοὺς ἐν παραβολαῖς ἔλεγεν
αὐτοῖς, Πῶς δύναται Σατανᾶς Σατανᾶν ἐκβάλλειν; ²⁴ καὶ ἐὰν
βασιλεία ἐφ' ἑαυτὴν μερισθῇ, οὐ δύναται σταθῆναι ἡ βασιλεία
ἐκείνη· ²⁵ καὶ ἐὰν οἰκία ἐφ' ἑαυτὴν μερισθῇ, οὐ δυνήσεται ἡ οἰκία
ἐκείνη σταθῆναι. ²⁶ καὶ εἰ ὁ Σατανᾶς ἀνέστη ἐφ' ἑαυτὸν καὶ
ἐμερίσθη, οὐ δύναται στῆναι ἀλλὰ τέλος ἔχει.

²⁷ Ἀλλ' οὐ δύναται οὐδεὶς εἰς τὴν οἰκίαν τοῦ ἰσχυροῦ
εἰσελθὼν τὰ σκεύη αὐτοῦ διαρπάσαι ἐὰν μὴ πρῶτον τὸν ἰσχυρὸν
δήσῃ, καὶ τότε τὴν οἰκίαν αὐτοῦ διαρπάσει.

²⁸ Ἀμὴν λέγω ὑμῖν ὅτι πάντα ἀφεθήσεται τοῖς υἱοῖς τῶν
ἀνθρώπων, τὰ ἁμαρτήματα καὶ αἱ βλασφημίαι ὅσα ἐὰν
βλασφημήσωσιν· ²⁹ ὃς δ' ἂν βλασφημήσῃ εἰς τὸ πνεῦμα τὸ
ἅγιον οὐκ ἔχει ἄφεσιν εἰς τὸν αἰῶνα, ἀλλὰ ἔνοχός ἐστιν αἰωνίου
ἁμαρτήματος,

³⁰ Ὅτι ἔλεγον, Πνεῦμα ἀκάθαρτον ἔχει.

True relatives   ³¹ Καὶ ἔρχεται ἡ μήτηρ αὐτοῦ καὶ οἱ ἀδελφοὶ αὐτοῦ καὶ ἔξω
στήκοντες ἀπέστειλαν πρὸς αὐτὸν καλοῦντες αὐτόν. ³² καὶ
ἐκάθητο περὶ αὐτὸν ὄχλος, καὶ λέγουσιν αὐτῷ, Ἰδοὺ ἡ μήτηρ
σου καὶ οἱ ἀδελφοί σου [καὶ αἱ ἀδελφαί σου] ἔξω ζητοῦσίν σε.

³³ Καὶ ἀποκριθεὶς αὐτοῖς λέγει, Τίς ἐστιν ἡ μήτηρ μου καὶ οἱ
ἀδελφοί;

³⁴ Καὶ περιβλεψάμενος τοὺς περὶ αὐτὸν κύκλῳ καθημένους
λέγει, Ἴδε ἡ μήτηρ μου καὶ οἱ ἀδελφοί μου. ³⁵ ὃς ἂν ποιήσῃ τὸ
θέλημα τοῦ θεοῦ, οὗτος ἀδελφός μου καὶ ἀδελφὴ καὶ μήτηρ
ἐστίν.

---

32. *And sisters:* omitted in most MSS, including the two earliest, but also in
Mark 6:3.

• **3:23.** *Riddles:* the same Greek term can be translated *parables*, but the following sayings are not in the form of "parables" (§4.4; §6.5).

• **3:27.** *A powerful man's house:* since Jesus is the "more powerful" one (1:7), Mark's riddle is an analogy: in an exorcism Jesus "ties up" Satan and releases those "under his control."

• **3:28.** *I swear to you:* the first instance in Mark of a formula used only by Jesus when making a solemn declaration (§5.2). The serious topic here is the ultimate *blasphemy:* uttering slander against *the holy spirit.* Since *the holy spirit* defines what Jesus does (1:8), the one *eternal sin* is to slander Jesus.

• **3:30.** Apparently another narrative aside,

²³And after calling them over, he would speak to them in riddles: "How can Satan drive out Satan? ²⁴After all, if a government is divided against itself, that government cannot endure. ²⁵And if a household is divided against itself, that household won't be able to survive. ²⁶So if Satan rebels against himself and is divided, he cannot endure but is done for.

²⁷"No one can enter a powerful man's house to steal his belongings unless he first ties him up. Only then does he loot his house.

²⁸"I swear to you, all offenses and whatever blasphemies humankind might blaspheme will be forgiven them. ²⁹But whoever blasphemes against the holy spirit is never ever forgiven, but is guilty of an eternal sin."

(³⁰Remember, it was they who had started the accusation, "He is controlled by an unclean spirit.")

³¹Then his mother and his brothers arrive. While still outside, they send in and ask for him. ³²A crowd was sitting around him, and they say to him, "Look, your mother and your brothers [and sisters] are outside looking for you."

True relatives

³³In response he says to them: "My mother and brothers—who ever are they?"

³⁴And looking right at those seated around him in a circle, he says, "Here are my mother and my brothers. ³⁵Whoever does God's will, that's my brother and sister and mother!"

---

even though Mark does not use the Greek conjunction *gar* (§6.1). *The accusation*: repeats the earlier charge from v. 22 and further identifies "unclean spirits" as "demons" (1:34). For Mark this is the accusation that *blasphemes against the holy spirit* (v. 29).

• **3:31.** *His mother and his brothers*: the first mention of Jesus' family members, some of whom are named in 6:3. Mark presents Jesus as distancing himself from them, perhaps implying a critique of the role of

Jesus' relatives in the early church. Since *brothers* was commonly used by Christians for each other, this anecdote may also preserve the early church's claim that Jesus sanctioned the inclusion of non-Jews.

• **3:35.** *God's will*: the same as *what God wants* (14:36), in the form of "what one does." In the traditional Judean understanding, *God's will* is most clearly set forth in the Hebrew Bible, as interpreted by the Pharisees. However, Jesus will explicitly reject that mode of interpretation (7:5–13).

4 Καὶ πάλιν ἤρξατο διδάσκειν παρὰ τὴν θάλασσαν. καὶ συνάγεται πρὸς αὐτὸν ὄχλος πλεῖστος, ὥστε αὐτὸν εἰς πλοῖον ἐμβάντα καθῆσθαι ἐν τῇ θαλάσσῃ, καὶ πᾶς ὁ ὄχλος πρὸς τὴν θάλασσαν ἐπὶ τῆς γῆς ἦσαν. ²Καὶ ἐδίδασκεν αὐτοὺς ἐν παραβολαῖς πολλά, καὶ ἔλεγεν αὐτοῖς ἐν τῇ διδαχῇ αὐτοῦ,

³ Ἀκούετε. ἰδοὺ ἐξῆλθεν ὁ σπείρων σπεῖραι. ⁴καὶ ἐγένετο ἐν τῷ σπείρειν ὃ μὲν ἔπεσεν παρὰ τὴν ὁδόν, καὶ ἦλθεν τὰ πετεινὰ καὶ κατέφαγεν αὐτό. ⁵καὶ ἄλλο ἔπεσεν ἐπὶ τὸ πετρῶδες ὅπου οὐκ εἶχεν γῆν πολλήν, καὶ εὐθὺς ἐξανέτειλεν διὰ τὸ μὴ ἔχειν βάθος γῆς· ⁶καὶ ὅτε ἀνέτειλεν ὁ ἥλιος ἐκαυματίσθη, καὶ διὰ τὸ μὴ ἔχειν ῥίζαν ἐξηράνθη. ⁷καὶ ἄλλο ἔπεσεν εἰς τὰς ἀκάνθας, καὶ ἀνέβησαν αἱ ἄκανθαι καὶ συνέπνιξαν αὐτό, καὶ καρπὸν οὐκ ἔδωκεν. ⁸καὶ ἄλλα ἔπεσεν εἰς τὴν γῆν τὴν καλήν, καὶ ἐδίδου καρπὸν ἀναβαίνοντα καὶ αὐξανόμενα, καὶ ἔφερεν ἐν τριάκοντα καὶ ἐν ἑξήκοντα καὶ ἐν ἑκατόν.

⁹Καὶ ἔλεγεν, Ὃς ἔχει ὦτα ἀκούειν ἀκουέτω.

Secret of God's imperial rule

¹⁰Καὶ ὅτε ἐγένετο κατὰ μόνας, ἠρώτων αὐτὸν οἱ περὶ αὐτὸν σὺν τοῖς δώδεκα τὰς παραβολάς. ¹¹καὶ ἔλεγεν αὐτοῖς, Ὑμῖν τὸ μυστήριον δέδοται τῆς βασιλείας τοῦ θεοῦ· ἐκείνοις δὲ τοῖς ἔξω ἐν παραβολαῖς τὰ πάντα γίνεται, ¹²ἵνα

βλέποντες βλέπωσιν
καὶ μὴ ἴδωσιν,
καὶ ἀκούοντες ἀκούωσιν
καὶ μὴ συνιῶσιν,
μήποτε ἐπιστρέψωσιν καὶ ἀφεθῇ αὐτοῖς.

Understanding the sower

¹³Καὶ λέγει αὐτοῖς, Οὐκ οἴδατε τὴν παραβολὴν ταύτην, καὶ πῶς πάσας τὰς παραβολὰς γνώσεσθε; ¹⁴ὁ σπείρων τὸν λόγον

---

9. One early MS adds: *Whoever has a mind should put it to work.*

• **4:1–34.** The first extended discourse in Mark, and the only one in addition to ch. 13, features Jesus as teller of parables. Mark treats the enigmatic quality of parables as evidence of the ironic nature of what Jesus is attempting to teach.

• **4:2.** *Parables:* here refers to sayings in the form of a parabolic story, different than the enigmatic riddle in 3:23 (§4.4; §6.5).

• **4:3.** *Listen to this!* a call to attention that echoes the Judean call to worship, *Hear, Israel!* (Mark 12:29). *This sower:* Mark envisions a typical peasant farmer casting seeds by hand from a pouch. A wooden plough was then used to turn the seeds under the

soil, where conditions permitted. The kinds of soil conditions described are quite realistic for that terrain. Wheat was the most likely grain crop; it would have been planted in the fall for late spring harvest.

• **4:8.** *A yield of thirty:* apparently meaning "thirty times the amount sown." A tenfold yield would have been a good harvest.

• **4:9.** *Anyone with two good ears:* anyone capable of hearing. This admonition was used particularly after sayings that warranted further explanation (4:23; 7:16).

• **4:11.** *The secret:* part of the irony about God's imperial rule (1:15) being a riddle (§3.5), so everything *in parables* comes to

4 Once again he started to teach beside the sea. An enormous crowd gathers around him, so he climbs into a boat and sits there on the water facing the huge crowd on the shore.

²He would then teach them many things in parables. In the course of his teaching he would tell them:

³Listen to this! This sower went out to sow. ⁴While he was sowing, some seed fell along the path, and the birds came and ate it up. ⁵Other seed fell on rocky ground where there wasn't much soil, and it came up right away because the soil had no depth. ⁶But when the sun came up it was scorched, and because it had no root it withered. ⁷Still other seed fell among thorns, and the thorns came up and choked it, so that it produced no fruit. ⁸Finally, some seed fell on good earth and started producing fruit. The seed sprouted and grew: one part had a yield of thirty, another part sixty, and a third part one hundred.

⁹And as usual he said: "Anyone here with two good ears had better listen!"

¹⁰Whenever he went off by himself, those close to him with the twelve would ask him about the parables. ¹¹And he would say to them: "You have been given the secret of God's imperial rule; but to those outside everything is presented in parables, ¹²so that

Secret of God's imperial rule

They may look with eyes wide open
but never quite see,
and may listen with ears attuned
but never quite understand,
otherwise they might turn around and find forgiveness!"

¹³Then he says to them: "You don't get this parable, so how are you going to understand other parables? ¹⁴The 'sower' is

Understanding the sower

---

mean *riddles* again (§2.3; §4.4; §4.5; §6.5). *Those outside*: an important category defined by Mark: those for whom Jesus' teaching remains a riddle are by definition those outside God's imperial rule.

• **4:12.** A bold use of Isa 6:9–10, but not directly quoting either Hebrew or LXX. The opening *so that* may have been influenced by Judean interpretation of Isa 6:6–10, or Mark may have shortened it from *so that the scripture might be fulfilled*, a common theme in Matthew (for example 13:14), but not in Mark. It would soften the present text, which, as it stands, means that the parables ironically prevent some people

from understanding. Indeed, Isaiah claims that his calling was specifically to present his message in such a way that people would not understand it. For Mark the Isaiah text justifies Jesus' teaching style, which required "insider" explanations. *Eyes wide open* and *ears attuned*: the theme of seeing and hearing, but "never quite understanding," is important throughout the rest of the first half of Mark, and provides the framework for the central section (8:22–10:52).

• **4:13.** *You don't get it*: could be a question, *Don't you get it?* The translation *get it* captures the sense of "have insight," or "see

σπείρει. ¹⁵οὗτοι δέ εἰσιν οἱ παρὰ τὴν ὁδὸν ὅπου σπείρεται ὁ λόγος, καὶ ὅταν ἀκούσωσιν εὐθὺς ἔρχεται ὁ Σατανᾶς καὶ αἴρει τὸν λόγον τὸν ἐσπαρμένον εἰς αὐτούς. ¹⁶καὶ οὗτοί εἰσιν οἱ ἐπὶ τὰ πετρώδη σπειρόμενοι, οἳ ὅταν ἀκούσωσιν τὸν λόγον εὐθὺς μετὰ χαρᾶς λαμβάνουσιν αὐτόν, ¹⁷καὶ οὐκ ἔχουσιν ῥίζαν ἐν ἑαυτοῖς ἀλλὰ πρόσκαιροί εἰσιν· εἶτα γενομένης θλίψεως ἢ διωγμοῦ διὰ τὸν λόγον εὐθὺς σκανδαλίζονται. ¹⁸καὶ ἄλλοι εἰσὶν οἱ εἰς τὰς ἀκάνθας σπειρόμενοι· οὗτοί εἰσιν οἱ τὸν λόγον ἀκούσαντες, ¹⁹καὶ αἱ μέριμναι τοῦ αἰῶνος καὶ ἡ ἀπάτη τοῦ πλούτου καὶ αἱ περὶ τὰ λοιπὰ ἐπιθυμίαι εἰσπορευόμεναι συμπνίγουσιν τὸν λόγον, καὶ ἄκαρπος γίνεται. ²⁰καὶ ἐκεῖνοί εἰσιν οἱ ἐπὶ τὴν γῆν τὴν καλὴν σπαρέντες, οἵτινες ἀκούουσιν τὸν λόγον καὶ παραδέχονται καὶ καρποφοροῦσιν ἐν τριάκοντα καὶ ἐν ἑξήκοντα καὶ ἐν ἑκατόν.

Lamp & bushel   ²¹Καὶ ἔλεγεν αὐτοῖς, Μήτι ἔρχεται ὁ λύχνος ἵνα ὑπὸ τὸν μόδιον τεθῇ ἢ ὑπὸ τὴν κλίνην; οὐχ ἵνα ἐπὶ τὴν λυχνίαν τεθῇ;

²²Οὐ γάρ ἐστίν τι κρυπτὸν ἐὰν μὴ ἵνα φανερωθῇ, οὐδὲ ἐγένετο ἀπόκρυφον ἀλλ' ἵνα ἔλθῃ εἰς φανερόν.

²³Εἴ τις ἔχει ὦτα ἀκούειν ἀκουέτω.

Measure   ²⁴Καὶ ἔλεγεν αὐτοῖς, Βλέπετε τί ἀκούετε. ἐν ᾧ μέτρῳ μετρεῖτε
for measure   μετρηθήσεται ὑμῖν καὶ προστεθήσεται ὑμῖν.

²⁵Ὃς γὰρ ἔχει, δοθήσεται αὐτῷ· καὶ ὃς οὐκ ἔχει, καὶ ὃ ἔχει ἀρθήσεται ἀπ' αὐτοῦ.

Seed & harvest   ²⁶Καὶ ἔλεγεν,

Οὕτως ἐστὶν ἡ βασιλεία τοῦ θεοῦ ὡς ἄνθρωπος βάλῃ τὸν σπόρον ἐπὶ τῆς γῆς ²⁷καὶ καθεύδῃ καὶ ἐγείρηται νύκτα καὶ ἡμέραν, καὶ ὁ σπόρος βλαστᾷ καὶ μηκύνηται ὡς οὐκ οἶδεν αὐτός. ²⁸αὐτομάτη ἡ γῆ καρποφορεῖ, πρῶτον χόρτον, εἶτεν στάχυν, εἶτεν πλήρη σῖτον ἐν τῷ στάχυϊ. ²⁹ὅταν δὲ παραδοῖ ὁ καρπός, εὐθὺς ἀποστέλλει τὸ δρέπανον, ὅτι παρέστηκεν ὁ θερισμός.

---

the light," as distinct from *understand*, in the sense of "figure out," learn by studying. This fits the contrast Mark has made between Jesus' approach and that of "scholars" (1:22).

• **4:14–20.** This kind of interpretation of parables is associated with the allegorical method used by the early church. Each detail of the parabolic story was assumed to be a hidden code for something significantly Christian.

• **4:15.** This description fits the opponents, who never give Jesus' message a chance (3:22).

• **4:16–17.** The ones on *rocky ground* who listen joyously, but under duress are *easily*

'sowing' the message. [15]The first group are the ones 'along the path': here the message 'is sown,' but when they hear, Satan comes right along and steals the message that has been 'sown' into them. [16]The second group are the ones sown 'on rocky ground.' Whenever they listen to the message, right away they receive it happily. [17]Yet they do not have their own 'root' and so are short-lived. When distress or persecution comes because of the message, such a person becomes easily shaken right away. [18]And the third group are those sown 'among the thorns.' These are the ones who have listened to the message, [19]but the worries of the age and the seductiveness of wealth and the yearning for everything else come and 'choke' the message and they become 'fruitless.' [20]And the final group are the ones sown 'on good earth.' They are the ones who listen to the message and take it in and 'produce fruit, here thirty, there sixty, and there one hundred.'"

[21]And he would say to them: "Since when is the lamp brought in to be put under the bushel basket or under the bed? It's put on the lampstand, isn't it?

Lamp & bushel

[22]"After all, there is nothing hidden except to be brought to light, nor anything secreted away that won't be exposed.

[23]"If anyone here has two good ears, use them!"

[24]And he went on to say to them: "Pay attention to what you hear! The measure you use will be the measure used on you, and then some.

Measure for measure

[25]"In fact, to those who have, more will be given, and from those who don't have, even what they do have will be taken away!"

[26]And he would say:

Seed & harvest

God's imperial rule is like this: Suppose someone sows seed on the ground, [27]and sleeps and rises night and day, and the seed sprouts and matures, although the sower is unaware of it. [28]The earth produces fruit on its own, first a shoot, then a head, then mature grain on the head. [29]But when the grain ripens, all of a sudden (that farmer) sends for the sickle, because it's harvest time.

---

shaken, ironically includes Peter, the "Rock" (3:16; §3.5), who resolutely fails to see himself is such descriptions (14:29).

• **4:19.** The hindrance of wealth typifies the person with good intentions, who nonetheless did not become a follower, because he would not relinquish his money (10:22).

• **4:21.** *He would say to them*: also in vv. 26,

30, and the variation in v. 24, *he went on to say*, are a Markan way of continuing the discourse by adding another saying that was originally independent.

• **4:22.** This saying seems to forecast the failure of Jesus' attempt to avoid exposure (3:12).

• **4:23.** A variation of v. 9.

Mustard seed

³⁰Καὶ ἔλεγεν,

Πῶς ὁμοιώσωμεν τὴν βασιλείαν τοῦ θεοῦ, ἢ ἐν τίνι αὐτὴν παραβολῇ θῶμεν; ³¹ὡς κόκκῳ σινάπεως, ὃς ὅταν σπαρῇ ἐπὶ τῆς γῆς, μικρότερον ὂν πάντων τῶν σπερμάτων τῶν ἐπὶ τῆς γῆς, ³²καὶ ὅταν σπαρῇ, ἀναβαίνει καὶ γίνεται μεῖζον πάντων τῶν λαχάνων καὶ ποιεῖ κλάδους μεγάλους, ὥστε δύνασθαι ὑπὸ τὴν σκιὰν αὐτοῦ τὰ πετεινὰ τοῦ οὐρανοῦ κατασκηνοῦν.

Only in parables

³³Καὶ τοιαύταις παραβολαῖς πολλαῖς ἐλάλει αὐτοῖς τὸν λόγον, καθὼς ἠδύναντο ἀκούειν· ³⁴χωρὶς δὲ παραβολῆς οὐκ ἐλάλει αὐτοῖς, κατ᾽ ἰδίαν δὲ τοῖς ἰδίοις μαθηταῖς ἐπέλυεν πάντα.

Rebuking
wind & wave

³⁵Καὶ λέγει αὐτοῖς ἐν ἐκείνῃ τῇ ἡμέρᾳ ὀψίας γενομένης, Διέλθωμεν εἰς τὸ πέραν.

³⁶Καὶ ἀφέντες τὸν ὄχλον παραλαμβάνουσιν αὐτὸν ὡς ἦν ἐν τῷ πλοίῳ, καὶ ἄλλα πλοῖα ἦν μετ᾽ αὐτοῦ. ³⁷καὶ γίνεται λαῖλαψ μεγάλη ἀνέμου, καὶ τὰ κύματα ἐπέβαλλεν εἰς τὸ πλοῖον, ὥστε ἤδη γεμίζεσθαι τὸ πλοῖον. ³⁸καὶ αὐτὸς ἦν ἐν τῇ πρύμνῃ ἐπὶ τὸ προσκεφάλαιον καθεύδων· καὶ ἐγείρουσιν αὐτὸν καὶ λέγουσιν αὐτῷ,

Διδάσκαλε, οὐ μέλει σοι ὅτι ἀπολλύμεθα;

³⁹Καὶ διεγερθεὶς ἐπετίμησεν τῷ ἀνέμῳ καὶ εἶπεν τῇ θαλάσσῃ, Σιώπα, πεφίμωσο.

Καὶ ἐκόπασεν ὁ ἄνεμος, καὶ ἐγένετο γαλήνη μεγάλη.

⁴⁰Καὶ εἶπεν αὐτοῖς, Τί δειλοί ἐστε; οὔπω ἔχετε πίστιν;

⁴¹Καὶ ἐφοβήθησαν φόβον μέγαν, καὶ ἔλεγον πρὸς ἀλλήλους, Τίς ἄρα οὗτός ἐστιν ὅτι καὶ ὁ ἄνεμος καὶ ἡ θάλασσα ὑπακούει αὐτῷ;

---

40. *You still don't trust, do you?* Many, mostly later, MSS read *How is it you don't trust?*

• **4:31–32.** The mustard plant could become 8–10 feet tall, but suggesting its branches could shade the birds seems to be an ironical twist on the Old Testament image of an empire that is like a mighty [cedar] tree in whose shade the birds rest (Ezek 17:22–24; 31:5–6; Dan 4:7–9). God's empire of course would be the greatest of all empires, like a mighty mustard plant!

• **4:34.** This definition complements the previous one about outsiders (v. 11). *His own disciples*: defined as those who have parables "spelled out" to them, whereas for others Jesus' teaching remains "in parables," unexplained, and therefore, not understood. However, Mark's story does not present those who are already "disciples" as the ones who naturally come to understand

³⁰And he would say:

To what should we compare God's imperial rule, or what parable should we use for it? ³¹Consider the mustard seed: When it is sown on the ground, though it is the smallest of all the seeds on the earth, ³²—yet when it is sown, it comes up, and becomes the biggest of all garden plants, and produces branches, so that the birds of the sky can nest in its shade.

³³And with the help of many such parables he would speak his message to them according to their ability to comprehend. ³⁴Yet he would not say anything to them except by way of parable, but would spell everything out in private to his own disciples.

³⁵Later in the day, when evening had come, he says to them, "Let's go across to the other side."

³⁶After sending the crowd away, they took him along since he was in the boat, and other boats accompanied him. ³⁷Then a great squall comes up and the waves begin to pound against the boat, so that the boat suddenly began to fill up. ³⁸He was in the stern sleeping on a cushion. And they wake him up and say to him,

"Teacher, don't you care that we are going to drown?"

³⁹Then he got up and rebuked the wind and said to the sea, "Be quiet, shut up!"

The wind then died down and there was a great calm.

⁴⁰He said to them: "Why are you so cowardly? You still don't trust, do you?"

⁴¹And they were completely terrified and would say to one another, "Who can this fellow be, that even the wind and the sea obey him?"

---

what Jesus explains.

• **4:35–41.** The voyage across the sea of Galilee provides transition for the first time to territory that was predominantly pagan. The stormy crossing is also used by Mark as a test for the readiness of the disciples.

• **4:39.** *He rebuked the wind*: echoes Israel's celebration of the exodus story: the Lord "rebuked" the sea and led the Israelites to safety (Ps 106:9; for more on Mark's use of exodus language, see §4.2; §4.10). *Be quiet, shut up!*: exorcism language used for controlling evil forces (1:25; 10:48).

• **4:41.** *Who can this fellow be?* This question by the *cowardly* disciples (v. 40) only confirms that they "don't get it" (v. 13), but rather face the challenge ahead already *terrified* (§4.7).

5 Καὶ ἦλθον εἰς τὸ πέραν τῆς θαλάσσης εἰς τὴν χώραν τῶν Γερασηνῶν. ²καὶ ἐξελθόντος αὐτοῦ ἐκ τοῦ πλοίου εὐθὺς ὑπήντησεν αὐτῷ ἐκ τῶν μνημείων ἄνθρωπος ἐν πνεύματι ἀκαθάρτῳ, ³ὃς τὴν κατοίκησιν εἶχεν ἐν τοῖς μνήμασιν· καὶ οὐδὲ ἁλύσει οὐκέτι οὐδεὶς ἐδύνατο αὐτὸν δῆσαι, ⁴διὰ τὸ αὐτὸν πολλάκις πέδαις καὶ ἁλύσεσιν δεδέσθαι καὶ διεσπάσθαι ὑπ’ αὐτοῦ τὰς ἁλύσεις καὶ τὰς πέδας συντετρῖφθαι, καὶ οὐδεὶς ἴσχυεν αὐτὸν δαμάσαι· ⁵καὶ διὰ παντὸς νυκτὸς καὶ ἡμέρας ἐν τοῖς μνήμασιν καὶ ἐν τοῖς ὄρεσιν ἦν κράζων καὶ κατακόπτων ἑαυτὸν λίθοις. ⁶καὶ ἰδὼν τὸν Ἰησοῦν ἀπὸ μακρόθεν ἔδραμεν καὶ προσεκύνησεν αὐτῷ, ⁷καὶ κράξας φωνῇ μεγάλῃ λέγει,

Τί ἐμοὶ καὶ σοί, Ἰησοῦ υἱὲ τοῦ θεοῦ τοῦ ὑψίστου; ὁρκίζω σε τὸν θεόν, μή με βασανίσῃς. ⁸ἔλεγεν γὰρ αὐτῷ, Ἔξελθε τὸ πνεῦμα τὸ ἀκάθαρτον ἐκ τοῦ ἀνθρώπου.

⁹Καὶ ἐπηρώτα αὐτόν, Τί ὄνομά σοι;

Καὶ λέγει αὐτῷ, Λεγιὼν ὄνομά μοι, ὅτι πολλοί ἐσμεν. ¹⁰Καὶ παρεκάλει αὐτὸν πολλὰ ἵνα μὴ αὐτοὺς ἀποστείλῃ ἔξω τῆς χώρας.

¹¹Ἦν δὲ ἐκεῖ πρὸς τῷ ὄρει ἀγέλη χοίρων μεγάλη βοσκομένη· ¹²καὶ παρεκάλεσαν αὐτὸν λέγοντες, Πέμψον ἡμᾶς εἰς τοὺς χοίρους, ἵνα εἰς αὐτοὺς εἰσέλθωμεν.

¹³Καὶ ἐπέτρεψεν αὐτοῖς. καὶ ἐξελθόντα τὰ πνεύματα τὰ ἀκάθαρτα εἰσῆλθον εἰς τοὺς χοίρους, καὶ ὥρμησεν ἡ ἀγέλη κατὰ τοῦ κρημνοῦ εἰς τὴν θάλασσαν, ὡς δισχίλιοι, καὶ ἐπνίγοντο ἐν τῇ θαλάσσῃ. ¹⁴καὶ οἱ βόσκοντες αὐτοὺς ἔφυγον καὶ ἀπήγγειλαν εἰς τὴν πόλιν καὶ εἰς τοὺς ἀγρούς·

Καὶ ἦλθον ἰδεῖν τί ἐστιν τὸ γεγονός. ¹⁵καὶ ἔρχονται πρὸς τὸν Ἰησοῦν, καὶ θεωροῦσιν τὸν δαιμονιζόμενον καθήμενον ἱματισμένον καὶ σωφρονοῦντα, τὸν ἐσχηκότα τὸν λεγιῶνα, καὶ ἐφοβήθησαν. ¹⁶καὶ διηγήσαντο αὐτοῖς οἱ ἰδόντες πῶς ἐγένετο τῷ δαιμονιζομένῳ καὶ περὶ τῶν χοίρων. ¹⁷καὶ ἤρξαντο παρακαλεῖν αὐτὸν ἀπελθεῖν ἀπὸ τῶν ὁρίων αὐτῶν.

---

1. *Gerasenes:* MSS vary between *Gadarenes* (preferred in Matthew), *Gerasenes* (preferred also in Luke), and *Gergesenes*, apparently an attempted correction. The earliest MSS of Mark agree on *Gerasenes*.

• **5:1–20.** The first story Mark tells in a foreign setting is an exorcism, similar to the first story that begins Jesus' activity in his native environment (1:21–28).

• **5:1.** *The other side of the sea:* puts Jesus in foreign territory for the first time. The location is unclear (see textual note). Gerasa was a large town in the hills 30 miles southeast of the seacoast, whereas Gadara was a small town only 6 miles inland. The location of Gergesa is unknown, but often guessed to be a coastal village. The uncertainty suggests that later copiers of Mark were searching for a geographical location much closer to shore than Gerasa.

• **5:2.** *Tombs:* cave-like chambers found or cut in rock formations, usually large enough to

5 And they came to the other side of the sea, to the region of the Gerasenes. ²And when he got out of the boat, suddenly a person controlled by an unclean spirit came from the tombs to accost him. ³This man made his home in the tombs, and no one was able to bind him, not even with a chain, ⁴because, though he had often been bound with fetters and with chains, he would break the fetters and pull the chains apart, and nobody had the strength to subdue him. ⁵And day and night he would howl among the tombs and across the hills and keep bruising himself on the stones. ⁶And when he saw Jesus from a distance, he ran up and knelt before him ⁷and, shouting at the top of his voice, he says,

The Demon of Gerasa

"What do you want with me, Jesus, you son of the most high God? For God's sake, don't torment me!" ⁸—because he had been saying to it: "Come out of that fellow, you filthy spirit!"

⁹And ⟨Jesus⟩ started questioning him: "What's your name?"

"My name is Legion," he says, "for there are many of us."

¹⁰And it kept begging him over and over not to expel them from their territory.

¹¹Now over there by the mountain a large herd of pigs was feeding. ¹²And so they bargained with him: "Send us over to the pigs so we may enter them!"

¹³And he agreed. And then the unclean spirits came out and entered the pigs, and the herd rushed down the bluff into the sea, about two thousand of them, and drowned in the sea. ¹⁴And the herdsmen ran off and reported it in town and out in the country.

And they went out to see what had happened. ¹⁵And they come to Jesus and notice the demoniac sitting with his clothes on and with his wits about him, the one who had harbored Legion, and they were scared. ¹⁶And those who had seen told them what had happened to the demoniac, and all about the pigs. ¹⁷And they started begging him to go away from their

---

bury entire families. Often the skeletons were later reburied, so the tomb could be continuously reused. Burial places were considered "unclean" and therefore located outside the borders of towns and cities. Abandoned tombs would have been natural places for "unclean" persons to find shelter.

• **5:4.** *Fetters:* ankle shackles joined by *chains* to hobble otherwise uncontrollable persons, probably suffering from severe mental illness, attributed to "unclean spirits."

• **5:7.** The words are very similar to the first exorcism (1:24), only more severe, since this foreign setting is stereotypically re-

garded as exceedingly "unclean."

• **5:9.** *Legion:* a Roman army unit with as many as 6000 soldiers. Four legions were stationed in nearby Syria at the time. Since pork epitomizes "unclean" for a Judean, the large number of pigs also characterizes how "unclean" this foreign area was.

• **5:13.** The Legion *drowned in the sea:* seems to echo the exodus story that rejoices when Pharaoh's army is "swallowed up in the sea" (Exod 15:4). Thus there may be a critique included here of the Roman occupation army. Removing all the pigs would also symbolically "cleanse" a pagan area.

¹⁸καὶ ἐμβαίνοντος αὐτοῦ εἰς τὸ πλοῖον παρεκάλει αὐτὸν ὁ δαιμονισθεὶς ἵνα μετ᾽ αὐτοῦ ᾖ. ¹⁹καὶ οὐκ ἀφῆκεν αὐτόν, ἀλλὰ λέγει αὐτῷ, Ὕπαγε εἰς τὸν οἶκόν σου πρὸς τοὺς σούς, καὶ ἀπάγγειλον αὐτοῖς ὅσα ὁ κύριός σοι πεποίηκεν καὶ ἠλέησέν σε. ²⁰Καὶ ἀπῆλθεν καὶ ἤρξατο κηρύσσειν ἐν τῇ Δεκαπόλει ὅσα ἐποίησεν αὐτῷ ὁ Ἰησοῦς, καὶ πάντες ἐθαύμαζον.

Jairus' daughter   ²¹Καὶ διαπεράσαντος τοῦ Ἰησοῦ πάλιν εἰς τὸ πέραν συνήχθη ὄχλος πολὺς ἐπ᾽ αὐτόν, καὶ ἦν παρὰ τὴν θάλασσαν. ²²καὶ ἔρχεται εἷς τῶν ἀρχισυναγώγων, ὀνόματι Ἰάϊρος, καὶ ἰδὼν αὐτὸν πίπτει πρὸς τοὺς πόδας αὐτοῦ ²³καὶ παρακαλεῖ αὐτὸν πολλὰ λέγων ὅτι Τὸ θυγάτριόν μου ἐσχάτως ἔχει, ἵνα ἐλθὼν ἐπιθῇς τὰς χεῖρας αὐτῇ ἵνα σωθῇ καὶ ζήσῃ. ²⁴Καὶ ἀπῆλθεν μετ᾽ αὐτοῦ.

Jesus cures   Καὶ ἠκολούθει αὐτῷ ὄχλος πολύς, καὶ συνέθλιβον αὐτόν.
a woman   ²⁵καὶ γυνὴ οὖσα ἐν ῥύσει αἵματος δώδεκα ἔτη ²⁶καὶ πολλὰ παθοῦσα ὑπὸ πολλῶν ἰατρῶν καὶ δαπανήσασα τὰ παρ᾽ αὐτῆς πάντα καὶ μηδὲν ὠφεληθεῖσα ἀλλὰ μᾶλλον εἰς τὸ χεῖρον ἐλθοῦσα, ²⁷ἀκούσασα περὶ τοῦ Ἰησοῦ, ἐλθοῦσα ἐν τῷ ὄχλῳ ὄπισθεν ἥψατο τοῦ ἱματίου αὐτοῦ· ²⁸ἔλεγεν γὰρ ὅτι Ἐὰν ἅψωμαι κἂν τῶν ἱματίων αὐτοῦ σωθήσομαι. ²⁹καὶ εὐθὺς ἐξηράνθη ἡ πηγὴ τοῦ αἵματος αὐτῆς, καὶ ἔγνω τῷ σώματι ὅτι ἴαται ἀπὸ τῆς μάστιγος.

³⁰Καὶ εὐθὺς ὁ Ἰησοῦς ἐπιγνοὺς ἐν ἑαυτῷ τὴν ἐξ αὐτοῦ δύναμιν ἐξελθοῦσαν ἐπιστραφεὶς ἐν τῷ ὄχλῳ ἔλεγεν, Τίς μου ἥψατο τῶν ἱματίων;

³¹Καὶ ἔλεγον αὐτῷ οἱ μαθηταὶ αὐτοῦ, Βλέπεις τὸν ὄχλον συνθλίβοντά σε, καὶ λέγεις, Τίς μου ἥψατο;

³²Καὶ περιεβλέπετο ἰδεῖν τὴν τοῦτο ποιήσασαν. ³³ἡ δὲ γυνὴ φοβηθεῖσα καὶ τρέμουσα, εἰδυῖα ὃ γέγονεν αὐτῇ, ἦλθεν καὶ προσέπεσεν αὐτῷ καὶ εἶπεν αὐτῷ πᾶσαν τὴν ἀλήθειαν. ³⁴Ὁ δὲ εἶπεν αὐτῇ, Θυγάτηρ, ἡ πίστις σου σέσωκέν σε· ὕπαγε εἰς εἰρήνην, καὶ ἴσθι ὑγιὴς ἀπὸ τῆς μάστιγός σου.

---

21. After *crossed over* some MSS add *in a boat.*

- **5:19.** *Go . . . tell*: in striking contrast to the secrecy motif elsewhere (§4.4), possibly because this is the first story set in foreign territory. *Patron*: the generic sense of *lord* or *master* (§6.4), one who provides for and protects someone of lesser social status and economic means.

- **5:20.** *Decapolis*: the area north of Perea (described at 3:8), named after the "ten cities" in the region east of Galilee and the Jordan River, including Gerasa and Gadara (see v. 1).

- **5:21–43.** Mark embeds one healing story inside another, with common features connecting the two: each is about a Judean female in whose story "twelve years" plays an important role.

- **5:22.** *Synagogue officials*: presiders responsible for arranging the weekly sabbath day services (1:21).

region. ¹⁸And as ⟨Jesus⟩ was getting into the boat, the ex-demoniac kept pleading with him to let him go along. ¹⁹And he would not let him, but says to him, "Go home to your people and tell them what your patron has done for you—how he has shown mercy to you."

²⁰And he went away and started spreading the news in the Decapolis about what Jesus had done for him, and everybody would marvel.

²¹When Jesus had again crossed over to the other side, a large crowd gathered around him, and he was beside the sea. ²²And one of the synagogue officials comes, Jairus by name, and as soon as he sees him, he falls at his feet ²³and pleads with him and begs, "My little daughter is on the verge of death, so come and put your hands on her so she may be cured and live!"

²⁴And ⟨Jesus⟩ set out with him.

Jairus' daughter

And a large crowd started following and shoving against him. ²⁵And there was a woman who had had a vaginal flow for twelve years, ²⁶who had suffered much under many doctors, and who had spent everything she had, but hadn't been helped at all, but instead had gotten worse. ²⁷When ⟨this woman⟩ heard about Jesus, she came up from behind in the crowd and touched his cloak. (²⁸No doubt she had been figuring, "If I could just touch his clothes, I'll be cured!") ²⁹And the vaginal flow stopped instantly, and she sensed in her body that she was cured of her illness.

Jesus cures
a woman

³⁰And suddenly, because Jesus realized that power had drained out of him, he turned around and started asking the crowd, "Who touched my clothes?"

³¹And his disciples said to him, "You see the crowd jostling you around and you're asking, 'Who touched me?'"

³²And he started looking around to see who had done this. ³³Although the woman was afraid and trembling—she realized what she had done—she came and fell down before him and told him the whole truth.

³⁴He said to her, "Daughter, your trust has cured you. Go in peace, and farewell to your illness."

• **5:23.** *Little daughter*: term of affection not restricted to age.

• **5:25.** *Vaginal flow*: not regular monthly menstruation, but abnormal vaginal bleeding. Both conditions make a woman ritually unclean (Leviticus 15). *Twelve years*: this detail emphasizes a perpetual state of uncleanness, like leprosy (1:40), but it also ties this story with the one that follows (v. 42; §3.3).

• **5:27.** *Cloak*: any outer garment.

• **5:34.** *Your trust has cured you*: Mark's earlier theme of trust (1:15; 2:5; 4:40) is now directly tied to Jesus' concern to "save life" (3:4; 8:35). *Cure* and *save* are two different senses of the same Greek word, preserved in English in "salve" and "salvage."

³⁵ Ἔτι αὐτοῦ λαλοῦντος ἔρχονται ἀπὸ τοῦ ἀρχισυναγώγου λέγοντες ὅτι Ἡ θυγάτηρ σου ἀπέθανεν· τί ἔτι σκύλλεις τὸν διδάσκαλον; ³⁶ Ὁ δὲ Ἰησοῦς παρακούσας τὸν λόγον λαλούμενον λέγει τῷ ἀρχισυναγώγῳ, Μὴ φοβοῦ, μόνον πίστευε. ³⁷ Καὶ οὐκ ἀφῆκεν οὐδένα μετ᾽ αὐτοῦ συνακολουθῆσαι εἰ μὴ τὸν Πέτρον καὶ Ἰάκωβον καὶ Ἰωάννην τὸν ἀδελφὸν Ἰακώβου. ³⁸ καὶ ἔρχονται εἰς τὸν οἶκον τοῦ ἀρχισυναγώγου, καὶ θεωρεῖ θόρυβον καὶ κλαίοντας καὶ ἀλαλάζοντας πολλά, ³⁹ καὶ εἰσελθὼν λέγει αὐτοῖς, Τί θορυβεῖσθε καὶ κλαίετε; τὸ παιδίον οὐκ ἀπέθανεν ἀλλὰ καθεύδει. ⁴⁰ Καὶ κατεγέλων αὐτοῦ. αὐτὸς δὲ ἐκβαλὼν πάντας παραλαμβάνει τὸν πατέρα τοῦ παιδίου καὶ τὴν μητέρα καὶ τοὺς μετ᾽ αὐτοῦ, καὶ εἰσπορεύεται ὅπου ἦν τὸ παιδίον· ⁴¹ καὶ κρατήσας τῆς χειρὸς τοῦ παιδίου λέγει αὐτῇ, Ταλιθα κουμ, ὅ ἐστιν μεθερμηνευόμενον Τὸ κοράσιον, σοὶ λέγω, ἔγειρε. ⁴² καὶ εὐθὺς ἀνέστη τὸ κοράσιον καὶ περιεπάτει.

Ἦν γὰρ ἐτῶν δώδεκα.

Καὶ ἐξέστησαν εὐθὺς ἐκστάσει μεγάλῃ. ⁴³ καὶ διεστείλατο αὐτοῖς πολλὰ ἵνα μηδεὶς γνοῖ τοῦτο, καὶ εἶπεν δοθῆναι αὐτῇ φαγεῖν.

• **5:41.** *Talitha koum*: in Aramaic, Jesus' native language. Mark's use of Aramaic (also in 3:17; 7:11, 34; 14:36; 15:34), which is not retained in Matthew and Luke, can be seen as evidence of Mark's use of early sources. To Greek-speaking Christians, for-

Jairus' daughter dies

³⁵While he was still speaking, the synagogue official's people approach and say, "Your daughter has died; why keep bothering the teacher?"

³⁶When Jesus overheard this conversation, he says to the synagogue official, "Don't be afraid, just have trust!"

³⁷And he wouldn't let anyone follow along with him except Peter and James and John, James' brother. ³⁸When they come to the house of the synagogue official, he notices a lot of clamor and people crying and wailing, ³⁹and he goes in and says to them, "Why are you carrying on like this? The child hasn't died but is asleep."

⁴⁰And they started laughing at him. But he runs everyone out and takes the child's father and her mother and his companions and goes in where the child is. ⁴¹And he takes the child by the hand and says to her, "*talitha koum*" (which means, "Little girl," I say to you, "Get up!"). ⁴²And the little girl got right up and started walking around.

(Incidentally, she was twelve years old.)

And they were downright ecstatic. ⁴³And he gave them strict orders that no one should learn about this, and he told them to give her something to eat.

---

eign words in miracle stories may also have had the quality of "Abracadabra."

• **5:42.** *Twelve years old*: the age of transition to early adulthood, soon after which a young woman was usually "betrothed" to be married a year later.

6 Καὶ ἐξῆλθεν ἐκεῖθεν, καὶ ἔρχεται εἰς τὴν πατρίδα αὐτοῦ, καὶ ἀκολουθοῦσιν αὐτῷ οἱ μαθηταὶ αὐτοῦ. ²καὶ γενομένου σαββάτου ἤρξατο διδάσκειν ἐν τῇ συναγωγῇ· καὶ πολλοὶ ἀκούοντες ἐξεπλήσσοντο λέγοντες, Πόθεν τούτῳ ταῦτα, καὶ τίς ἡ σοφία ἡ δοθεῖσα τούτῳ καὶ αἱ δυνάμεις τοιαῦται διὰ τῶν χειρῶν αὐτοῦ γινόμεναι; ³οὐχ οὗτός ἐστιν ὁ τέκτων, ὁ υἱὸς τῆς Μαρίας καὶ ἀδελφὸς Ἰακώβου καὶ Ἰωσῆτος καὶ Ἰούδα καὶ Σίμωνος; καὶ οὐκ εἰσὶν αἱ ἀδελφαὶ αὐτοῦ ὧδε πρὸς ἡμᾶς; καὶ ἐσκανδαλίζοντο ἐν αὐτῷ.

⁴Καὶ ἔλεγεν αὐτοῖς ὁ Ἰησοῦς ὅτι Οὐκ ἔστιν προφήτης ἄτιμος εἰ μὴ ἐν τῇ πατρίδι αὐτοῦ καὶ ἐν τοῖς συγγενεῦσιν αὐτοῦ καὶ ἐν τῇ οἰκίᾳ αὐτοῦ.

⁵Καὶ οὐκ ἐδύνατο ἐκεῖ ποιῆσαι οὐδεμίαν δύναμιν, εἰ μὴ ὀλίγοις ἀρρώστοις ἐπιθεὶς τὰς χεῖρας ἐθεράπευσεν· ⁶καὶ ἐθαύμαζεν διὰ τὴν ἀπιστίαν αὐτῶν. καὶ περιῆγεν τὰς κώμας κύκλῳ διδάσκων.

⁷Καὶ προσκαλεῖται τοὺς δώδεκα, καὶ ἤρξατο αὐτοὺς ἀποστέλλειν δύο δύο, καὶ ἐδίδου αὐτοῖς ἐξουσίαν τῶν πνευμάτων τῶν ἀκαθάρτων· ⁸καὶ παρήγγειλεν αὐτοῖς ἵνα μηδὲν ἄρωσιν εἰς ὁδὸν εἰ μὴ ῥάβδον μόνον, μὴ ἄρτον, μὴ πήραν, μὴ εἰς τὴν ζώνην χαλκόν, ⁹ἀλλὰ ὑποδεδεμένους σανδάλια καὶ μὴ ἐνδύσασθαι δύο χιτῶνας. ¹⁰καὶ ἔλεγεν αὐτοῖς, Ὅπου ἐὰν εἰσέλθητε εἰς οἰκίαν, ἐκεῖ μένετε ἕως ἂν ἐξέλθητε ἐκεῖθεν. ¹¹καὶ ὃς ἂν τόπος μὴ δέξηται ὑμᾶς μηδὲ ἀκούσωσιν ὑμῶν, ἐκπορευόμενοι ἐκεῖθεν ἐκτινάξατε τὸν χοῦν τὸν ὑποκάτω τῶν ποδῶν ὑμῶν εἰς μαρτύριον αὐτοῖς.

¹²Καὶ ἐξελθόντες ἐκήρυξαν ἵνα μετανοῶσιν, ¹³καὶ δαιμόνια πολλὰ ἐξέβαλλον, καὶ ἤλειφον ἐλαίῳ πολλοὺς ἀρρώστους καὶ ἐθεράπευον.

---

2. And "Who gave him the right to perform such miracles:" some MSS read so that he has the right to perform even such miracles. 3. Some MSS read Isn't this the son of the carpenter and Mary? (closer to Matt 13:55). 6. He was always shocked: a few of the oldest MSS read he became shocked.

• 6:1–34. Mark returns to the setting of Jesus' hometown to reinforce Jesus' distancing himself from his "relatives" (as at 3:31–35). Then the attention is again on "the twelve." This time they provide the framework for the story about what finally happened to John the Baptizer.

• 6:2. Wisdom: the teachings of the "wise," often preserved in short memorable sayings, mostly in timeless proverbs: "Nobody pours young wine into old wineskins" (2:22). However, only unconventional wisdom ("aphorisms") astounds an audience into wondering about its source. Especially in Mark, Jesus' aphorisms tend to be sub-

versive: "Among you, whoever wants to become great must be your servant" (10:43). Miracles: from the word for "power" (5:30), emphasizing Jesus' ability and authority to do such things, rather than that they are "unexplainable."

• 6:3. The carpenter, Mary's son: both occur only here in the New Testament; the carpenter's son is unique to Matt 13:55. Mary's son is most unusual in a Judean setting, but Mark has no mention of Joseph, Mary's "husband." This expression could be part of Mark's theology that Jesus' only father is God (1:11; 9:7; 14:36; 15:39). It could also be an insult implying illegit-

6 Then he left that place, and he comes to his hometown, and his disciples follow him. ²When the sabbath day arrived, he started teaching in the synagogue; and many who heard him were astounded and said so: "Where's he getting this?" and "What's the source of all this wisdom?" and "Who gave him the right to perform such miracles? ³This is the carpenter, isn't it? Isn't he Mary's son? And who are his brothers, if not James and Judas and Simon? And who are his sisters, if not our neighbors?" And they were resentful of him.

⁴Jesus used to tell them: "No prophet goes without respect, except on his home turf and among his relatives and at home!"

⁵He was unable to perform a single miracle there, except that he did cure a few by laying hands on them, ⁶though he was always shocked at their lack of trust. And he used to go around the villages, teaching in a circuit.

No respect at home

⁷Then he summoned the twelve and started sending them out in pairs and giving them authority over unclean spirits. ⁸And he instructed them not to take anything on the road, except a staff: no bread, no knapsack, no spending money, ⁹but to wear sandals, and to wear no more than one shirt. ¹⁰And he went on to say to them: "Wherever you enter someone's house, stay there until you leave town. ¹¹And whatever place does not welcome you or listen to you, get out of there and shake the dust off your feet in witness against them."

Instructions for the road

¹²So they set out and announced that people should turn their lives around, ¹³and they often drove out demons, and they anointed many sick people with oil and healed ⟨them⟩.

---

imacy, since Mark has no stories explaining Jesus' birth. *His brothers* and *sisters* are mentioned in 3:31–33. *Resentful:* suggests being offended, even provoked (14:27, 29).

• **6:4.** The saying about a prophet's lack of respect became a popular Judean saying, but there is no version of it attested earlier than the time of Jesus.

• **6:7.** *The twelve:* the group was formed earlier for this purpose (3:14–15).

• **6:8.** *Staff:* or wooden stick, commonly carried by cross-country travelers, useful both on rough terrain and as protection against wild animals. *Knapsack:* could be used by wandering philosophers to beg for money.

• **6:9.** *Sandals:* leather soles attached to the feet by straps (1:7), commonly worn when journeying, especially a distance, as already implied by the "staff" (v. 8). The require-

ment to wear sandals also would distinguish the disciples from the wandering philosophers of the time who went around barefoot. Another tradition contains the opposite requirements: neither staff nor sandals are allowed (Matt 10:10; Luke 9:3; 10:4), which may reflect either a sense of greater austerity, or an attempt to imitate the wandering philosophers.

• **6:11.** When leaving pagan territory, Judeans shook off the "unclean" dust before returning home, giving this gesture a judgmental quality of *witness against* someone. The situation is reversed here as these instructions are given to Jesus' followers to use against their own neighbors.

• **6:12.** The disciples' preaching continues a central theme of Jesus' message, as summarized by Mark, *change your ways* (1:15).

¹⁴Καὶ ἤκουσεν ὁ βασιλεὺς Ἡρῴδης, φανερὸν γὰρ ἐγένετο τὸ ὄνομα αὐτοῦ, καὶ ἔλεγον ὅτι Ἰωάννης ὁ βαπτίζων ἐγήγερται ἐκ νεκρῶν, καὶ διὰ τοῦτο ἐνεργοῦσιν αἱ δυνάμεις ἐν αὐτῷ. ¹⁵ἄλλοι δὲ ἔλεγον ὅτι Ἡλίας ἐστίν· ἄλλοι δὲ ἔλεγον ὅτι προφήτης ὡς εἷς τῶν προφητῶν. ¹⁶Ἀκούσας δὲ ὁ Ἡρῴδης ἔλεγεν, Ὃν ἐγὼ ἀπεκεφάλισα Ἰωάννην, οὗτος ἠγέρθη.

¹⁷Αὐτὸς γὰρ ὁ Ἡρῴδης ἀποστείλας ἐκράτησεν τὸν Ἰωάννην καὶ ἔδησεν αὐτὸν ἐν φυλακῇ διὰ Ἡρῳδιάδα τὴν γυναῖκα Φιλίππου τοῦ ἀδελφοῦ αὐτοῦ, ὅτι αὐτὴν ἐγάμησεν· ¹⁸ἔλεγεν γὰρ ὁ Ἰωάννης τῷ Ἡρῴδῃ ὅτι Οὐκ ἔξεστίν σοι ἔχειν τὴν γυναῖκα τοῦ ἀδελφοῦ σου.

¹⁹Ἡ δὲ Ἡρῳδιὰς ἐνεῖχεν αὐτῷ καὶ ἤθελεν αὐτὸν ἀποκτεῖναι, καὶ οὐκ ἠδύνατο· ²⁰ὁ γὰρ Ἡρῴδης ἐφοβεῖτο τὸν Ἰωάννην, εἰδὼς αὐτὸν ἄνδρα δίκαιον καὶ ἅγιον, καὶ συνετήρει αὐτόν, καὶ ἀκούσας αὐτοῦ πολλὰ ἐποίει, καὶ ἡδέως αὐτοῦ ἤκουεν.

²¹Καὶ γενομένης ἡμέρας εὐκαίρου ὅτε Ἡρῴδης τοῖς γενεσίοις αὐτοῦ δεῖπνον ἐποίησεν τοῖς μεγιστᾶσιν αὐτοῦ καὶ τοῖς χιλιάρχοις καὶ τοῖς πρώτοις τῆς Γαλιλαίας, ²²καὶ εἰσελθούσης τῆς θυγατρὸς αὐτῆς τῆς Ἡρῳδιάδος καὶ ὀρχησαμένης, ἤρεσεν τῷ Ἡρῴδῃ καὶ τοῖς συνανακειμένοις. εἶπεν ὁ βασιλεὺς τῷ κορασίῳ, Αἴτησόν με ὃ ἐὰν θέλῃς, καὶ δώσω σοι· ²³καὶ ὤμοσεν αὐτῇ, Ὅ τι ἐὰν αἰτήσῃς δώσω σοι ἕως ἡμίσους τῆς βασιλείας μου.

²⁴Καὶ ἐξελθοῦσα εἶπεν τῇ μητρὶ αὐτῆς, Τί αἰτήσωμαι; Ἡ δὲ εἶπεν, Τὴν κεφαλὴν Ἰωάννου τοῦ βαπτίζοντος.

²⁵Καὶ εἰσελθοῦσα εὐθὺς μετὰ σπουδῆς πρὸς τὸν βασιλέα ᾐτήσατο λέγουσα, Θέλω ἵνα ἐξαυτῆς δῷς μοι ἐπὶ πίνακι τὴν κεφαλὴν Ἰωάννου τοῦ βαπτιστοῦ.

²⁶Καὶ περίλυπος γενόμενος ὁ βασιλεὺς διὰ τοὺς ὅρκους καὶ τοὺς ἀνακειμένους οὐκ ἠθέλησεν ἀθετῆσαι αὐτήν· ²⁷καὶ εὐθὺς ἀποστείλας ὁ βασιλεὺς σπεκουλάτορα ἐπέταξεν ἐνέγκαι τὴν κεφαλὴν αὐτοῦ. καὶ ἀπελθὼν ἀπεκεφάλισεν αὐτὸν ἐν τῇ φυλακῇ

---

14. People (indefinite they): some MSS have he, that is, Herod. **22.** The daughter of Herodias: some of the earliest MSS have his daughter Herodias.

• **6:14.** King Herod: Herod Antipas, son of Herod the Great, not properly a king, but the tetrarch of Galilee and Perea during Jesus' lifetime. Raised from the dead: Pharisees did promote belief in resurrection, but this could mean simply, "He's another John the Baptizer."

• **6:15.** These same speculations are repeated later by the disciples (8:28). Elijah was prominent in such speculation because he

was associated with the preparation for the messianic age (Mal 4:5). Mark has already associated the image of Elijah with John (Mark 1:6).

• **6:17.** Herodias actually had been the wife of Antipas' half-brother Herod, rather than his half-brother Philip. The Herodian family tree was very complicated because it was a real-life "soap opera." Antipas' father, Herod, had had ten wives, the first five

[14]King Herod heard about it—by now, ⟨Jesus'⟩ reputation had become well known—and people kept saying that John the Baptizer had been raised from the dead and that, as a consequence, miraculous powers were at work in him. [15] Some spread the rumor that he was Elijah, while others reported that he was a prophet like one of the prophets.

[16]When Herod got wind of it, he started declaring, "John, the one I beheaded, has been raised!"

[17]Earlier Herod himself had sent someone to arrest John and put him in chains in a dungeon, on account of Herodias, his brother Philip's wife, because he had married her. [18]You see, John had said to Herod, "It is not right for you to have your brother's wife!"

[19]So Herodias nursed a grudge against him and wanted to eliminate him, but she couldn't manage it, [20]because Herod was afraid of John. He knew that he was an upright and holy man, and so protected him, and, although he listened to him frequently, he was very confused, yet he listened to him eagerly.

[21]Now a festival day came, when Herod gave a banquet on his birthday for his courtiers, and his commanders, and the leading citizens of Galilee. [22]And the daughter of Herodias came in and captivated Herod and his dinner guests by dancing. The king said to the girl, "Ask me for whatever you wish and I'll grant it to you!" [23]Then he swore an oath to her: "I'll grant you whatever you ask for, up to half my domain!"

[24]She went out and said to her mother, "What should I ask for?"

And she replied, "The head of John the Baptist!"

[25]She promptly hastened back and made her request: "I want you to give me the head of John the Baptist on a platter, right now!"

[26]The king grew regretful, but, on account of his oaths and the dinner guests, he didn't want to refuse her. [27]So right away the king sent for the executioner and commanded him to bring his head. And he went away and beheaded ⟨John⟩ in prison.

Herod beheads John

---

giving him seven sons, the first three of which Herod had executed for treason. Herodias was the daughter of one of the executed half-brothers, so she was also the niece of both her husbands, but marrying a niece was a common practice at the time, even encouraged. She left her first husband, who did not share her political ambitions, and Herod Antipas (v. 14) divorced his first wife, the daughter of a neighboring king, in order to marry her. Philip was actually married to Herodias' daughter (v.22) from her first marriage, elsewhere named Salome.

• **6:18.** Lev 18:16 forbids sexual relations between brother-in-law and sister-in-law; Lev 20:21 calls it an "impurity" that shall not produce children.

• **6:22.** *The daughter of Herodias:* could be read as *her daughter Herodias,* but v. 24 supports *the daughter of.*

²⁸καὶ ἤνεγκεν τὴν κεφαλὴν αὐτοῦ ἐπὶ πίνακι καὶ ἔδωκεν αὐτὴν τῷ κορασίῳ, καὶ τὸ κοράσιον ἔδωκεν αὐτὴν τῇ μητρὶ αὐτῆς. ²⁹καὶ ἀκούσαντες οἱ μαθηταὶ αὐτοῦ ἦλθον καὶ ἦραν τὸ πτῶμα αὐτοῦ καὶ ἔθηκαν αὐτὸ ἐν μνημείῳ.

The twelve report

³⁰Καὶ συνάγονται οἱ ἀπόστολοι πρὸς τὸν Ἰησοῦν, καὶ ἀπήγγειλαν αὐτῷ πάντα ὅσα ἐποίησαν καὶ ὅσα ἐδίδαξαν. ³¹Καὶ λέγει αὐτοῖς, Δεῦτε ὑμεῖς αὐτοὶ κατ᾽ ἰδίαν εἰς ἔρημον τόπον καὶ ἀναπαύσασθε ὀλίγον.

Ἦσαν γὰρ οἱ ἐρχόμενοι καὶ οἱ ὑπάγοντες πολλοί, καὶ οὐδὲ φαγεῖν εὐκαίρουν. ³²Καὶ ἀπῆλθον ἐν τῷ πλοίῳ εἰς ἔρημον τόπον κατ᾽ ἰδίαν. ³³καὶ εἶδον αὐτοὺς ὑπάγοντας καὶ ἐπέγνωσαν πολλοί, καὶ πεζῇ ἀπὸ πασῶν τῶν πόλεων συνέδραμον ἐκεῖ καὶ προῆλθον αὐτούς. ³⁴καὶ ἐξελθὼν εἶδεν πολὺν ὄχλον, καὶ ἐσπλαγχνίσθη ἐπ᾽ αὐτοὺς ὅτι ἦσαν ὡς πρόβατα μὴ ἔχοντα ποιμένα, καὶ ἤρξατο διδάσκειν αὐτοὺς πολλά.

Loaves & fish for 5,000

³⁵Καὶ ἤδη ὥρας πολλῆς γενομένης προσελθόντες αὐτῷ οἱ μαθηταὶ αὐτοῦ ἔλεγον ὅτι Ἔρημός ἐστιν ὁ τόπος, καὶ ἤδη ὥρα πολλή· ³⁶ἀπόλυσον αὐτούς, ἵνα ἀπελθόντες εἰς τοὺς κύκλῳ ἀγροὺς καὶ κώμας ἀγοράσωσιν ἑαυτοῖς τί φάγωσιν. ³⁷Ὁ δὲ ἀποκριθεὶς εἶπεν αὐτοῖς, Δότε αὐτοῖς ὑμεῖς φαγεῖν.

Καὶ λέγουσιν αὐτῷ, Ἀπελθόντες ἀγοράσωμεν δηναρίων διακοσίων ἄρτους καὶ δώσωμεν αὐτοῖς φαγεῖν; ³⁸Ὁ δὲ λέγει αὐτοῖς, Πόσους ἄρτους ἔχετε; ὑπάγετε ἴδετε.

Καὶ γνόντες λέγουσιν, Πέντε, καὶ δύο ἰχθύας. ³⁹Καὶ ἐπέταξεν αὐτοῖς ἀνακλῖναι πάντας συμπόσια συμπόσια ἐπὶ τῷ χλωρῷ χόρτῳ. ⁴⁰καὶ ἀνέπεσαν πρασιαὶ πρασιαὶ κατὰ ἑκατὸν καὶ κατὰ πεντήκοντα. ⁴¹καὶ λαβὼν τοὺς πέντε ἄρτους καὶ τοὺς δύο ἰχθύας ἀναβλέψας εἰς τὸν οὐρανὸν εὐλόγησεν καὶ κατέκλασεν τοὺς ἄρτους καὶ ἐδίδου τοῖς μαθηταῖς αὐτοῦ ἵνα παρατιθῶσιν αὐτοῖς, καὶ τοὺς δύο ἰχθύας ἐμέρισεν πᾶσιν. ⁴²καὶ ἔφαγον πάντες καὶ ἐχορτάσθησαν· ⁴³καὶ ἦραν κλάσματα δώδεκα κοφίνων πληρώματα καὶ ἀπὸ τῶν ἰχθύων. ⁴⁴καὶ ἦσαν οἱ φαγόντες τοὺς ἄρτους πεντακισχίλιοι ἄνδρες.

• **6:29.** Mark's conclusion seems meant to indicate what good *disciples* do when their master has been executed, in contrast to Jesus' disciples abandoning him (14:50).

• **6:30.** *The apostles:* only here in Mark, when they have returned from apostle-like activity (vv. 7-13). Because of the abrupt ending of Mark's gospel at 16:8, this is Mark's only anticipation of the disciples' future role in the life of the church.

• **6:34.** The exodus image of *a huge crowd* in a *desolate* place (v. 35) is reinforced by calling them *sheep without a shepherd*. Moses used this description for the Israelites in the wilderness (Num 27:17) when he asked for a successor. God appointed Joshua (in Greek, *Jesus*). The prophets developed more fully the image of the king as shepherd of the sheep, culminating in Zechariah's use of it in judgment against the king, a text used in Mark 14:27.

• **6:35–52.** The first of two times that Mark

²⁸He brought his head on a platter and presented it to the girl, and the girl gave it to her mother. ²⁹When his disciples heard about it, they came and got his body and put it in a tomb.

³⁰Then the apostles regroup around Jesus and they reported to him everything that they had done and taught.

³¹And he says to them: "You come privately to an isolated place and rest a little."

(Remember, many were coming and going and they didn't even have a chance to eat.)

³²So they went away in the boat privately to an isolated place. ³³But many noticed them leaving and figured it out and raced there on foot from all the towns and got there ahead of them. ³⁴When he came ashore, he saw a huge crowd and was moved by them, because they 'resembled sheep without a shepherd,' and he started teaching them at length.

³⁵And when the hour had already grown late, his disciples would approach him and say, "This place is desolate and it's late. ³⁶Send them away so that they can go to the farms and villages around here to buy something to eat."

³⁷But in response he said to them: "Give them something to eat yourselves!"

And they say to him: "Are we to go out and buy half a year's wages worth of bread and donate it for their meal?!"

³⁸So he says to them: "How many loaves do you have? Go look."

And when they find out, they say, "Five, and two fish."

³⁹Next he instructed them all to sit down and eat, some over here, some over there, on the green grass. ⁴⁰So they sat down group by group, in hundreds and in fifties. ⁴¹And he took the five loaves and the two fish, looked up to the sky, gave a blessing, and broke the bread apart, and started giving it to his disciples to pass around to them, and even the two fish they shared with everybody. ⁴²Everybody had more than enough to eat. ⁴³Then they picked up twelve baskets full of leftovers, including some fish. ⁴⁴And the number of men who had some bread came to five thousand.

---

pairs a feeding story with a boat trip (also in 8:1–21).
- **6:37.** *Half a year's wages*: Greek has *two hundred denarii*, a denarius being about a day's pay (Matt 20:2).
- **6:40.** *Group by group*: could imply the custom used at passover meals, or simply for ease of distribution.
- **6:41.** The sequence, *took, gave a blessing, broke, and started giving*, is the same as at the last supper (14:22). The traditional

Judean *blessing* before a meal is: "Blessed are you, O Lord our God, Ruler of the universe, who brings forth bread from the earth."
- **6:42.** *More than enough to eat*: echoes the description of the promised land at the end of the exodus journey: *you shall have more than enough to eat* (Deut 8:10). Thus this story ends at it began (v. 34), reminiscent of the exodus story.

Jesus departs

⁴⁵Καὶ εὐθὺς ἠνάγκασεν τοὺς μαθητὰς αὐτοῦ ἐμβῆναι εἰς τὸ πλοῖον καὶ προάγειν εἰς τὸ πέραν πρὸς Βηθσαϊδάν, ἕως αὐτὸς ἀπολύει τὸν ὄχλον. ⁴⁶καὶ ἀποταξάμενος αὐτοῖς ἀπῆλθεν εἰς τὸ ὄρος προσεύξασθαι.

Jesus walks on water

⁴⁷Καὶ ὀψίας γενομένης ἦν τὸ πλοῖον ἐν μέσῳ τῆς θαλάσσης, καὶ αὐτὸς μόνος ἐπὶ τῆς γῆς. ⁴⁸καὶ ἰδὼν αὐτοὺς βασανιζομένους ἐν τῷ ἐλαύνειν, ἦν γὰρ ὁ ἄνεμος ἐναντίος αὐτοῖς, περὶ τετάρτην φυλακὴν τῆς νυκτὸς ἔρχεται πρὸς αὐτοὺς περιπατῶν ἐπὶ τῆς θαλάσσης· καὶ ἤθελεν παρελθεῖν αὐτούς. ⁴⁹οἱ δὲ ἰδόντες αὐτὸν ἐπὶ τῆς θαλάσσης περιπατοῦντα ἔδοξαν ὅτι φάντασμά ἐστιν, καὶ ἀνέκραξαν· ⁵⁰πάντες γὰρ αὐτὸν εἶδον καὶ ἐταράχθησαν. ὁ δὲ εὐθὺς ἐλάλησεν μετ᾿ αὐτῶν, καὶ λέγει αὐτοῖς, Θαρσεῖτε, ἐγώ εἰμι· μὴ φοβεῖσθε. ⁵¹καὶ ἀνέβη πρὸς αὐτοὺς εἰς τὸ πλοῖον, καὶ ἐκόπασεν ὁ ἄνεμος. καὶ λίαν ἐκ περισσοῦ ἐν ἑαυτοῖς ἐξίσταντο, ⁵²οὐ γὰρ συνῆκαν ἐπὶ τοῖς ἄρτοις, ἀλλ᾿ ἦν αὐτῶν ἡ καρδία πεπωρωμένη.

Cure of the sick

⁵³Καὶ διαπεράσαντες ἐπὶ τὴν γῆν ἦλθον εἰς Γεννησαρὲτ καὶ προσωρμίσθησαν. ⁵⁴καὶ ἐξελθόντων αὐτῶν ἐκ τοῦ πλοίου εὐθὺς ἐπιγνόντες αὐτὸν ⁵⁵περιέδραμον ὅλην τὴν χώραν ἐκείνην καὶ ἤρξαντο ἐπὶ τοῖς κραβάττοις τοὺς κακῶς ἔχοντας περιφέρειν ὅπου ἤκουον ὅτι ἐστίν. ⁵⁶καὶ ὅπου ἂν εἰσεπορεύετο εἰς κώμας ἢ εἰς πόλεις ἢ εἰς ἀγροὺς ἐν ταῖς ἀγοραῖς ἐτίθεσαν τοὺς ἀσθενοῦντας, καὶ παρεκάλουν αὐτὸν ἵνα κἂν τοῦ κρασπέδου τοῦ ἱματίου αὐτοῦ ἅψωνται· καὶ ὅσοι ἂν ἥψαντο αὐτοῦ ἐσῴζοντο.

---

44. *Bread* is omitted in some of the early MSS.

• **6:45.** *Bethsaida*: located on the east bank where the Jordan River enters the Sea of Galilee from the north, so it is just outside of Galilee, a return to pagan territory. This journey gets detoured, but they do arrive in Bethsaida, abruptly, at 8:22.

• **6:47–51.** Another sea-crossing story with heightened details from the first one (4:35–41), including the exodus motif and the disciples failure to comprehend.

• **6:50.** *Take heart*: imitates Moses at the exodus sea-crossing (Exod 14:13), when the Israelites "were in great fear" of the Egyptians as they approached "the sea." *It's me*: the common way to answer, "Who's there?" However, it also echoes God's instructions to Moses: Just call me "I am," as an explanation of the name *Yahweh* (Exod 3:14; also utilized in Isa 43:10).

• **6:52.** *Obstinate*: the strongest language Mark uses for the disciples, earlier used for Jesus' opponents (3:5).

⁴⁵And right away he made his disciples embark in the boat and go ahead to the opposite shore toward Bethsaida, while he himself dispersed the crowd. ⁴⁶And once he got away from them, he went off to the mountain to pray.

Jesus departs

⁴⁷When evening came, the boat was in the middle of the sea, and he was alone on the land. ⁴⁸When he saw they were having a rough time making headway, because the wind was against them, at about three o'clock in the morning he comes toward them walking on the sea and intending to go past them. ⁴⁹But when they saw him walking on the sea, they thought he was a ghost and they cried out. ⁵⁰By now they all saw him and were terrified. But right away he spoke with them and says to them: "Take heart, it's me! Don't be afraid." ⁵¹And he climbed into the boat with them, and the wind died down. By this time they were completely dumbfounded. (⁵²You see, they hadn't understood about the loaves; they were being obstinate.)

Jesus walks on water

⁵³Once they had crossed over to land, they landed at Gennesaret and dropped anchor. ⁵⁴As soon as they had gotten out of the boat, people recognized him right away, ⁵⁵and they ran around over the whole area and started bringing those who were ill on mats to wherever he was rumored to be. ⁵⁶And wherever he would go, into villages, or towns, or onto farms, they would lay out the sick in the marketplaces and beg him to let them touch the fringe of his cloak. And all those who managed to touch it were cured!

Cure of the sick

• **6:53–56.** Another Markan summary providing transition to the next extended section.

• **6:53.** *Gennesaret*: usually located on the west bank of the Sea of Galilee, below Capernaum, so they would have landed in the opposite direction from their destination (v. 45). However, the verb *crossed over* in 5:21 meant a complete crossing, which here would mean the eastern shore opposite Galilee. Mark may have been careless about the geographical designation, as elsewhere (7:31; 8:10, 13).

• **6:56.** *The fringe of his cloak*: tassels attached to the corners of the outer garment (Deut 22:12), as a reminder to do "all the commandments of the Lord" (Num 15:38–39). Mark thus pictures Jesus in typically Judean garments. *Cured* by touching: apparently understood as a transference of power (5:28, 30), since the Greek word here for *sick* also has the sense "weak."

*Rules for
handwashing*

7 Καὶ συνάγονται πρὸς αὐτὸν οἱ Φαρισαῖοι καί τινες τῶν
γραμματέων ἐλθόντες ἀπὸ Ἱεροσολύμων ²καὶ ἰδόντες τινὰς τῶν
μαθητῶν αὐτοῦ ὅτι κοιναῖς χερσίν, τοῦτ᾽ ἔστιν ἀνίπτοις,
ἐσθίουσιν τοὺς ἄρτους ³ οἱ γὰρ Φαρισαῖοι καὶ πάντες οἱ Ἰουδαῖοι
ἐὰν μὴ πυγμῇ νίψωνται τὰς χεῖρας οὐκ ἐσθίουσιν, κρατοῦντες
τὴν παράδοσιν τῶν πρεσβυτέρων, ⁴καὶ ἀπ᾽ ἀγορᾶς ἐὰν μὴ
βαπτίσωνται οὐκ ἐσθίουσιν, καὶ ἄλλα πολλά ἐστιν ἃ παρέλαβον
κρατεῖν, βαπτισμοὺς ποτηρίων καὶ ξεστῶν καὶ χαλκίων ⁵καὶ
ἐπερωτῶσιν αὐτὸν οἱ Φαρισαῖοι καὶ οἱ γραμματεῖς, Διὰ τί οὐ
περιπατοῦσιν οἱ μαθηταί σου κατὰ τὴν παράδοσιν τῶν
πρεσβυτέρων, ἀλλὰ κοιναῖς χερσὶν ἐσθίουσιν τὸν ἄρτον;
⁶Ὁ δὲ εἶπεν αὐτοῖς, Καλῶς ἐπροφήτευσεν Ἠσαΐας περὶ
ὑμῶν τῶν ὑποκριτῶν, ὡς γέγραπται ὅτι

Οὗτος ὁ λαὸς τοῖς χείλεσίν με τιμᾷ,
ἡ δὲ καρδία αὐτῶν πόρρω ἀπέχει ἀπ᾽ ἐμοῦ·
⁷μάτην δὲ σέβονταί με,
διδάσκοντες διδασκαλίας ἐντάλματα ἀνθρώπων.

⁸ἀφέντες τὴν ἐντολὴν τοῦ θεοῦ κρατεῖτε τὴν παράδοσιν τῶν
ἀνθρώπων.
⁹Καὶ ἔλεγεν αὐτοῖς, Καλῶς ἀθετεῖτε τὴν ἐντολὴν τοῦ θεοῦ,
ἵνα τὴν παράδοσιν ὑμῶν στήσητε. ¹⁰Μωϋσῆς γὰρ εἶπεν, Τίμα
τὸν πατέρα σου καὶ τὴν μητέρα σου, καί, Ὁ κακολογῶν πατέρα
ἢ μητέρα θανάτῳ τελευτάτω· ¹¹ὑμεῖς δὲ λέγετε, Ἐὰν εἴπῃ

---

3. *In a particular way:* some early MSS read *often*.   4. *Kettles:* most later
MSS add *and beds*, here could mean eating couches, suggesting *tables*, or
could be addressing the concerns of Leviticus 15 for purifying where an
"unclean" person sat.   9. *Establish:* the earliest MSS have *keep*.

• **7:1–23.** The matter of purity regulations is
now addressed in a direct way. The uncertainty about the geographical references at
6:45, 53, make it unclear whether Mark
locates this story in or outside Galilee.

• **7:2.** *Defiled hands:* hands that may have
touched something considered impure by
the religious code (Lev 15:11). The Pharisaic practice was to assume all people had
"defiled hands" before every meal, and
therefore, should never eat *without washing
their hands* according to the proper procedure of the Pharisees. This was more
than mere hygiene.

• **7:3.** *The Judeans generally:* these requirements had always been binding for priests,
but the Pharisees argued that the common
folk were obligated to perform these washings, an interpretation Jesus apparently

rejected. Whether *Judeans generally* in the
time of Jesus followed the Pharisaic practices regarding handwashing is actually
doubtful. This is most likely a Markan
stereotype from his own day, reflecting the
attitude of Christians from pagan backgrounds towards those from Judean backgrounds. *In a particular way:* the Greek
expression, derived from the word "fist," is
unclear in this context. It could mean "up
to the wrist," or "with the hands cupped,"
or "with a fistful of water," or something
unknown to us, so it is best left unspecified.
The tradition of the elders: the oral tradition
promoted by the Pharisees regarding how
to interpret the written Torah. The Pharisees regarded both the oral law and the
written as equally derived from Moses.
Concern in the oral law with the trans-

7 The Pharisees gather around him, along with some of the scholars, who had come from Jerusalem. ²When they notice some of his disciples eating their meal with defiled hands, that is to say, without washing their hands (³you see, the Pharisees and the Judeans generally wouldn't think of eating without first washing their hands in a particular way, always observing the tradition of the elders, ⁴and they won't eat when they get back from the marketplace without washing again, and there are many other traditions they cherish, such as the washing of cups and jugs and kettles) , ⁵the Pharisees and the scholars start questioning him: "Why don't your disciples live up to the tradition of the elders, instead of eating bread with defiled hands?"

Rules for handwashing

⁶And he answered them: "How accurately Isaiah depicted you phonies when he wrote:

This people honors me with their lips,
but their heart stays far away from me.
⁷Their worship of me is empty,
because they insist on teachings that are human commandments.

⁸You have set aside God's commandment and hold fast to human tradition!"

⁹Or he would say to them: "How expert you've become at putting aside God's commandment to establish your own tradition. ¹⁰For instance, Moses said, 'Honor your father and your mother' and 'Those who curse their father or mother will surely die.' ¹¹But you say, 'If people say to their father or mother,

---

ference of impurity was even greater in the time of Mark's gospel than it was in the time of Jesus, when interpretations of the purity regulations were not yet fully codified.

- **7:4.** *Cups and jugs and kettles*: in the cycle of impurity, "unclean" containers would defile the water in them, which in turn would defile the food or hands the water was meant to "cleanse."

- **7:5.** *Your disciples*: as in the earlier controversy with the Pharisees over fasting (2:18), the accusation is not made directly against Jesus, but against his disciples, which suggests this may reflect a later dispute between Pharisees and Christians.

- **7:6.** *Phonies*: suggests "not what they appear to be," by someone else's standards; the traditional translation *hypocrites* implies

insincere intentions, which is not the issue here. Isa 29:13 makes this point only when quoted from the LXX translation. The Hebrew text is not well suited for this purpose: "Because this people . . . honors me with their lips, and their heart is far away from me, and their worship of me is a commandment taught by humans, therefore [I will punish them]." The reliance on the LXX text suggests this is a later, Christian argument.

- **7:10.** *Moses said*: introduces commands found in the Torah (Penteteuch), here from Exod 20:12; 21:17; repeated in Deut 5:16; Lev 20:9. *Honor*: was interpreted by the rabbis to mean "provide for."

- **7:11.** The context suggests the taking of an oath: "I declare, 'Whatever . . . to be *Korban*,'" which Mark explains as *conse-*

ἄνθρωπος τῷ πατρὶ ἢ τῇ μητρί, Κορβᾶν, ὅ ἐστιν, Δῶρον, ὃ ἐὰν
ἐξ ἐμοῦ ὠφεληθῇς, ¹²οὐκέτι ἀφίετε αὐτὸν οὐδὲν ποιῆσαι τῷ
πατρὶ ἢ τῇ μητρί, ¹³ἀκυροῦντες τὸν λόγον τοῦ θεοῦ τῇ
παραδόσει ὑμῶν ᾗ παρεδώκατε· καὶ παρόμοια τοιαῦτα πολλὰ
ποιεῖτε.

What comes out defiles

¹⁴Καὶ προσκαλεσάμενος πάλιν τὸν ὄχλον ἔλεγεν αὐτοῖς,
Ἀκούσατέ μου πάντες καὶ σύνετε. ¹⁵οὐδέν ἐστιν ἔξωθεν τοῦ
ἀνθρώπου εἰσπορευόμενον εἰς αὐτὸν ὃ δύναται κοινῶσαι αὐτόν·
ἀλλὰ τὰ ἐκ τοῦ ἀνθρώπου ἐκπορευόμενά ἐστιν τὰ κοινοῦντα τὸν
ἄνθρωπον. [¹⁶εἴ τις ἔχει ὦτα ἀκούειν ἀκουέτω.]

¹⁷Καὶ ὅτε εἰσῆλθεν εἰς οἶκον ἀπὸ τοῦ ὄχλου, ἐπηρώτων αὐτὸν
οἱ μαθηταὶ αὐτοῦ τὴν παραβολήν. ¹⁸καὶ λέγει αὐτοῖς, Οὕτως καὶ
ὑμεῖς ἀσύνετοί ἐστε; οὐ νοεῖτε ὅτι πᾶν τὸ ἔξωθεν εἰσπορευόμενον
εἰς τὸν ἄνθρωπον οὐ δύναται αὐτὸν κοινῶσαι, ¹⁹ὅτι οὐκ
εἰσπορεύεται αὐτοῦ εἰς τὴν καρδίαν ἀλλ᾽ εἰς τὴν κοιλίαν, καὶ εἰς
τὸν ἀφεδρῶνα ἐκπορεύεται; καθαρίζων πάντα τὰ βρώματα.

²⁰Ἔλεγεν δὲ ὅτι Τὸ ἐκ τοῦ ἀνθρώπου ἐκπορευόμενον ἐκεῖνο
κοινοῖ τὸν ἄνθρωπον· ²¹ἔσωθεν γὰρ ἐκ τῆς καρδίας τῶν
ἀνθρώπων οἱ διαλογισμοὶ οἱ κακοὶ ἐκπορεύονται, πορνεῖαι,
κλοπαί, φόνοι, ²²μοιχεῖαι, πλεονεξίαι, πονηρίαι, δόλος,
ἀσέλγεια, ὀφθαλμὸς πονηρός, βλασφημία, ὑπερηφανία,
ἀφροσύνη· ²³πάντα ταῦτα τὰ πονηρὰ ἔσωθεν ἐκπορεύεται καὶ
κοινοῖ τὸν ἄνθρωπον.

Greek woman's daughter

²⁴Ἐκεῖθεν δὲ ἀναστὰς ἀπῆλθεν εἰς τὰ ὅρια Τύρου. καὶ
εἰσελθὼν εἰς οἰκίαν οὐδένα ἤθελεν γνῶναι, καὶ οὐκ ἠδυνήθη
λαθεῖν· ²⁵ἀλλ᾽ εὐθὺς ἀκούσασα γυνὴ περὶ αὐτοῦ, ἧς εἶχεν τὸ
θυγάτριον αὐτῆς πνεῦμα ἀκάθαρτον, ἐλθοῦσα προσέπεσεν πρὸς
τοὺς πόδας αὐτοῦ· ²⁶ἡ δὲ γυνὴ ἦν Ἑλληνίς, Συροφοινίκισσα τῷ
γένει· καὶ ἠρώτα αὐτὸν ἵνα τὸ δαιμόνιον ἐκβάλῃ ἐκ τῆς θυγατρὸς
αὐτῆς. ²⁷καὶ ἔλεγεν αὐτῇ, Ἄφες πρῶτον χορτασθῆναι τὰ τέκνα,

---

16. This verse is not found in the earliest MSS.　　**19.** *Outhouse:* one early
MS substitutes *sewer.*

---

crated to God. The conflict arises because
the Torah also commands that any oath
must be kept (Num 30:2; Deut 23:21).
Later rabbis ruled that the command to
"honor father and mother" took precedence
over any conflicting obligations.

• **7:15.** This saying has the distinctive charac-
teristics of a subversive aphorism, the kind
of "wisdom" saying typical of Jesus (6:2),
since it takes the category "defile" and gives
it a significantly different meaning. *Defile:*
the opposite of "make, or treat as, holy,"
the central objective of the religious practices
promoted by the Pharisees. An even more
explicit version of the saying is in v. 18.

• **7:16.** This saying, missing in the earliest
surviving MSS, was commonly used after
parables (4:9) and aphorisms (4:23) that
warranted further explanation. Thus it
could easily have been added here later.

• **7:17.** *Riddle:* the Greek is *parabole*, but this
is a puzzling saying (see 3:23), not a
parabolic story (§6.5).

• **7:18.** *Dim-witted:* another of Mark's unflat-
tering characterizations of the disciples
(§4.5). *Nothing from outside can defile:* even
more explicit than v. 15, this version of the
saying directly undercuts all Pharisaic concerns about food and eating regulations.

• **7:19.** *This is how:* inferred from the context

"Whatever I might have spent to support you is *korban*"' (which means "consecrated to God"), [12]you no longer let those persons do anything for their father or mother. [13]So you end up invalidating God's word with your own tradition, which you then perpetuate. And you do all kinds of other things like that!"

[14]Once again he summoned the crowd and would say to them: "Listen to me, all of you, and try to understand! [15]It's not what goes into a person from the outside that can defile; rather it's what comes out of the person that defiles. [[16]If anyone has two good ears, use them!]"

What comes out
defiles

[17]When he entered a house away from the crowd, his disciples started questioning him about the riddle. [18]And he says to them: "Are you as dim-witted as the rest? Don't you realize that nothing from outside can defile by going into a person, [19]because it doesn't get to the heart but passes into the stomach, and comes out in the outhouse?" (This is how everything we eat is purified.)

[20]And he went on to say: "It's what comes out of a person that defiles. [21]For from out of the human heart issue wicked intentions: sexual immorality, thefts, murders, [22]adulteries, envies, wickedness, deceit, promiscuity, an evil eye, blasphemy, arrogance, lack of good sense. [23]All these evil things come from the inside out and defile the person."

[24]From there he got up and went away to the regions of Tyre. Whenever he visited a house he wanted no one to know, but he could not escape notice. [25]Instead, suddenly a woman whose daughter had an unclean spirit heard about him, and came and fell down at his feet. [26]The woman was a Greek, by race a Phoenician from Syria. And she started asking him to drive the demon out of her daughter. [27]He responded to her like this:

Greek woman's
daughter

---

to be the function of the Greek dangling participle, "purifying," here rendered *is purified*. It has a masculine ending, which could refer back to Jesus in v. 18, implying: "By saying this, he was purifying everything we eat." This would then be the early Christian interpretation of what Jesus taught about dietary regulations: "nothing is unclean in itself" (Rom 14:14), and "what God has made clean, you must not call impure" (Acts 10:15; 11:9). Some MSS change the ending of the participle in an attempt to remove the apparent ambiguity. SV reads the Greek participle in its immediate context as Mark's ironical comment about the natural digestive process just described.

• **7:20.** Jesus substitutes ethical concerns for

purity regulations.

• **7:21–22.** All but one of these "vices" are found somewhere in the LXX version of the Old Testament; so this is a rather commonplace list. *Wicked intentions*: provides the basis for the following list of six plural nouns and six singular nouns, likely meant to cover the common moral sins. *An evil eye*: may suggest "greedy."

• **7:24–37.** Mark presents several healing stories outside Galilee.

• **7:26.** *A Phoenician from Syria*: the old coastal region of Phoenicia, including the main cities of Tyre (v. 24) and Sidon (v. 31), was now part of the Roman province of Syria.

• **7:27.** *Dogs*: the Greek suggests *puppies*, or, as in v. 28, pets *under the table*. Jesus may

οὐ γάρ ἐστιν καλὸν λαβεῖν τὸν ἄρτον τῶν τέκνων καὶ τοῖς κυναρίοις βαλεῖν. ²⁸ Ἡ δὲ ἀπεκρίθη καὶ λέγει αὐτῷ, Κύριε, καὶ τὰ κυνάρια ὑποκάτω τῆς τραπέζης ἐσθίουσιν ἀπὸ τῶν ψιχίων τῶν παιδίων. ²⁹ Καὶ εἶπεν αὐτῇ, Διὰ τοῦτον τὸν λόγον ὕπαγε, ἐξελήλυθεν ἐκ τῆς θυγατρός σου τὸ δαιμόνιον. ³⁰ Καὶ ἀπελθοῦσα εἰς τὸν οἶκον αὐτῆς εὗρεν τὸ παιδίον βεβλημένον ἐπὶ τὴν κλίνην καὶ τὸ δαιμόνιον ἐξεληλυθός.

Deaf mute ³¹ Καὶ πάλιν ἐξελθὼν ἐκ τῶν ὁρίων Τύρου ἦλθεν διὰ Σιδῶνος εἰς τὴν θάλασσαν τῆς Γαλιλαίας ἀνὰ μέσον τῶν ὁρίων Δεκαπόλεως. ³² Καὶ φέρουσιν αὐτῷ κωφὸν καὶ μογιλάλον, καὶ παρακαλοῦσιν αὐτὸν ἵνα ἐπιθῇ αὐτῷ τὴν χεῖρα. ³³ καὶ ἀπολαβόμενος αὐτὸν ἀπὸ τοῦ ὄχλου κατ᾽ ἰδίαν ἔβαλεν τοὺς δακτύλους αὐτοῦ εἰς τὰ ὦτα αὐτοῦ καὶ πτύσας ἥψατο τῆς γλώσσης αὐτοῦ, ³⁴ καὶ ἀναβλέψας εἰς τὸν οὐρανὸν ἐστέναξεν, καὶ λέγει αὐτῷ, Εφφαθα, ὅ ἐστιν, Διανοίχθητι. ³⁵ καὶ εὐθέως ἠνοίγησαν αὐτοῦ αἱ ἀκοαί, καὶ ἐλύθη ὁ δεσμὸς τῆς γλώσσης αὐτοῦ, καὶ ἐλάλει ὀρθῶς. ³⁶ καὶ διεστείλατο αὐτοῖς ἵνα μηδενὶ λέγωσιν· ὅσον δὲ αὐτοῖς διεστέλλετο, αὐτοὶ μᾶλλον περισσότερον ἐκήρυσσον. ³⁷ Καὶ ὑπερπερισσῶς ἐξεπλήσσοντο λέγοντες, Καλῶς πάντα πεποίηκεν· καὶ τοὺς κωφοὺς ποιεῖ ἀκούειν καὶ τοὺς ἀλάλους λαλεῖν.

---

28. *Sir:* some early MSS read *Yes, Sir.*   **31.** *The regions of Tyre and traveled through Sidon:* many, mostly later, MSS read *The regions of Tyre and Sidon and went.*

---

be repeating a popular Judean slur about pagans.

• **7:28.** *Sir:* translates *kyrie*, the polite way to address someone of higher social rank. But it also means "master/patron" (5:19), and is used in the LXX for "the Lord" (1:3). There is ambiguity and irony in this address—she may only be being polite by

"Let the children be fed first, since it isn't good to take bread out of children's mouths and throw it to the dogs!"

²⁸But as a rejoinder she says to him: "Sir, even the dogs under the table get to eat scraps dropped by children!"

²⁹Then he said to her: "For that retort, be on your way, the demon has come out of your daughter."

³⁰She returned home and found the child lying on the bed and the demon gone.

³¹Then he left the regions of Tyre and traveled through Sidon to the Sea of Galilee, through the middle of the region known as the Decapolis.   *Deaf mute*

³²And they bring him a deaf mute and plead with him to lay his hand on him. ³³Taking him aside from the crowd in private, he stuck his fingers into the man's ears and spat and touched his tongue. ³⁴And looking up to the sky, he groaned and says to him, "*ephphatha*" (which means, "Be opened!"). ³⁵And his ears opened up, and right away his speech impediment was removed, and he started speaking properly. ³⁶Then he ordered them to tell no one. But no matter how much he enjoined them, they spread it around all the more.

³⁷And they were completely dumbfounded. "He's done everything and has done it quite well," they said; "he even makes the deaf hear and the mute speak!"

---

saying *kyrie* ("sir"), but the reader recognizes the greater truth: Jesus is indeed "master," and will become "Lord" (for more discussion of translating *kyrios*, see §6.4).

• **7:31.** This is an awkward journey, since Sidon is 22 miles north of Tyre, in the opposition direction from the Sea of Galilee and the Decapolis.

• **7:33.** The technique, including he *spat*, was a common healing "remedy," though Judeans considered the use of spittle "unclean."

• **7:34.** *Ephphatha*: in Jesus' native language, Aramaic, similar to the special term remembered in an earlier healing story (5:41).

• **7:37.** *The deaf hear and the mute speak*: describes what was expected to happen when God "will come and save us" (Isa 35:4–6 LXX).

Loaves & fish
for 4,000

8 Ἐν ἐκείναις ταῖς ἡμέραις πάλιν πολλοῦ ὄχλου ὄντος καὶ μὴ ἐχόντων τί φάγωσιν, προσκαλεσάμενος τοὺς μαθητὰς λέγει αὐτοῖς, ²Σπλαγχνίζομαι ἐπὶ τὸν ὄχλον ὅτι ἤδη ἡμέραι τρεῖς προσμένουσίν μοι καὶ οὐκ ἔχουσιν τί φάγωσιν· ³καὶ ἐὰν ἀπολύσω αὐτοὺς νήστεις εἰς οἶκον αὐτῶν, ἐκλυθήσονται ἐν τῇ ὁδῷ· καί τινες αὐτῶν ἀπὸ μακρόθεν ἥκασιν.

⁴Καὶ ἀπεκρίθησαν αὐτῷ οἱ μαθηταὶ αὐτοῦ ὅτι Πόθεν τούτους δυνήσεταί τις ὧδε χορτάσαι ἄρτων ἐπ᾽ ἐρημίας; ⁵Καὶ ἠρώτα αὐτούς, Πόσους ἔχετε ἄρτους; Οἱ δὲ εἶπαν, Ἑπτά.

⁶Καὶ παραγγέλλει τῷ ὄχλῳ ἀναπεσεῖν ἐπὶ τῆς γῆς· καὶ λαβὼν τοὺς ἑπτὰ ἄρτους εὐχαριστήσας ἔκλασεν καὶ ἐδίδου τοῖς μαθηταῖς αὐτοῦ ἵνα παρατιθῶσιν καὶ παρέθηκαν τῷ ὄχλῳ. ⁷καὶ εἶχον ἰχθύδια ὀλίγα· καὶ εὐλογήσας αὐτὰ εἶπεν καὶ ταῦτα παρατιθέναι. ⁸καὶ ἔφαγον καὶ ἐχορτάσθησαν, καὶ ἦραν περισσεύματα κλασμάτων ἑπτὰ σπυρίδας. ⁹ἦσαν δὲ ὡς τετρακισχίλιοι. καὶ ἀπέλυσεν αὐτούς.

Demand for
a sign

¹⁰Καὶ εὐθὺς ἐμβὰς εἰς τὸ πλοῖον μετὰ τῶν μαθητῶν αὐτοῦ ἦλθεν εἰς τὰ μέρη Δαλμανουθά. ¹¹καὶ ἐξῆλθον οἱ Φαρισαῖοι καὶ ἤρξαντο συζητεῖν αὐτῷ, ζητοῦντες παρ᾽ αὐτοῦ σημεῖον ἀπὸ τοῦ οὐρανοῦ, πειράζοντες αὐτόν. ¹²καὶ ἀναστενάξας τῷ πνεύματι αὐτοῦ λέγει, Τί ἡ γενεὰ αὕτη ζητεῖ σημεῖον; ἀμὴν λέγω ὑμῖν, εἰ δοθήσεται τῇ γενεᾷ ταύτῃ σημεῖον.

¹³Καὶ ἀφεὶς αὐτοὺς πάλιν ἐμβὰς ἀπῆλθεν εἰς τὸ πέραν.

Bread & leaven

¹⁴Καὶ ἐπελάθοντο λαβεῖν ἄρτους, καὶ εἰ μὴ ἕνα ἄρτον οὐκ εἶχον μεθ᾽ ἑαυτῶν ἐν τῷ πλοίῳ. ¹⁵καὶ διεστέλλετο αὐτοῖς λέγων, Ὁρᾶτε, βλέπετε ἀπὸ τῆς ζύμης τῶν Φαρισαίων καὶ τῆς ζύμης Ἡρῴδου.

¹⁶Καὶ διελογίζοντο πρὸς ἀλλήλους ὅτι ἄρτους οὐκ ἔχουσιν. ¹⁷καὶ γνοὺς λέγει αὐτοῖς, Τί διαλογίζεσθε ὅτι ἄρτους οὐκ ἔχετε;

---

7. *Blessed them:* some MSS omit *them*, so *gave a blessing*, in the Jewish sense of blessing God (6:41).   10. *Dalmanoutha:* MSS vary considerably in spelling and substitutions of *Magada* (from Matt 15:39) or *Magdala.* 15. *Herod:* some MSS read *Herodians* (3:6; 12:13).

• **8:1–21.** The first half of Mark's story culminates with the second combination of feeding story and boat trip (6:35–52), this time apparently while Jesus is still outside Galilee.

• **8:4.** The disciples had already seen a demonstration of how to feed people in a *desolate place* (6:35–44), but *they hadn't understood* (6:52).

• **8:6.** *Gave thanks:* equivalent to *gave a blessing* (6:41).

• **8:7.** *Blessed them:* or *gave a blessing for them.*

• **8:10.** *Dalmanoutha:* unknown location not mentioned elsewhere; sometimes associated with *Magdala,* a town on the western shore of the Sea of Galilee.

• **8:11.** *A sign in the sky:* some activity or event that would authenticate that God is the source of what Jesus does. Mark has already suggested that Jesus' opponents are incapable of recognizing such a sign, because they have accused Jesus of being in league with Satan (3:22).

• **8:12.** *I swear to God:* the formula for a

8 And once again during that same period, when there was a huge crowd without anything to eat, he calls the disciples aside and says to them: ²"I feel sorry for the crowd, because they have already spent three days with me and haven't had anything to eat. ³If I send these people home hungry, they will collapse on the road—in fact some of them have come from quite a distance."

Loaves & fish for 4,000

⁴And his disciples answered him, "How can anyone feed these people bread out here in this desolate place?"

⁵And he started asking them, "How many loaves do you have?"

They replied, "Seven."

⁶Then he orders the crowd to sit down on the ground. And he took the seven loaves, gave thanks, and broke them into pieces, and started giving ⟨them⟩ to his disciples to hand out; and they passed them around to the crowd. ⁷They also had a few small fish. When he had blessed them, he told them to hand those out as well. ⁸They had more than enough to eat. Then they picked up seven big baskets of leftover scraps. ⁹There were about four thousand people there. Then he started sending them away.

¹⁰And he got right into the boat with his disciples and went to the Dalmanoutha district. ¹¹The Pharisees came out and started to argue with him. To test him, they demanded a sign in the sky. ¹²He groaned under his breath and says: "Why does this generation insist on a sign? I swear to God, no sign will be given this generation!"

Demand for a sign

¹³And turning his back on them, he got back in the boat and crossed over to the other side.

¹⁴They forgot to bring any bread and had nothing with them in the boat except one loaf. ¹⁵Then he started giving them directives: "Look," he says, "watch out for the leaven of the Pharisees and the leaven of Herod!"

Bread & leaven

¹⁶They began looking quizzically at one another because they didn't have any bread. ¹⁷And because he was aware of this, he

---

solemn declaration (3:28) here introduces an oath (§5.2).

• **8:13.** *The other side*: from which direction is uncertain. Since v. 10 does not mention a crossing, Dalmanoutha could be on the eastern shore, with v. 13 the crossing back to the western, Galilean side. However, Dalmanoutha is usually associated with Magdala on the west coast, making this the third, and last, trip across to the east, parallel to the two stormy crossings that already showed the disciples' failure to

understand (4:35–41; 6:45–52).

• **8:14.** *Bread*: or *loaves*, brings back the topic the disciples had been obstinate about before (6:52).

• **8:15.** *Leaven*: yeast added to bread dough, except during Passover (14:1). Jesus here uses the image symbolically, as did the Judean rabbis, for something that corrupts people. Linking the Pharisees to Herod reminds the reader of the conspiracy in 3:6.

• **8:16–17.** *Looking quizzically* and *puzzling*: the disciples' response to Jesus' saying

οὔπω νοεῖτε οὐδὲ συνίετε; πεπωρωμένην ἔχετε τὴν καρδίαν ὑμῶν; 18 ὀφθαλμοὺς ἔχοντες οὐ βλέπετε καὶ ὦτα ἔχοντες οὐκ ἀκούετε; καὶ οὐ μνημονεύετε, 19 ὅτε τοὺς πέντε ἄρτους ἔκλασα εἰς τοὺς πεντακισχιλίους, πόσους κοφίνους κλασμάτων πλήρεις ἤρατε;

Λέγουσιν αὐτῷ, Δώδεκα.

20 Ὅτε τοὺς ἑπτὰ εἰς τοὺς τετρακισχιλίους, πόσων σπυρίδων πληρώματα κλασμάτων ἤρατε;

Καὶ λέγουσιν, Ἑπτά.

21 Καὶ ἔλεγεν αὐτοῖς, Οὔπω συνίετε;

A blind man receives his sight

22 Καὶ ἔρχονται εἰς Βηθσαϊδάν. καὶ φέρουσιν αὐτῷ τυφλὸν καὶ παρακαλοῦσιν αὐτὸν ἵνα αὐτοῦ ἅψηται. 23 καὶ ἐπιλαβόμενος τῆς χειρὸς τοῦ τυφλοῦ ἐξήνεγκεν αὐτὸν ἔξω τῆς κώμης, καὶ πτύσας εἰς τὰ ὄμματα αὐτοῦ, ἐπιθεὶς τὰς χεῖρας αὐτῷ, ἐπηρώτα αὐτόν, Εἴ τι βλέπεις;

24 Καὶ ἀναβλέψας ἔλεγεν, Βλέπω τοὺς ἀνθρώπους, ὅτι ὡς δένδρα ὁρῶ περιπατοῦντας.

25 Εἶτα πάλιν ἐπέθηκεν τὰς χεῖρας ἐπὶ τοὺς ὀφθαλμοὺς αὐτοῦ, καὶ διέβλεψεν, καὶ ἀπεκατέστη, καὶ ἐνέβλεπεν τηλαυγῶς ἅπαντα. 26 καὶ ἀπέστειλεν αὐτὸν εἰς οἶκον αὐτοῦ λέγων, Μηδὲ εἰς τὴν κώμην εἰσέλθῃς.

What are people saying?

27 Καὶ ἐξῆλθεν ὁ Ἰησοῦς καὶ οἱ μαθηταὶ αὐτοῦ εἰς τὰς κώμας Καισαρείας τῆς Φιλίππου· καὶ ἐν τῇ ὁδῷ ἐπηρώτα τοὺς μαθητὰς αὐτοῦ λέγων αὐτοῖς, Τίνα με λέγουσιν οἱ ἄνθρωποι εἶναι;

28 Οἱ δὲ εἶπαν αὐτῷ λέγοντες ὅτι Ἰωάννην τὸν βαπτιστήν, καὶ ἄλλοι, Ἠλίαν, ἄλλοι δὲ ὅτι εἷς τῶν προφητῶν.

---

26. *Don't bother to go back to the village:* most later MSS add *and don't tell anyone in the village,* probably derived from other stories in Mark (1:44; 3:12; 8:30); some MSS read the first part as, *Go to your home.*

---

about the leaven (v. 15) is reminiscent of the way the scholars "silently wondered" and "entertained questions" (2:6, 8), when Jesus talked about forgiving sins. Mark thus treats both sayings as equally enigmatic.

• **8:17.** *Just dense* a condition similar to *obstinate* (6:52), and more serious than the earlier charge that the disciples *don't get it* (4:13).

• **8:18.** *You still don't see; you still don't hear!:* this devastating critique echoes Jesus' definition of outsiders—people who remain in a world of parables. The words also echo Jeremiah's description of "foolish and senseless people" who are stubborn (Jer 5:21, 23), and Ezekiel's description of

"rebellious" people (Ezek 12:2).

• **8:19–20.** *Baskets:* two different kinds suggested in Greek; the first for a Judean wicker basket, the second for a large matbasket commonly used for supplies. These distinctions were made in the original feeding stories (6:43; 8:8), possibly as part of the contrast between the Judean and pagan settings of the two stories, reinforced here by the numbers *five* and *twelve* with the former, and *seven* with the latter.

• **8:21.** *Still don't understand:* a resounding reiteration of the earlier *still haven't got the point* (v. 17). The third, and final, trip across the sea leaves the disciples in the same state of failure to understand as did

says to them: "Why are you puzzling about your lack of bread? You still aren't using your heads, are you? You still haven't got the point, have you? Are you just dense? ¹⁸Though you have eyes, you still don't see, and though you have ears, you still don't hear! Don't you even remember ¹⁹how many baskets full of scraps you picked up when I broke up the five loaves for the five thousand?"

"Twelve," they reply to him.

²⁰"When I broke up the seven loaves for the four thousand, how many big baskets full of scraps did you pick up?"

And they say, "Seven."

²¹And he repeats: "You still don't understand, do you?"

²²They come to Bethsaida, and they bring him a blind person, and plead with him to touch him. ²³He took the blind man by the hand and led him out of the village. And he spat into his eyes, and placed his hands on him, and started questioning him: "Do you see anything?"

A blind man receives his sight

²⁴When his sight began to come back, the first thing he said was: "I see human figures, as though they were trees walking around."

²⁵Then he put his hands over his eyes a second time. And he opened his eyes, and his sight was restored, and he saw everything clearly. ²⁶And he sent him home, saying, "Don't bother to go back to the village!"

²⁷Jesus and his disciples set out for the villages of Caesarea Philippi. On the road he started questioning his disciples, asking them, "What are people saying about me?"

What are people saying?

²⁸In response they said to him, "⟨Some say, 'You are⟩ John the Baptist,' and others 'Elijah,' but others 'One of the prophets.'"

---

the first two trips (4:40-41; 6:51-52).

• **8:22-26.** A story of a blind person seeing is matched with a similar one in 10:46-52 to form the framework for the middle section of Mark's story.

• **8:23.** *Spat into his eyes:* for healing (7:33).

• **8:25.** *A second time:* an unusual detail in a healing story. The result, *he saw everything clearly*, is in striking contrast to the continuing "blindness" of the disciples in the rest of this section (§4.5).

• **8:27–9:29.** The first of three sequences in which Jesus announces forthcoming suffering, the disciples demonstrate their failure to understand, and Jesus engages in further teaching.

• **8:27.** *The villages of:* implies "in the area surrounding." *Caesarea Philippi:* in the hill-country northeast of Galilee, in the territory of Philip (6:17), who rebuilt the city and renamed it after the emperor. It was outside of the area of current Judean influence, but it also represented the northern border of the ancient Israelite nation. Mark thus presents Jesus as journeying to Jerusalem across the entire length of the former "promised land." Without explanation, Mark presents Jesus as suddenly interested in the question of his own identity, a forbidden topic in the first half of the story (1:34; 3:12).

• **8:28.** *One of the prophets:* probably has the

²⁹Καὶ αὐτὸς ἐπηρώτα αὐτούς, Ὑμεῖς δὲ τίνα με λέγετε εἶναι; Ἀποκριθεὶς ὁ Πέτρος λέγει αὐτῷ, Σὺ εἶ ὁ Χριστός. ³⁰καὶ ἐπετίμησεν αὐτοῖς ἵνα μηδενὶ λέγωσιν περὶ αὐτοῦ.

Son of Adam
destined to suffer

³¹Καὶ ἤρξατο διδάσκειν αὐτοὺς ὅτι δεῖ τὸν υἱὸν τοῦ ἀνθρώπου πολλὰ παθεῖν καὶ ἀποδοκιμασθῆναι ὑπὸ τῶν πρεσβυτέρων καὶ τῶν ἀρχιερέων καὶ τῶν γραμματέων καὶ ἀποκτανθῆναι καὶ μετὰ τρεῖς ἡμέρας ἀναστῆναι· ³²καὶ παρρησίᾳ τὸν λόγον ἐλάλει. καὶ προσλαβόμενος ὁ Πέτρος αὐτὸν ἤρξατο ἐπιτιμᾶν αὐτῷ. ³³ὁ δὲ ἐπιστραφεὶς καὶ ἰδὼν τοὺς μαθητὰς αὐτοῦ ἐπετίμησεν Πέτρῳ καὶ λέγει, Ὕπαγε ὀπίσω μου, Σατανᾶ, ὅτι οὐ φρονεῖς τὰ τοῦ θεοῦ ἀλλὰ τὰ τῶν ἀνθρώπων.

Saving &
losing life

³⁴Καὶ προσκαλεσάμενος τὸν ὄχλον σὺν τοῖς μαθηταῖς αὐτοῦ εἶπεν αὐτοῖς, Εἴ τις θέλει ὀπίσω μου ἀκολουθεῖν, ἀπαρνησάσθω ἑαυτὸν καὶ ἀράτω τὸν σταυρὸν αὐτοῦ καὶ ἀκολουθείτω μοι. ³⁵ὃς γὰρ ἐὰν θέλῃ τὴν ψυχὴν αὐτοῦ σῶσαι ἀπολέσει αὐτήν· ὃς δ' ἂν ἀπολέσει τὴν ψυχὴν αὐτοῦ ἕνεκεν [ἐμοῦ καὶ] τοῦ εὐαγγελίου σώσει αὐτήν. ³⁶τί γὰρ ὠφελεῖ ἄνθρωπον κερδῆσαι τὸν κόσμον ὅλον καὶ ζημιωθῆναι τὴν ψυχὴν αὐτοῦ; ³⁷τί γὰρ δοῖ ἄνθρωπος ἀντάλλαγμα τῆς ψυχῆς αὐτοῦ;

³⁸Ὃς γὰρ ἐὰν ἐπαισχυνθῇ με καὶ τοὺς ἐμοὺς λόγους ἐν τῇ γενεᾷ ταύτῃ τῇ μοιχαλίδι καὶ ἁμαρτωλῷ, καὶ ὁ υἱὸς τοῦ ἀνθρώπου ἐπαισχυνθήσεται αὐτὸν ὅταν ἔλθῃ ἐν τῇ δόξῃ τοῦ πατρὸς αὐτοῦ μετὰ τῶν ἀγγέλων τῶν ἁγίων.

9 ¹καὶ ἔλεγεν αὐτοῖς, Ἀμὴν λέγω ὑμῖν ὅτι εἰσίν τινες ὧδε τῶν ἑστηκότων οἵτινες οὐ μὴ γεύσωνται θανάτου ἕως ἂν ἴδωσιν τὴν βασιλείαν τοῦ θεοῦ ἐληλυθυῖαν ἐν δυνάμει.

---

31. *After three days:* some MSS read *on the third day,* following Matthew and Luke, who also have *be raised,* which corresponds to the actual resurrection story (Mark 16:6).   **35.** *For my sake and:* Greek *emou kai* is omitted in several, including the earliest, MSS, but is included in this saying in Matt 16:25 and Luke 9:24.

sense, *Just another prophet.*

• **8:29.** *The Anointed:* mentioned for the first time since the opening line (1:1). It appears to answer also the disciples' earlier question: "Who can this fellow be?" (4:41).

• **8:30.** *He warned them:* as he did the "unclean spirits" who called him "son of God" (3:12). Treating "the Anointed" this same way further links the two terms.

• **8:31.** *Son of Adam:* used earlier to justify

Jesus' actions (2:10, 28), now becomes Jesus' preferred way to talk about what would happen to himself, repeated in 9:31 and, in greater detail, in 10:33. These summaries outline the same tradition of the "good news" Paul preached: Christ died for our sins and was buried and was raised on the third day (1 Cor 15:1–4). *The elders and the ranking priests and the scholars:* the constituent groups of the Sanhedrin, the

²⁹But he continued to press them, "What about you, who do you say I am?"

Peter responds to him, "You are the Anointed!" ³⁰And he warned them not to tell anyone about him.

³¹He started teaching them that the son of Adam was destined to suffer a great deal, and be rejected by the elders and the ranking priests and the scholars, and be killed, and after three days rise. ³²And he would say this openly. And Peter took him aside and began to lecture him. ³³But he turned, noticed his disciples, and reprimanded Peter verbally: "Get out of my sight, you Satan, you, because you're not thinking in God's terms, but in human terms."

Son of Adam destined to suffer

³⁴After he called the crowd together with his disciples, he said to them: "Those who want to come after me should deny themselves, pick up their cross, and follow me! ³⁵Remember, those who try to save their own life are going to lose it, but those who lose their life [for my sake and] for the sake of the good news are going to save it. ³⁶After all, what good does it do a person to acquire the whole world and pay for it with life? ³⁷Or, what would a person give in exchange for life?

Saving & losing life

³⁸"Moreover, those who are ashamed of me and my message in this adulterous and sinful generation, of them the son of Adam will likewise be ashamed when he comes in his Father's glory accompanied by holy angels!"

9 ¹And he used to tell them: "I swear to you: Some of those standing here won't ever taste death before they see God's imperial rule set in with power!"

Jerusalem Council, which functioned like a supreme court on all Judean internal matters. *The elders* were heads of important families; *the ranking priests* were authorities in the temple; *the scholars* were legal experts (2:6).

- **8:33.** *Get out of my sight:* ironically, the Greek is the same as for, *Go follow me* (rather than oppose me). *You Satan, you:* treats as a temptation by opposing forces (1:13) Peter's refusal to accept rejection by the Jerusalem authorities as part of Jesus' description of "the Anointed."
- **8:34.** *Pick up their cross:* suggests accepting martyrdom. *Follow me:* the original call to the disciples (1:17, 20) now becomes a way to define Christians.

- **8:38.** *Son of Adam:* just used in the description of Jesus' forthcoming suffering (v. 31), but "coming in glory with angels" is the language of the final judgment. The imagery is derived from Dan 7:13–14, where a human figure comes on the clouds to the deity and receives glory and dominion for ever (also used in 13:26).
- **9:1.** *I swear to you:* introduces oath-like statements (3:38), which are often about something that *won't ever* happen (§5.2). *God's imperial rule set in with power:* describes what was "closing in" at the beginning of the story (1:15) as being accomplished in the lifetime of some of Jesus' followers.

Jesus
transformed

9 ²Καὶ μετὰ ἡμέρας ἓξ παραλαμβάνει ὁ Ἰησοῦς τὸν Πέτρον καὶ τὸν Ἰάκωβον καὶ τὸν Ἰωάννην, καὶ ἀναφέρει αὐτοὺς εἰς ὄρος ὑψηλὸν κατ' ἰδίαν μόνους. καὶ μετεμορφώθη ἔμπροσθεν αὐτῶν, ³καὶ τὰ ἱμάτια αὐτοῦ ἐγένετο στίλβοντα λευκὰ λίαν οἷα γναφεὺς ἐπὶ τῆς γῆς οὐ δύναται οὕτως λευκᾶναι. ⁴καὶ ὤφθη αὐτοῖς Ἠλίας σὺν Μωϋσεῖ, καὶ ἦσαν συλλαλοῦντες τῷ Ἰησοῦ. ⁵καὶ ἀποκριθεὶς ὁ Πέτρος λέγει τῷ Ἰησοῦ, Ῥαββί, καλόν ἐστιν ἡμᾶς ὧδε εἶναι, καὶ ποιήσωμεν τρεῖς σκηνάς, σοὶ μίαν καὶ Μωϋσεῖ μίαν καὶ Ἠλίᾳ μίαν. ⁶οὐ γὰρ ᾔδει τί ἀποκριθῇ, ἔκφοβοι γὰρ ἐγένοντο.

⁷Καὶ ἐγένετο νεφέλη ἐπισκιάζουσα αὐτοῖς, καὶ ἐγένετο φωνὴ ἐκ τῆς νεφέλης, Οὗτός ἐστιν ὁ υἱός μου ὁ ἀγαπητός, ἀκούετε αὐτοῦ. ⁸καὶ ἐξάπινα περιβλεψάμενοι οὐκέτι οὐδένα εἶδον ἀλλὰ τὸν Ἰησοῦν μόνον μεθ' ἑαυτῶν.

Elijah
must come

⁹Καὶ καταβαινόντων αὐτῶν ἐκ τοῦ ὄρους διεστείλατο αὐτοῖς ἵνα μηδενὶ ἃ εἶδον διηγήσωνται, εἰ μὴ ὅταν ὁ υἱὸς τοῦ ἀνθρώπου ἐκ νεκρῶν ἀναστῇ.

¹⁰Καὶ τὸν λόγον ἐκράτησαν πρὸς ἑαυτοὺς συζητοῦντες τί ἐστιν τὸ ἐκ νεκρῶν ἀναστῆναι. ¹¹καὶ ἐπηρώτων αὐτὸν λέγοντες, Ὅτι λέγουσιν οἱ γραμματεῖς ὅτι Ἠλίαν δεῖ ἐλθεῖν πρῶτον;

¹²Ὁ δὲ ἔφη αὐτοῖς, Ἠλίας μὲν ἐλθὼν πρῶτον ἀποκαθιστάνει πάντα, καὶ πῶς γέγραπται ἐπὶ τὸν υἱὸν τοῦ ἀνθρώπου ἵνα πολλὰ πάθῃ καὶ ἐξουδενηθῇ; ¹³ἀλλὰ λέγω ὑμῖν ὅτι καὶ Ἠλίας ἐλήλυθεν, καὶ ἐποίησαν αὐτῷ ὅσα ἤθελον, καθὼς γέγραπται ἐπ' αὐτόν.

---

5. *Let's:* some MSS read, *Do you want us to?*

• **9:2-13.** The transfiguration scene is in some ways similar to an appearance of Jesus after the resurrection, but Mark's abrupt ending (16:8) does not allow for any such story at that point.

• **9:2.** *Six days later:* unusually specific for Mark. It parallels Moses' experience on Mt. Sinai: "The clouds covered it for six days; and on the seventh day [the Lord] called to Moses out of the cloud" (Exod 24:16). It is unclear whether this is could be the direct fulfillment of v. 1, or whether a more public "seeing" is expected.

• **9:3.** *Intensely brilliant white:* reflects the radiance of God's glory, like Moses on Sinai:

"the skin of his face shone because he had been talking with God" (Exod 38:29).

• **9:4.** Since Elijah went directly to heaven (2 Kgs 2:11) and Moses had no known burial place (Deut 34:6), both were legendary figures who avoided death. They were also major prophetic figures. Moses was the only prophet who had talked with God "face to face" (Deut 34:10), and Elijah had escaped to Moses' mountain and encountered the voice of God (1 Kgs 19:9, 13). The speculation about future prophets was based on Moses (Mark 9:7) and Elijah (1:6; 6:15; 9:11).

• **9:5.** *Rabbi:* Hebrew for "my master," used

9 ²Six days later, Jesus takes Peter and James and John along and leads them off by themselves to a lofty mountain. He was transformed in front of them, ³and his clothes became an intensely brilliant white, whiter than any laundry on earth could make them. ⁴Elijah appeared to them, with Moses, and they were conversing with Jesus. ⁵Peter responds by saying to Jesus, "Rabbi, it's a good thing we're here. In fact, why not set up three tents, one for you, and one for Moses, and one for Elijah!" (⁶You see, he didn't know how else to respond, since they were terrified.)

⁷And a cloud moved in and cast a shadow over them, and a voice came out of the cloud: "This is my favored son, listen to him!" ⁸Suddenly, as they looked around, they saw no one, but were alone with Jesus.

⁹And as they were walking down the mountain he instructed them not to describe what they had seen to anyone, until the son of Adam rise from the dead.

¹⁰And they kept it to themselves, puzzling over what this could mean, this 'rising from the dead.' ¹¹And they started questioning him: "The scholars claim, don't they, that Elijah must come first?"

¹²He would respond to them, "Of course Elijah comes first to restore everything. So, how does scripture claim that the son of Adam will suffer greatly and be the object of scorn? ¹³On the other hand, I tell you that Elijah in fact has come, and they had their way with him, just as the scriptures indicate."

Jesus transformed

Elijah must come

---

by disciples to address their teachers, especially after the time of Jesus. In Mark only Peter (11:21) and Judas (14:45) address Jesus this way (see also 10:51). *Tents*: could refer to the shelters set up for the Judean Feast of Tabernacles, the annual harvest festival commemorating the tents used during the exodus, or to the Tent of Meeting described during Moses' Sinai encounter (Exodus 26), where later Moses would meet with God during the exodus, or it could suggest a desire to prolong the experience by setting up camp.

- **9:7.** *This is my favored son*: similar to the words at Jesus' baptism (1:11), except this time they are directed to the disciples, rather than to Jesus. *Listen to him*: echoes Deut 18:15, "God will raise up for you a prophet like [Moses]—listen to him."

- **9:11.** *The scholars claim*: based on Mal 4:5, "I will send you the prophet Elijah before the great and terrible day of the Lord comes."

- **9:12.** *Scripture* does not explicitly make this claim, but Christians had favorite texts (§2.1), such as Isaiah 53 and Psalm 22, which both mention *scorn* (Isa 53:3; Ps 22:6).

- **9:13.** *Elijah has come*: must refer to John the Baptizer, as Mark presents him (1:6). *As the scriptures indicate*: nowhere is the suffering of Elijah a direct theme in scripture. One parallel between John and Elijah is the role of the daughter of Herodias in the death of John (6:14–29) and Jezebel's threat to the life of Elijah (1 Kgs 19:1–2, 10).

The mute spirit ¹⁴Καὶ ἐλθόντες πρὸς τοὺς μαθητὰς εἶδον ὄχλον πολὺν περὶ αὐτοὺς καὶ γραμματεῖς συζητοῦντας πρὸς αὐτούς. ¹⁵καὶ εὐθὺς πᾶς ὁ ὄχλος ἰδόντες αὐτὸν ἐξεθαμβήθησαν, καὶ προστρέχοντες ἠσπάζοντο αὐτόν. ¹⁶καὶ ἐπηρώτησεν αὐτούς, Τί συζητεῖτε πρὸς αὐτούς;

¹⁷Καὶ ἀπεκρίθη αὐτῷ εἷς ἐκ τοῦ ὄχλου, Διδάσκαλε, ἤνεγκα τὸν υἱόν μου πρὸς σέ, ἔχοντα πνεῦμα ἄλαλον· ¹⁸καὶ ὅπου ἐὰν αὐτὸν καταλάβῃ ῥήσσει αὐτόν, καὶ ἀφρίζει καὶ τρίζει τοὺς ὀδόντας καὶ ξηραίνεται· καὶ εἶπα τοῖς μαθηταῖς σου ἵνα αὐτὸ ἐκβάλωσιν, καὶ οὐκ ἴσχυσαν.

¹⁹Ὁ δὲ ἀποκριθεὶς αὐτοῖς λέγει, Ὦ γενεὰ ἄπιστος, ἕως πότε πρὸς ὑμᾶς ἔσομαι; ἕως πότε ἀνέξομαι ὑμῶν; φέρετε αὐτὸν πρός με.

²⁰Καὶ ἤνεγκαν αὐτὸν πρὸς αὐτόν. καὶ ἰδὼν αὐτὸν τὸ πνεῦμα εὐθὺς συνεσπάραξεν αὐτόν, καὶ πεσὼν ἐπὶ τῆς γῆς ἐκυλίετο ἀφρίζων. ²¹καὶ ἐπηρώτησεν τὸν πατέρα αὐτοῦ, Πόσος χρόνος ἐστὶν ὡς τοῦτο γέγονεν αὐτῷ;

Ὁ δὲ εἶπεν, Ἐκ παιδιόθεν· ²²καὶ πολλάκις καὶ εἰς πῦρ αὐτὸν ἔβαλεν καὶ εἰς ὕδατα ἵνα ἀπολέσῃ αὐτόν· ἀλλ' εἴ τι δύνῃ, βοήθησον ἡμῖν σπλαγχνισθεὶς ἐφ' ἡμᾶς.

²³Ὁ δὲ Ἰησοῦς εἶπεν αὐτῷ, Τὸ Εἰ δύνῃ, πάντα δυνατὰ τῷ πιστεύοντι.

²⁴Εὐθὺς κράξας ὁ πατὴρ τοῦ παιδίου ἔλεγεν, Πιστεύω· βοήθει μου τῇ ἀπιστίᾳ.

²⁵Ἰδὼν δὲ ὁ Ἰησοῦς ὅτι ἐπισυντρέχει ὄχλος ἐπετίμησεν τῷ πνεύματι τῷ ἀκαθάρτῳ λέγων αὐτῷ, Τὸ ἄλαλον καὶ κωφὸν πνεῦμα, ἐγὼ ἐπιτάσσω σοι, ἔξελθε ἐξ αὐτοῦ καὶ μηκέτι εἰσέλθῃς εἰς αὐτόν.

²⁶Καὶ κράξας καὶ πολλὰ σπαράξας ἐξῆλθεν· καὶ ἐγένετο ὡσεὶ νεκρός, ὥστε τοὺς πολλοὺς λέγειν ὅτι ἀπέθανεν. ²⁷ὁ δὲ Ἰησοῦς κρατήσας τῆς χειρὸς αὐτοῦ ἤγειρεν αὐτόν, καὶ ἀνέστη.

²⁸Καὶ εἰσελθόντος αὐτοῦ εἰς οἶκον οἱ μαθηταὶ αὐτοῦ κατ' ἰδίαν ἐπηρώτων αὐτόν, Ὅτι ἡμεῖς οὐκ ἠδυνήθημεν ἐκβαλεῖν αὐτό;

²⁹Καὶ εἶπεν αὐτοῖς, Τοῦτο τὸ γένος ἐν οὐδενὶ δύναται ἐξελθεῖν εἰ μὴ ἐν προσευχῇ.

---

23. *What you do mean, 'If you can':* many MSS read, *If you can have trust,* missing the context that Jesus is repeating what the father has said.   **24.** After *cried out* later MSS add *with tears.*   **29.** Later MSS add *and fasting* at the end, reflecting a later church practice.

• **9:14–29.** Mark is apparently following the exodus sequence, where Moses descends from the mountain to find the people have lost their trust (Exod 32:15–20).

• **9:18.** The disciples' inability here is in contrast to their already having done similar

¹⁴When they rejoined the disciples, they saw a huge crowd surrounding them and scholars arguing with them. ¹⁵And all of a sudden, when the whole crowd caught sight of him, they were alarmed and rushed up to meet him. ¹⁶He asked them, "Why are you bothering to argue with them?"

¹⁷And one person from the crowd answered him, "Teacher, I brought my son to you, because he has a mute spirit. ¹⁸Whenever it takes him over, it knocks him down, and he foams at the mouth and grinds his teeth and stiffens up. I spoke to your disciples about having them drive it out, but they couldn't."

¹⁹In response he says, "You distrustful lot, how long must I associate with you? How long must I put up with you? Bring him over to me!"

²⁰And they brought him over to him. And when the spirit noticed him, right away it threw him into convulsions, and he fell to the ground, and kept rolling around, foaming at the mouth. ²¹And ⟨Jesus⟩ asked his father, "How long has he been like this?"

He replied, "Ever since he was a child. ²²Frequently it has thrown him into fire and into water to destroy him. So if you can do anything, take pity on us and help us!"

²³Jesus said to him, "What do you mean, 'If you can'? All things are possible for the one who trusts."

²⁴Right away the father of the child cried out and said, "I do trust! Help my lack of trust!"

²⁵When Jesus saw that the crowd was about to mob them, he rebuked the unclean spirit, and commands it, "Deaf and mute spirit, I command you, get out of him and don't ever go back inside him!"

²⁶And after he shrieked and went into a series of convulsions, it came out. And he took on the appearance of a corpse, so that the rumor went around that he had died. ²⁷But Jesus took hold of his hand and raised him, and there he stood.

²⁸And when he had gone home, his disciples started questioning him privately: "Why couldn't we drive it out?"

²⁹He said to them, "The only thing that can drive this kind out is prayer."

---

healings (6:13).

• **9:19.** *Distrustful lot:* those who lack trust (4:40), in contrast with the trust demonstrated by those who get cured (2:5; 5:34), as again in this story (vv. 23–24). Moses had used similar language about his generation (Deut 32:5, 20). *How long:* a complaint God makes against the people during the exodus (Num 14:27).

• **9:23.** *What do you mean:* makes explicit that Jesus is repeating back to the father the words, "If you can." Mark's readers understand that the crucial factor in a healing is not Jesus' ability, but trust (6:5–6). As soon as the child's father hears Jesus say, "trust," he affirms that indeed he does, which singles him out from the "distrustful lot" that he is among (v. 19).

Son of Adam
will die & rise

³⁰Κἀκεῖθεν ἐξελθόντες παρεπορεύοντο διὰ τῆς Γαλιλαίας, καὶ οὐκ ἤθελεν ἵνα τις γνοῖ· ³¹ἐδίδασκεν γὰρ τοὺς μαθητὰς αὐτοῦ καὶ ἔλεγεν αὐτοῖς ὅτι Ὁ υἱὸς τοῦ ἀνθρώπου παραδίδοται εἰς χεῖρας ἀνθρώπων, καὶ ἀποκτενοῦσιν αὐτόν, καὶ ἀποκτανθεὶς μετὰ τρεῖς ἡμέρας ἀναστήσεται. ³²οἱ δὲ ἠγνόουν τὸ ῥῆμα, καὶ ἐφοβοῦντο αὐτὸν ἐπερωτῆσαι.

Number one
is last

³³Καὶ ἦλθον εἰς Καφαρναούμ. καὶ ἐν τῇ οἰκίᾳ γενόμενος ἐπηρώτα αὐτούς, Τί ἐν τῇ ὁδῷ διελογίζεσθε; ³⁴οἱ δὲ ἐσιώπων, πρὸς ἀλλήλους γὰρ διελέχθησαν ἐν τῇ ὁδῷ τίς μείζων.

³⁵Καὶ καθίσας ἐφώνησεν τοὺς δώδεκα καὶ λέγει αὐτοῖς, Εἴ τις θέλει πρῶτος εἶναι ἔσται πάντων ἔσχατος καὶ πάντων διάκονος.

³⁶Καὶ λαβὼν παιδίον ἔστησεν αὐτὸ ἐν μέσῳ αὐτῶν καὶ ἐναγκαλισάμενος αὐτὸ εἶπεν αὐτοῖς, ³⁷Ὃς ἂν ἓν τῶν τοιούτων παιδίων δέξηται ἐπὶ τῷ ὀνόματί μου, ἐμὲ δέχεται· καὶ ὃς ἂν ἐμὲ δέχηται, οὐκ ἐμὲ δέχεται ἀλλὰ τὸν ἀποστείλαντά με.

For & against

³⁸Ἔφη αὐτῷ ὁ Ἰωάννης, Διδάσκαλε, εἴδομέν τινα ἐν τῷ ὀνόματί σου ἐκβάλλοντα δαιμόνια, καὶ ἐκωλύομεν αὐτόν, ὅτι οὐκ ἠκολούθει ἡμῖν.

³⁹Ὁ δὲ Ἰησοῦς εἶπεν, Μὴ κωλύετε αὐτόν, οὐδεὶς γάρ ἐστιν ὃς ποιήσει δύναμιν ἐπὶ τῷ ὀνόματί μου καὶ δυνήσεται ταχὺ κακολογῆσαί με· ⁴⁰ὃς γὰρ οὐκ ἔστιν καθ᾽ ἡμῶν, ὑπὲρ ἡμῶν ἐστιν. ⁴¹ὃς γὰρ ἂν ποτίσῃ ὑμᾶς ποτήριον ὕδατος ἐν ὀνόματι ὅτι Χριστοῦ ἐστε, ἀμὴν λέγω ὑμῖν ὅτι οὐ μὴ ἀπολέσῃ τὸν μισθὸν αὐτοῦ.

Hand, foot
& eye

⁴²Καὶ ὃς ἂν σκανδαλίσῃ ἕνα τῶν μικρῶν τούτων τῶν πιστευόντων, καλόν ἐστιν αὐτῷ μᾶλλον εἰ περίκειται μύλος ὀνικὸς περὶ τὸν τράχηλον αὐτοῦ καὶ βέβληται εἰς τὴν θάλασσαν.

⁴³Καὶ ἐὰν σκανδαλίζῃ σε ἡ χείρ σου, ἀπόκοψον αὐτήν· καλόν ἐστίν σε κυλλὸν εἰσελθεῖν εἰς τὴν ζωὴν ἢ τὰς δύο χεῖρας ἔχοντα ἀπελθεῖν εἰς τὴν γέενναν, εἰς τὸ πῦρ τὸ ἄσβεστον.[⁴⁴]

⁴⁵Καὶ ἐὰν ὁ πούς σου σκανδαλίζῃ σε, ἀπόκοψον αὐτόν· καλόν ἐστίν σε εἰσελθεῖν εἰς τὴν ζωὴν χωλὸν ἢ τοὺς δύο πόδας ἔχοντα βληθῆναι εἰς τὴν γέενναν.[⁴⁶]

---

42. *Trusting souls:* most MSS read *souls who trust in me* (Matt 18:6).
44, 46. Many later MSS introduce v. 48 at both of these places as well.

- **9:30–10:31.** The second of three sequences (the first began at 8:27) featuring: a prediction of suffering, the disciples' failure to understand, Jesus' teaching.
- **9:30.** The journey begun at the northern border (8:27) now reaches Jesus' home area, Galilee.
- **9:31.** A repeat of 8:31 (§3.2). *Turned over to his enemies:* echoes the description of Judas

as the one who *turned him in* (3:19).
- **9:32.** *Never* and *always* are implied by verbs in the imperfect tense (§6.2).
- **9:35.** *Sat down and called:* suggests almost a formal setting for teaching. The issue of leadership must have become a crisis after Jesus' death (see also 10:42–44).
- **9:36.** *Her:* the Greek does not indicate the sex of the child.

³⁰They left there and started going through Galilee, and he did not want anyone to know. ³¹Remember, he was instructing his disciples and telling them: "The son of Adam is being turned over to his enemies, and they will end up killing him. And three days after he is killed he will rise!" ³²But they never understood this remark, and always dreaded to ask him ⟨about it⟩.

Son of Adam will die & rise

³³And they came to Capernaum. When he got home, he started questioning them, "What were you arguing about on the road?" ³⁴They fell completely silent, because on the road they had been bickering about who was greatest.

Number one is last

³⁵He sat down and called the twelve and says to them: "If anyone wants to be 'number one,' that person has to be last of all and servant of all!"

³⁶And he took a child and had her stand in front of them, and he put his arm around her, and he said to them: ³⁷"Whoever accepts a child like this in my name is accepting me. And whoever accepts me is not so much accepting me as the one who sent me."

³⁸John said to him, "Teacher, we saw someone driving out demons in your name, so we tried to stop him, because he wasn't one of our adherents."

For & against

³⁹Jesus responded: "Don't stop him! After all, no one who performs a miracle in my name will turn around the next moment and curse me. ⁴⁰In fact, whoever is not against us is on our side. ⁴¹By the same token, whoever gives you a cup of water to drink because you carry the name of the Anointed, I swear to you, such persons certainly won't lose their reward!

⁴²"And those who mislead one of these little trusting souls would be better off if they were to have a millstone hung around their necks and were thrown into the sea!

Hand, foot & eye

⁴³"And if your hand gets you into trouble, cut it off! It is better for you to enter life maimed than to wind up in Gehenna, in the unquenchable fire, with both hands![⁴⁴]

⁴⁵"And if your foot gets you into trouble cut it off! It is better for you to enter life lame than to be thrown into Gehenna with both feet![⁴⁶]

• **9:38.** The issue here clearly seems to reflect a later Christian circumstance—someone practicing in the name of Jesus, who does not belong to the "in" group.

• **9:39.** *Curse*: in the general sense, *insult, abuse*, not *swear a curse*, as Peter does (14:51).

• **9:43–47.** What *gets you into trouble*: similar to what *misleads* you (v. 42). *Gehenna*: where the sacrifice refuse from the Jerusalem temple was burned; the perpetual fire was considered symbolic of the final judgment.

⁴⁷Καὶ ἐὰν ὁ ὀφθαλμός σου σκανδαλίζῃ σε, ἔκβαλε αὐτόν·
καλόν σέ ἐστιν μονόφθαλμον εἰσελθεῖν εἰς τὴν βασιλείαν τοῦ
θεοῦ ἢ δύο ὀφθαλμοὺς ἔχοντα βληθῆναι εἰς τὴν γέενναν, ⁴⁸ὅπου
ὁ σκώληξ αὐτῶν οὐ τελευτᾷ καὶ τὸ πῦρ οὐ σβέννυται·
⁴⁹Πᾶς γὰρ πυρὶ ἁλισθήσεται.
⁵⁰Καλὸν τὸ ἅλας· ἐὰν δὲ τὸ ἅλας ἄναλον γένηται, ἐν τίνι αὐτὸ
ἀρτύσετε;
Ἔχετε ἐν ἑαυτοῖς ἅλα, καὶ εἰρηνεύετε ἐν ἀλλήλοις.

---

49. Some MSS add: *And every sacrifice will be salted by fire*, apparently an
attempted explanation based on Lev 2:13, "Every sacrifice shall be
seasoned by salt."

⁴⁷"And if your eye gets you into trouble, rip it out! It is better for you to enter God's domain one-eyed than to be thrown into Gehenna with both eyes, ⁴⁸where the worm never dies and the fire never goes out!

⁴⁹"As you know, everyone there is salted by fire.

⁵⁰"Salt is good ⟨and salty⟩—if salt becomes bland, with what will you renew it?

"Maintain 'salt' among yourselves and be at peace with each other."

• **9:48.** From Isa 66:24, apparently came to mind here because of "fire" in the preceding sayings.

• **9:49–50.** Mark has formed a cluster of sayings by word association around *fire* and *salt*.

God's Imperial Rule

The traditional translation of the Greek phrase *Basileia tou theou, Kingdom of God,* was more appropriate to the age of King James I (1603–25; King James translation: 1611) than it is to our own in which inherited monarchies are more symbolic than political. The SV panel went in search of a term or phrase that would satisfy three basic requirements: (1) the phrase had to function as both verb and noun, to denote both an activity and a region; (2) the phrase had to specify that God's activity was absolute; there could be no suggestion of democracy or shared governance; (3) the phrase should have feeling tones of the ominous, of ultimate threat, of tyranny—associations going with the end of the age and the last judgment, since it often appears in such contexts.

Some panel members proposed *empire* as an appropriate ancient and modern counterpart, since it called to mind both the Roman Empire and the evil empires of the nineteenth and twentieth centures. But empire could not serve as a verb; for this purpose something like *rule* or *reign* was required. And Jesus' own use of the phrase, particularly in connection with his parables, called for a phrase that was perhaps less ominous, yet no less absolute. The happy solution the panel reached was to combine "imperial" with "rule" to gain the nuances of both terms.

When a spatial term is required by the context, it was decided to utilize *domain* because of its proximity to *dominion:* in his domain God's dominion is supreme.

Created male
& female

10 Καὶ ἐκεῖθεν ἀναστὰς ἔρχεται εἰς τὰ ὅρια τῆς Ἰουδαίας [καὶ] πέραν τοῦ Ἰορδάνου, καὶ συμπορεύονται πάλιν ὄχλοι πρὸς αὐτόν, καὶ ὡς εἰώθει πάλιν ἐδίδασκεν αὐτούς. ²καὶ [προσελθόντες Φαρισαῖοι] ἐπηρώτων αὐτὸν εἰ ἔξεστιν ἀνδρὶ γυναῖκα ἀπολῦσαι, πειράζοντες αὐτόν. ³ὁ δὲ ἀποκριθεὶς εἶπεν αὐτοῖς, Τί ὑμῖν ἐνετείλατο Μωϋσῆς; ⁴Οἱ δὲ εἶπαν, Ἐπέτρεψεν Μωϋσῆς βιβλίον ἀποστασίου γράψαι καὶ ἀπολῦσαι.

⁵Ὁ δὲ Ἰησοῦς εἶπεν αὐτοῖς, Πρὸς τὴν σκληροκαρδίαν ὑμῶν ἔγραψεν ὑμῖν τὴν ἐντολὴν ταύτην. ⁶ἀπὸ δὲ ἀρχῆς κτίσεως ἄρσεν καὶ θῆλυ ἐποίησεν [αὐτούς]· ⁷ἕνεκεν τούτου καταλείψει ἄνθρωπος τὸν πατέρα αὐτοῦ καὶ τὴν μητέρα [καὶ προσκολληθήσεται πρὸς τὴν γυναῖκα αὐτοῦ], ⁸καὶ ἔσονται οἱ δύο εἰς σάρκα μίαν· ὥστε οὐκέτι εἰσὶν δύο ἀλλὰ μία σάρξ. ⁹ὃ οὖν ὁ θεὸς συνέζευξεν ἄνθρωπος μὴ χωριζέτω.

¹⁰Καὶ εἰς τὴν οἰκίαν πάλιν οἱ μαθηταὶ περὶ τούτου ἐπηρώτων αὐτόν. ¹¹καὶ λέγει αὐτοῖς, Ὃς ἂν ἀπολύσῃ τὴν γυναῖκα αὐτοῦ καὶ γαμήσῃ ἄλλην μοιχᾶται ἐπ᾽ αὐτήν, ¹²καὶ ἐὰν αὐτὴ ἀπολύσασα τὸν ἄνδρα αὐτῆς γαμήσῃ ἄλλον μοιχᾶται.

Children in
God's domain

¹³Καὶ προσέφερον αὐτῷ παιδία ἵνα αὐτῶν ἅψηται· οἱ δὲ μαθηταὶ ἐπετίμησαν αὐτοῖς. ¹⁴ἰδὼν δὲ ὁ Ἰησοῦς ἠγανάκτησεν καὶ εἶπεν αὐτοῖς, Ἄφετε τὰ παιδία ἔρχεσθαι πρός με, μὴ κωλύετε αὐτά, τῶν γὰρ τοιούτων ἐστὶν ἡ βασιλεία τοῦ θεοῦ. ¹⁵ἀμὴν λέγω ὑμῖν, ὃς ἂν μὴ δέξηται τὴν βασιλείαν τοῦ θεοῦ ὡς παιδίον, οὐ μὴ εἰσέλθῃ εἰς αὐτήν. ¹⁶καὶ ἐναγκαλισάμενος αὐτὰ κατευλόγει τιθεὶς τὰς χεῖρας ἐπ᾽ αὐτά.

---

1. *Judea and across the Jordan:* some MSS omit *and* (as in Matt 19:1), so Judea proper is not included; other MSS read instead *Judea by way of the other side of the Jordan.*   **2.** *Pharisees approach him and:* omitted in some MSS, making *they* another indefinite *people.*   **6.** *God:* makes explicit the subject, and is read in most later MSS. *Them* is omitted in some MSS.   **7.** *And be united with his wife:* completes the quotation from Gen 2:24 (also in Matt 19:5), but is not in the earliest MSS.   **12.** *If she divorces her husband:* some MSS read, *If she leaves her husband,* suggesting a Judean milieu, where women had no divorce rights, unlike under Roman law.   **13.** *Scolded:* some MSS add a clarifying *those who brought.*

• **10:2.** Speaking out against divorce had cost John the Baptist his life (6:18), so pressing this issue with John's successor raises a volatile question.

• **10:4.** According to Deut 24:1, a husband could write *a writ of abandonment* to his

wife, if "she does not please him because he finds something objectionable about her" (NRSV). The two leading schools of rabbinic interpretation argued over the meaning of "something objectionable" as the basis for divorce. Jesus sides with neither one

10 And from there he gets up and goes to the territory of Judea [and] across the Jordan, and once again crowds gather around him. As usual, he started teaching them. ²And [Pharisees approach him and,] to test him, they ask whether a husband is permitted to divorce his wife. ³In response he puts a question to them: "What did Moses command you?"

Created male & female

⁴They replied: "Moses allowed one to prepare a writ of abandonment and thus to divorce the other party."

⁵Jesus said to them: "He gave you this injunction because you are obstinate. ⁶However, in the beginning, at the creation, 'God made [them] male and female.' ⁷'For this reason, a man will leave his father and mother [and be united with his wife], ⁸and the two will become one person,' so they are no longer two individuals but 'one person.' ⁹Therefore those God has coupled together, no one else should separate."

¹⁰And once again, as usual, when they got home, the disciples questioned him about this. ¹¹And he says to them: "Whoever divorces his wife and marries another commits adultery against her; ¹²and if she divorces her husband and marries another, she commits adultery."

¹³And they would bring children to him so he could lay hands on them, but the disciples scolded them. ¹⁴Then Jesus grew indignant when he saw this and said to them: "Let the children come up to me, don't try to stop them. After all, God's domain is peopled with such as these. ¹⁵I swear to you, whoever doesn't accept God's imperial rule the way a child would, certainly won't ever set foot in ⟨his domain⟩!" ¹⁶And he would put his arms around them and bless them, and lay his hands on them.

Children in God's domain

---

here (in contrast to Matt 5:32; 19:9). The *written* document ends the marriage contract, which had been signed at the betrothal (engagement), usually a year prior to the marriage. The contract specified the dowry, which reverted to the wife after divorce.

• **10:6–8.** Jesus' response combines the two creation accounts (Gen 1:27; 2:2) and treats them as more authoritative than Moses (v. 4). To use such a scholarly argument to defend a conservative position against divorce contrasts with the rather liberal picture Mark gives of Jesus on other issues, such as the sabbath day (2:24–28).

• **10:10.** The private setting is used by Mark to add later interpretation to sayings of Jesus (4:10). Both of the added sayings

remarkably give wives equal status with their husbands regarding divorce.

• **10:11.** *Against her*: has to mean the first wife, with whom the husband had become "one person" (v. 8).

• **10:12.** Since the Judean law did not provide for women to seek divorce, this scenario implies a Roman setting, which suggests a later Christian adaptation. However, Paul had earlier claimed that "the Lord" commanded: "If a wife gets divorced, she should remain unmarried" (1 Cor 7:11).

• **10:14–15.** *Domain*: translates *basileia* as a spatial image, a realm that one "enters" (see also vv. 23–25). Elsewhere, *imperial rule* is used when the image is God acting as emperor (see 1:15; §6.3).

Man with money

¹⁷Καὶ ἐκπορευομένου αὐτοῦ εἰς ὁδὸν προσδραμὼν εἷς καὶ γονυπετήσας αὐτὸν ἐπηρώτα αὐτόν, Διδάσκαλε ἀγαθέ, τί ποιήσω ἵνα ζωὴν αἰώνιον κληρονομήσω; ¹⁸ Ὁ δὲ Ἰησοῦς εἶπεν αὐτῷ, Τί με λέγεις ἀγαθόν; οὐδεὶς ἀγαθὸς εἰ μὴ εἷς ὁ θεός. ¹⁹τὰς ἐντολὰς οἶδας· Μὴ φονεύσῃς, Μὴ μοιχεύσῃς, Μὴ κλέψῃς, Μὴ ψευδομαρτυρήσῃς, Μὴ ἀποστερήσῃς, Τίμα τὸν πατέρα σου καὶ τὴν μητέρα. ²⁰ Ὁ δὲ ἔφη αὐτῷ, Διδάσκαλε, ταῦτα πάντα ἐφυλαξάμην ἐκ νεότητός μου. ²¹ Ὁ δὲ Ἰησοῦς ἐμβλέψας αὐτῷ ἠγάπησεν αὐτὸν καὶ εἶπεν αὐτῷ, Ἕν σε ὑστερεῖ· ὕπαγε ὅσα ἔχεις πώλησον καὶ δὸς τοῖς πτωχοῖς, καὶ ἕξεις θησαυρὸν ἐν οὐρανῷ, καὶ δεῦρο ἀκολούθει μοι. ²² Ὁ δὲ στυγνάσας ἐπὶ τῷ λόγῳ ἀπῆλθεν λυπούμενος, ἦν γὰρ ἔχων κτήματα πολλά.

Needle's eye

²³Καὶ περιβλεψάμενος ὁ Ἰησοῦς λέγει τοῖς μαθηταῖς αὐτοῦ, Πῶς δυσκόλως οἱ τὰ χρήματα ἔχοντες εἰς τὴν βασιλείαν τοῦ θεοῦ εἰσελεύσονται. ²⁴οἱ δὲ μαθηταὶ ἐθαμβοῦντο ἐπὶ τοῖς λόγοις αὐτοῦ.

Ὁ δὲ Ἰησοῦς πάλιν ἀποκριθεὶς λέγει αὐτοῖς, Τέκνα, πῶς δύσκολόν ἐστιν εἰς τὴν βασιλείαν τοῦ θεοῦ εἰσελθεῖν· ²⁵εὐκοπώτερόν ἐστιν κάμηλον διὰ τρυμαλιᾶς ῥαφίδος διελθεῖν ἢ πλούσιον εἰς τὴν βασιλείαν τοῦ θεοῦ εἰσελθεῖν. ²⁶Οἱ δὲ περισσῶς ἐξεπλήσσοντο λέγοντες πρὸς ἑαυτούς, Καὶ τίς δύναται σωθῆναι; ²⁷Ἐμβλέψας αὐτοῖς ὁ Ἰησοῦς λέγει, Παρὰ ἀνθρώποις ἀδύνατον ἀλλ' οὐ παρὰ θεῷ, πάντα γὰρ δυνατὰ παρὰ τῷ θεῷ. ²⁸Ἤρξατο λέγειν ὁ Πέτρος αὐτῷ, Ἰδοὺ ἡμεῖς ἀφήκαμεν πάντα καὶ ἠκολουθήκαμέν σοι. ²⁹Ἔφη ὁ Ἰησοῦς, Ἀμὴν λέγω ὑμῖν, οὐδείς ἐστιν ὃς ἀφῆκεν οἰκίαν ἢ ἀδελφοὺς ἢ ἀδελφὰς ἢ μητέρα ἢ πατέρα ἢ τέκνα ἢ ἀγροὺς ἕνεκεν ἐμοῦ καὶ ἕνεκεν τοῦ εὐαγγελίου, ³⁰ἐὰν μὴ λάβῃ ἑκατονταπλασίονα νῦν ἐν τῷ καιρῷ τούτῳ οἰκίας καὶ ἀδελφοὺς καὶ ἀδελφὰς καὶ μητέρας καὶ τέκνα καὶ ἀγροὺς μετὰ διωγμῶν, καὶ ἐν τῷ αἰῶνι τῷ ἐρσομένῳ ζωὴν αἰώνιον. ³¹Πολλοὶ δὲ ἔσονται πρῶτοι ἔσχατοι καὶ ἔσχατοι πρῶτοι.

---

19. *Do not defraud:* omitted in some MSS, not one of the ten commandments and not in Matt 19:18 or Luke 18:20.

• **10:19.** *The commandments:* the last six of the ten commandments are cited (Exodus 20; Deuteronomy 5), except the last two are reversed from their biblical order and "do not covet" is replaced by *do not defraud*, an appropriate interpretation in a situation where the issue is money. Jesus is thus pictured not as quoting scripture by rote,

17As he was traveling along the road, someone ran up, knelt before him, and started questioning him: "Good teacher, what do I have to do to inherit eternal life?"

Man with money

18Jesus said to him, "Why do you call me good? No one is good except for God alone. 19You know the commandments: 'You must not murder, you are not to commit adultery, you are not to steal, you are not to give false testimony, you are not to defraud, and you are to honor your father and mother.'"

20He said to him: "Teacher, I have observed all these things since I was a child!"

21Jesus loved him at first sight and said to him, "You are missing one thing: make your move, sell whatever you have and give ⟨the proceeds⟩ to the poor, and you will have treasure in heaven. And then come, follow me!"

22But stunned by this advice, he went away dejected, since he possessed a fortune.

23After looking around, Jesus says to his disciples, "How difficult it is for those who have money to enter God's domain!" 24The disciples were amazed at his words.

Needle's eye

In response Jesus repeats what he had said: "Children, how difficult it is to enter God's domain! 25It's easier for a camel to squeeze through a needle's eye, than for a wealthy person to get into God's domain!"

26And they were very perplexed, wondering to themselves, "Well then, who can be saved?"

27Jesus looks them in the eye and says, "For mortals it's impossible, but not for God; after all, everything's possible for God."

28Peter started lecturing him: "Look at us, we left everything to follow you!"

29Jesus said, "I swear to you, there is no one who has left home, or brothers, or sisters, or mother, or father, or children, or farms on my account and on account of the good news, 30who won't receive a hundred times as much now, in the present time, homes, and brothers, and sisters, and mothers, and children, and farms—including persecutions—and in the age to come, eternal life.

31"Many of the first will be last, and of the last many will be first."

---

but as giving a suitable variation.
- **10:21.** *Loved him at first sight*: combines two verbs, *looked at him and loved him.*
- **10:23–25.** *Domain*: a realm one "enters"
(see vv. 14–15).
- **10:30.** *A hundred times as much*: the yield of the best soil (4:8, 20).

Son of Adam will die & rise

³² Ἦσαν δὲ ἐν τῇ ὁδῷ ἀναβαίνοντες εἰς Ἱεροσόλυμα, καὶ ἦν προάγων αὐτοὺς ὁ Ἰησοῦς, καὶ ἐθαμβοῦντο, οἱ δὲ ἀκολουθοῦντες ἐφοβοῦντο. καὶ παραλαβὼν πάλιν τοὺς δώδεκα ἤρξατο αὐτοῖς λέγειν τὰ μέλλοντα αὐτῷ συμβαίνειν,

³³ Ὅτι Ἰδοὺ ἀναβαίνομεν εἰς Ἱεροσόλυμα, καὶ ὁ υἱὸς τοῦ ἀνθρώπου παραδοθήσεται τοῖς ἀρχιερεῦσιν καὶ τοῖς γραμματεῦσιν, καὶ κατακρινοῦσιν αὐτὸν θανάτῳ καὶ παραδώσουσιν αὐτὸν τοῖς ἔθνεσιν ³⁴ καὶ ἐμπαίξουσιν αὐτῷ καὶ ἐμπτύσουσιν αὐτῷ καὶ μαστιγώσουσιν αὐτὸν καὶ ἀποκτενοῦσιν, καὶ μετὰ τρεῖς ἡμέρας ἀναστήσεται.

Jesus' cup & baptism

³⁵ Καὶ προσπορεύονται αὐτῷ Ἰάκωβος καὶ Ἰωάννης οἱ υἱοὶ Ζεβεδαίου λέγοντες αὐτῷ, Διδάσκαλε, θέλομεν ἵνα ὃ ἐὰν αἰτήσωμέν σε ποιήσῃς ἡμῖν.

³⁶ Ὁ δὲ εἶπεν αὐτοῖς, Τί θέλετέ [με] ποιήσω ὑμῖν;

³⁷ Οἱ δὲ εἶπαν αὐτῷ, Δὸς ἡμῖν ἵνα εἷς σου ἐκ δεξιῶν καὶ εἷς ἐξ ἀριστερῶν καθίσωμεν ἐν τῇ δόξῃ σου.

³⁸ Ὁ δὲ Ἰησοῦς εἶπεν αὐτοῖς, Οὐκ οἴδατε τί αἰτεῖσθε. δύνασθε πιεῖν τὸ ποτήριον ὃ ἐγὼ πίνω, ἢ τὸ βάπτισμα ὃ ἐγὼ βαπτίζομαι βαπτισθῆναι;

³⁹ Οἱ δὲ εἶπαν αὐτῷ, Δυνάμεθα.

Ὁ δὲ Ἰησοῦς εἶπεν αὐτοῖς, Τὸ ποτήριον ὃ ἐγὼ πίνω πίεσθε καὶ τὸ βάπτισμα ὃ ἐγὼ βαπτίζομαι βαπτισθήσεσθε, ⁴⁰ τὸ δὲ καθίσαι ἐκ δεξιῶν μου ἢ ἐξ εὐωνύμων οὐκ ἔστιν ἐμὸν δοῦναι, ἀλλ᾽ οἷς ἡτοίμασται.

Number one is slave

⁴¹ Καὶ ἀκούσαντες οἱ δέκα ἤρξαντο ἀγανακτεῖν περὶ Ἰακώβου καὶ Ἰωάννου. ⁴² καὶ προσκαλεσάμενος αὐτοὺς ὁ Ἰησοῦς λέγει αὐτοῖς, Οἴδατε ὅτι οἱ δοκοῦντες ἄρχειν τῶν ἐθνῶν κατακυριεύουσιν αὐτῶν καὶ οἱ μεγάλοι αὐτῶν κατεξουσιάζουσιν αὐτῶν. ⁴³ οὐχ οὕτως δέ ἐστιν ἐν ὑμῖν· ἀλλ᾽ ὃς ἂν θέλῃ μέγας γενέσθαι ἐν ὑμῖν, ἔσται ὑμῶν διάκονος, ⁴⁴ καὶ ὃς ἂν θέλῃ ἐν ὑμῖν εἶναι πρῶτος, ἔσται πάντων δοῦλος· ⁴⁵ καὶ γὰρ ὁ υἱὸς τοῦ ἀνθρώπου οὐκ ἦλθεν διακονηθῆναι ἀλλὰ διακονῆσαι καὶ δοῦναι τὴν ψυχὴν αὐτοῦ λύτρον ἀντὶ πολλῶν.

---

32. *And others . . . frightened:* omitted in some MSS.   36. Greek *me* (*me*) is omitted in some MSS as redundant or awkward. Its presence in Greek parallels *you* (*se*) in v. 35. Both likely add emphasis.

- **10:32–45.** The third, and final, time (8:27; 9:30) to begin the sequence of predicted suffering, which the disciples do not comprehend, so Jesus teaches them.
- **10:33.** The third time for this announcement (8:31; 9:31) is the most explicit, with details that directly anticipate what will happen later (14:64–65; 15:15, 19–20, 31).
- **10:38.** *The cup that I'm drinking:* an image used by prophets for those who face suffering, "The cup of destruction, . . . drink it" (Ezek 23:33); "You have drunk from the hand of the Lord the cup of his fury . . . the cup of calamity, the cup of wrath" (Isa 51:17).
- **10:44.** *Slave:* a person who is owned as property by another person, who has absolute authority over the slave in all matters.

³²On the road going up to Jerusalem, Jesus was leading the way, they were apprehensive, and others who were following were frightened. Once again he took the twelve aside and started telling them what was going to happen to him:

Son of Adam will die & rise

³³"Listen, we're going up to Jerusalem, and the son of Adam will be turned over to the ranking priests and the scholars, and they will sentence him to death, and turn him over to foreigners, ³⁴and they will make fun of him, and spit on him, and flog him, and put ⟨him⟩ to death. Yet after three days he will rise!"

³⁵Then James and John, the sons of Zebedee, come up to him, and say to him, "Teacher, we want you to do for us whatever we ask!"

Jesus' cup & baptism

³⁶He said to them, "What do you want me to do for you?"

³⁷They reply to him, "In your glory, let one of us sit at your right hand, and the other at your left."

³⁸Jesus said to them, "You have no idea what you're asking for. Can you drink the cup that I'm drinking, or undergo the baptism I'm undergoing?"

³⁹They said to him, "We can!"

Jesus said to them, "The cup I'm drinking you'll be drinking, and the baptism I'm undergoing you'll be undergoing, ⁴⁰but as for sitting at my right or my left, that's not mine to grant, but belongs to those for whom it has been reserved."

⁴¹When they learned of it, the ten got annoyed with James and John. ⁴²So, calling them aside, Jesus says to them: "You know how those who supposedly rule over foreigners lord it over them, and how their strong men tyrannize them. ⁴³It's not going to be like that with you! With you, whoever wants to become great must be your servant, ⁴⁴and whoever among you wants to be 'number one' must be everybody's slave. ⁴⁵After all, the son of Adam didn't come to be served, but to serve, even to give his life as a ransom for many."

Number one is slave

Persons became slaves either by capture during war, indebtedness, punishment for crime, or as offspring of women who were slaves. Slaves provided the essential labor for domestic, business and public service, and probably constituted about one-third of the population in many areas of the Roman empire. A slave legally had only one master, the owner, though joint-ownership was possible. Thus to be slave *of everyone* is the ultimate expression of powerlessness. This radicalizes the earlier version in 9:35, "servant of all," and its corollary here in v.

43, "your servant." A *servant* renders personal service to another, such as did Peter's mother-in-law (1:31), irregardless of the relative social status of the two people.

• **10:45.** This saying is the culmination of the central section that began at 8:31 with the theme (§4.11) of the suffering of the *son of Adam* (9:31; 10:33) and the value of "giving one's life" (8:35–37). A *ransom*: the price paid to redeem a slave. This image was frequently used in the Old Testament to describe God's "redeeming" of Israel (e.g., Exod 15:13; Ps 106:10; Isa 43:1).

**Blind
Bartimaeus**

⁴⁶Καὶ ἔρχονται εἰς Ἰεριχώ. καὶ ἐκπορευομένου αὐτοῦ ἀπὸ Ἰεριχὼ καὶ τῶν μαθητῶν αὐτοῦ καὶ ὄχλου ἱκανοῦ ὁ υἱὸς Τιμαίου Βαρτιμαῖος τυφλὸς ἐκάθητο παρὰ τὴν ὁδὸν προσαιτῶν. ⁴⁷καὶ ἀκούσας ὅτι Ἰησοῦς ὁ Ναζαρηνός ἐστιν ἤρξατο κράζειν καὶ λέγειν, Υἱὲ Δαυὶδ Ἰησοῦ, ἐλέησόν με. ⁴⁸Καὶ ἐπετίμων αὐτῷ πολλοὶ ἵνα σιωπήσῃ· ὁ δὲ πολλῷ μᾶλλον ἔκραζεν, Υἱὲ Δαυίδ, ἐλέησόν με. ⁴⁹Καὶ στὰς ὁ Ἰησοῦς εἶπεν, Φωνήσατε αὐτόν. Καὶ φωνοῦσιν τὸν τυφλὸν λέγοντες αὐτῷ, Θάρσει, ἔγειρε, φωνεῖ σε. ⁵⁰ὁ δὲ ἀποβαλὼν τὸ ἱμάτιον αὐτοῦ ἀναπηδήσας ἦλθεν πρὸς τὸν Ἰησοῦν. ⁵¹Καὶ ἀποκριθεὶς αὐτῷ ὁ Ἰησοῦς εἶπεν, Τί σοι θέλεις ποιήσω; Ὁ δὲ τυφλὸς εἶπεν αὐτῷ, Ραββουνι, ἵνα ἀναβλέψω. ⁵²Καὶ ὁ Ἰησοῦς εἶπεν αὐτῷ, Ὕπαγε, ἡ πίστις σου σέσωκέν σε. καὶ εὐθὺς ἀνέβλεψεν, καὶ ἠκολούθει αὐτῷ ἐν τῇ ὁδῷ.

• **10:46–52.** This story of a blind person seeing again is paired with the one in 8:22–26 to form the framework for the middle section of Mark's gospel, which contrasted the disciples failure to "see" and understand.

• **10:46.** Bartimaeus: means son of Timaeus in Aramaic, so the explanatory phrase the son of Timaeus may be a latter addition.

• **10:47.** Nazarene: used for Jesus in the first public incident (for possible interpretations, see the note on 1:24).

• **10:47–48.** Son of David: a messianic title not actually used in the Hebrew Bible, and rejected later by Jesus (12:35). Its first recorded use is in the Psalms of Solomon,

first century B.C.E., "Lord, raise up for them their king, the son of David, to rule over your servant Israel" (17:21). The Davidic covenant promised the throne in Jerusalem to David's descendants forever (2 Sam 7:12–13).

• **10:51.** Rabbi: the Aramaic rabbouni, equivalent to Hebrew "rabbi" (9:5), "my master," popularized as an address for teachers.

• **10:52.** Your trust has cured you: identical to 5:34. On the road: this sections ends as it began (8:27). For Mark "the road" Jesus is on to Jerusalem is an extension of the way prepared by John (1:2–3; §4.1).

⁴⁶Then they come to Jericho. As he was leaving Jericho with his disciples and a sizable crowd, Bartimaeus, a blind beggar, the son of Timaeus, was sitting alongside the road. ⁴⁷When he learned that it was Jesus the Nazarene, he began to shout: "You son of David, Jesus, have mercy on me!"

⁴⁸And many kept yelling at him to shut up, but he shouted all the louder, "You son of David, have mercy on me!"

⁴⁹Jesus paused and said, "Tell him to come over here!"

They called to the blind man, "Be brave, get up, he's calling you!" ⁵⁰So he threw off his cloak, and jumped to his feet, and went over to Jesus.

⁵¹In response Jesus said, "What do you want me to do for you?"

The blind man said to him: "Rabbi, I want to see again!"

⁵²And Jesus said to him: "Be on your way, your trust has cured you." And right away he regained his sight, and he started following him on the road.

*Blind
Bartimaeus*

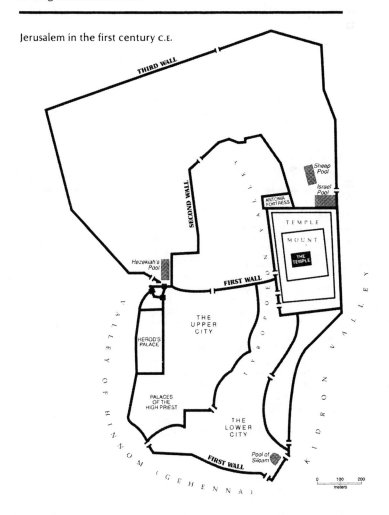

Jerusalem in the first century C.E.

Jesus enters
Jerusalem

11 Καὶ ὅτε ἐγγίζουσιν εἰς Ἱεροσόλυμα εἰς Βηθφαγὴ καὶ Βηθανίαν πρὸς τὸ Ὄρος τῶν Ἐλαιῶν, ἀποστέλλει δύο τῶν μαθητῶν αὐτοῦ ²καὶ λέγει αὐτοῖς, Ὑπάγετε εἰς τὴν κώμην τὴν κατέναντι ὑμῶν, καὶ εὐθὺς εἰσπορευόμενοι εἰς αὐτὴν εὑρήσετε πῶλον δεδεμένον ἐφ᾽ ὃν οὐδεὶς οὔπω ἀνθρώπων ἐκάθισεν· λύσατε αὐτὸν καὶ φέρετε. ³καὶ ἐάν τις ὑμῖν εἴπῃ, Τί ποιεῖτε τοῦτο; εἴπατε, Ὁ κύριος αὐτοῦ χρείαν ἔχει, καὶ εὐθὺς αὐτὸν ἀποστέλλει πάλιν ὧδε.

⁴Καὶ ἀπῆλθον καὶ εὗρον πῶλον δεδεμένον πρὸς θύραν ἔξω ἐπὶ τοῦ ἀμφόδου, καὶ λύουσιν αὐτόν. ⁵καί τινες τῶν ἐκεῖ ἑστηκότων ἔλεγον αὐτοῖς, Τί ποιεῖτε λύοντες τὸν πῶλον; ⁶οἱ δὲ εἶπαν αὐτοῖς καθὼς εἶπεν ὁ Ἰησοῦς· καὶ ἀφῆκαν αὐτούς.

⁷Καὶ φέρουσιν τὸν πῶλον πρὸς τὸν Ἰησοῦν, καὶ ἐπιβάλλουσιν αὐτῷ τὰ ἱμάτια αὐτῶν, καὶ ἐκάθισεν ἐπ᾽ αὐτόν. ⁸καὶ πολλοὶ τὰ ἱμάτια αὐτῶν ἔστρωσαν εἰς τὴν ὁδόν, ἄλλοι δὲ στιβάδας κόψαντες ἐκ τῶν ἀγρῶν. ⁹καὶ οἱ προάγοντες καὶ οἱ ἀκολουθοῦντες ἔκραζον,

Ὡσαννά·
εὐλογημένος ὁ ἐρχόμενος ἐν ὀνόματι κυρίου·
¹⁰ εὐλογημένη ἡ ἐρχομένη βασιλεία τοῦ πατρὸς ἡμῶν Δαυίδ·
Ὡσαννὰ ἐν τοῖς ὑψίστοις.

Fig tree
without figs

¹¹Καὶ εἰσῆλθεν εἰς Ἱεροσόλυμα εἰς τὸ ἱερόν· καὶ περιβλεψάμενος πάντα, ὀψίας ἤδη οὔσης τῆς ὥρας, ἐξῆλθεν εἰς Βηθανίαν μετὰ τῶν δώδεκα.

¹²Καὶ τῇ ἐπαύριον ἐξελθόντων αὐτῶν ἀπὸ Βηθανίας ἐπείνασεν. ¹³καὶ ἰδὼν συκῆν ἀπὸ μακρόθεν ἔχουσαν φύλλα ἦλθεν εἰ ἄρα τι εὑρήσει ἐν αὐτῇ, καὶ ἐλθὼν ἐπ᾽ αὐτὴν οὐδὲν εὗρεν

• **11:1–13:37.** Jesus' time in Jerusalem prior to preparation for Passover (14:1) is devoted by Mark almost entirely to activity associated with the temple.

• **11:1.** *The Mount of Olives*: overlooked the temple area from the east. In prophetic speculation this is the location from which "the Lord" goes forth for the final battle against Israel's enemies on the day of judgment (Zech 14:4). This made it a popular site for organizing freedom rallies against the Romans during the first century. However, Jesus had made it explicit that his procession was going to Jerusalem to face ridicule and death (10:33), so this scene is more likely a Markan satire of past political "triumphal processions," such as the Romans enjoyed.

• **11:2.** *A colt*: prescribed for a "just king and

savior" who brings peace, in Zech 9:9 (LXX), quoted in Matt 21:5, "Your king comes to you, humble and mounted on a donkey, on a colt."

• **11:3.** *Its master*: Greek *kyrios* can also be *the lord* (§6.4).

• **11:8.** Throwing their outer garments on the road is treatment for a king (2 Kgs 9:13); *leafy branches*: only in John (12:13) are they from "palm trees," a symbol of victory used by the Maccabean rulers in the second century B.C.E. (1 Macc 13:51; 2 Macc 10:7). In Mark they are cut *from the fields*, suggesting a rural crowd.

• **11:9.** *Hosanna!* An appeal in Aramaic: *Save us, now,* popular with holiday pilgrims entering Jerusalem. It is derived from Ps 118:25, which introduces the pilgrimage tribute that follows it. Psalm 118 is used at

11 When they get close to Jerusalem, near Bethphage and
Bethany at the Mount of Olives, he sends off two of his disciples
²with these instructions: "Go into the village across the way, and
right after you enter it, you'll find a colt tied up, one that has
never been ridden. Untie it and bring it here. ³If anyone questions you, 'Why are you doing this?' tell them, 'Its master has
need of it and he will send it back here right away.'"

⁴They set out and found a colt tied up at the door out on the
street, and they untie it. ⁵Some of the people standing around
started saying to them, "What do you think you're doing, unty-
ing that colt?" ⁶But they said just what Jesus had told them to
say, so they left them alone.

⁷So they bring the colt to Jesus, and they throw their cloaks
over it; then he got on it. ⁸And many people spread their cloaks
on the road, while others cut leafy branches from the fields.
⁹Those leading the way and those following kept shouting,

"Hosanna! Blessed is the one
who comes in the name of the Lord!"
¹⁰Blessed is the coming kingdom of our father David!
"Hosanna" in the highest!

¹¹And he went into Jerusalem to the temple area and took
stock of everything, but, since the hour was already late, he
returned to Bethany with the twelve.

¹²On the next day, as they were leaving Bethany, he got
hungry. ¹³So when he spotted a fig tree in the distance with
some leaves on it, he went up to it expecting to find something
on it. But when he got right up to it, he found nothing on it

Jesus enters Jerusalem

Fig tree without figs

---

the conclusion of the passover meal (14:26).

• **11:10.** *The coming kingdom of our father David:* not derived from any scripture. In pre-Christian Judean religion David is not called "our father" and David's kingdom is not talked about as "coming." In the expectation of Isaiah (9:7) "the throne of David and his kingdom" will be established again. Mark's unusual construction may be his stereotyped "Judean" response from a crowd that does not understand the nature of God's "imperial rule" (1:15).

• **11:11.** *Temple area:* the temple sanctuary was surrounded by a series of courtyards separated by walls to restrict access: only priests were allowed in the temple itself, only Judean males in the closest courtyard, Judean females limited to the next courtyard, and pagans only in the outer court-

yard, which during festival seasons would have been bustling with vendors and merchants (v. 15).

• **11:13.** *Fig tree:* often used symbolically in the Old Testament, especially by the prophets in announcing judgment on Israel's corrupt temple cult: "When I wanted to gather them, says the Lord, there are no grapes on the vine, nor figs on the fig tree; even the leaves are withered" (Jer 8:13 NRSV); "I will end . . . all her solemn feasts. And I will destroy . . . her fig-trees" (Hos 2:11–12); "their root is dried up, they shall bear no fruit" (Hos 9:16, LXX: "it was dried up [at] its roots, it certainly won't bear fruit again"); "Woe is me! For I have become like one who, after the summer fruit has been gathered, . . . finds no cluster to eat; there is no first-ripe fig for which I

εἰ μὴ φύλλα· ὁ γὰρ καιρὸς οὐκ ἦν σύκων. ¹⁴καὶ ἀποκριθεὶς εἶπεν αὐτῇ, Μηκέτι εἰς τὸν αἰῶνα ἐκ σοῦ μηδεὶς καρπὸν φάγοι. καὶ ἤκουον οἱ μαθηταὶ αὐτοῦ.

Temple as hideout

¹⁵Καὶ ἔρχονται εἰς ῾Ιεροσόλυμα. καὶ εἰσελθὼν εἰς τὸ ἱερὸν ἤρξατο ἐκβάλλειν τοὺς πωλοῦντας καὶ τοὺς ἀγοράζοντας ἐν τῷ ἱερῷ, καὶ τὰς τραπέζας τῶν κολλυβιστῶν καὶ τὰς καθέδρας τῶν πωλούντων τὰς περιστερὰς κατέστρεψεν, ¹⁶καὶ οὐκ ἤφιεν ἵνα τις διενέγκῃ σκεῦος διὰ τοῦ ἱεροῦ. ¹⁷καὶ ἐδίδασκεν καὶ ἔλεγεν αὐτοῖς, Οὐ γέγραπται ὅτι ῾Ο οἶκός μου οἶκος προσευχῆς κληθήσεται πᾶσιν τοῖς ἔθνεσιν; ὑμεῖς δὲ πεποιήκατε αὐτὸν ἡσπήλαιον λῃστῶν.

¹⁸Καὶ ἤκουσαν οἱ ἀρχιερεῖς καὶ οἱ γραμματεῖς, καὶ ἐζήτουν πῶς αὐτὸν ἀπολέσωσιν· ἐφοβοῦντο γὰρ αὐτόν, πᾶς γὰρ ὁ ὄχλος ἐξεπλήσσετο ἐπὶ τῇ διδαχῇ αὐτοῦ. ¹⁹καὶ ὅταν ὀψὲ ἐγένετο, ἐξεπορεύοντο ἔξω τῆς πόλεως.

Mountains into the sea

²⁰Καὶ παραπορευόμενοι πρωῒ εἶδον τὴν συκῆν ἐξηραμμένην ἐκ ῥιζῶν. ²¹καὶ ἀναμνησθεὶς ὁ Πέτρος λέγει αὐτῷ, ῾Ραββί, ἴδε ἡ συκῆ ἣν κατηράσω ἐξήρανται. ²²Καὶ ἀποκριθεὶς ὁ ᾿Ιησοῦς λέγει αὐτοῖς, Εἰ ἔχετε πίστιν θεοῦ, ²³ἀμὴν λέγω ὑμῖν ὅτι ὃς ἂν εἴπῃ τῷ ὄρει τούτῳ, ῎Αρθητι καὶ βλήθητι εἰς τὴν θάλασσαν, καὶ μὴ διακριθῇ ἐν τῇ καρδίᾳ αὐτοῦ ἀλλὰ πιστεύῃ ὅτι ὃ λαλεῖ γίνεται, ἔσται αὐτῷ. ²⁴διὰ τοῦτο λέγω

---

19. *They:* many MSS read *he*, similar to Mark 11:11 and Matt 21:17.
22. *Have trust:* some MSS read *If you have trust*, similar to Matt 21:21.

---

hunger" (Mic 7:1 NRSV). *It wasn't 'time':* an aside that reminds the reader that in this story *the 'time' is up* (1:15).

• **11:14.** The words of Jesus here capture a very emphatic, and for Mark an unusual, Greek construction used to express the strong wishes of a speaker that something never happen again. It is later called a curse (v. 21). Similar "curse" language is found in Acts 8:20, "May your money perish with you."

• **11:15.:** Jesus' action of "driving them out" echoes the language of Hos 9:15, "I will drive them out of my house" because of their wickedness, which is directly followed by the image of Israel as "dried up at its roots," no more to bear fruit (cited at v. 13). *Vendors* and *shoppers:* probably of livestock for sacrifices at the festival. *Bankers:* exchange foreign currency, which had images on it, for the temple coins required for proper offerings. Every Judean male was required to pay an annual half-shekel temple tax to support the daily sacrifice offered on behalf of all Judean people. The

local economy heavily depended on temple business and the temple treasury (12:41) was, in effect, a national bank. So Jesus' symbolic act was directed against the central institutions of his religion and culture. *Pigeon:* considered a "clean" bird, recommended for burnt offerings (Lev 1:14), especially for those who could not afford a larger animal offering (Lev 5:7).

• **11:16.** Mark's summary appears to reflect the prophecy, "There shall no longer be traders in the house of the Lord of hosts on that day" (Zech 14:21), which envisions a time when the entire temple area is purified. However, here v. 16 implies shutting down all the business activity associated with the temple. Of course that in fact happened when the Romans ended the temple's existence in 70 C.E.

• **11:17.** Mark again (as in 1:2–3) brings together several texts from the Greek Old Testament (LXX). These two involving prophetic critique of the temple offer an interpretation of Jesus' symbolic gesture in the temple area. *The scriptures:* quotes Isa

except some leaves. (You see, it wasn't 'time' for figs.) ¹⁴And he reacted by saying: "May no one so much as taste your fruit again!" And his disciples were listening.

¹⁵They come to Jerusalem. And he went into the temple and began chasing the vendors and shoppers out of the temple area, and he turned the bankers' tables upside down, along with the chairs of the pigeon merchants, ¹⁶and he wouldn't even let anyone carry a container through the temple area. ¹⁷Then he started teaching and would say to them: "Don't the scriptures say, 'My house is to be regarded as a house of prayer for all peoples'?—but you have turned it into 'a hideout for crooks'!"

Temple as hideout

¹⁸And the ranking priests and the scholars heard this and kept looking for a way to get rid of him. (The truth is that they stood in fear of him, and that the whole crowd was astonished at his teaching.) ¹⁹And when it grew dark, they made their way out of the city.

²⁰As they were walking along early one morning, they saw the fig tree withered from the roots up. ²¹And Peter remembered and says to him: "Rabbi, look, the fig tree you cursed has withered up!"

Mountains into the sea

²²In response Jesus says to them: "Have trust in God. ²³I swear to you, those who say to this mountain, 'Up with you and into the sea!' and do not waver in their conviction, but trust that what they say will happen, that's the way it will be. ²⁴This is why

---

56:7. *For all peoples*: the prophets criticized the religious leaders for their attitude toward pagans. Isaiah developed the image of Israel as "a light to the nations" (Isa 49:6; 51:4), probably building on the promise made in the covenant with Abraham and Sarah, that they would be father and mother of nations (Gen 17:4, 16). *Hideout for crooks*: from Jer 7:11, "crooks" originally suggested outlaw types who made no pretense to live by the Torah, but are then pictured as coming to the temple to make offerings in compliance with the Torah. Mark uses it against those who have taken over the courtyard for the pagans and turned it into a marketplace to make a profit for themselves. The term had taken on further political significance when Josephus used it to describe the militant revolutionaries who provoked the war with Rome (§1.3). These were the "zealots" who made the temple area their fortress ("hideout") against the Romans in 68-70 C.E. (further discussed at 13:18).

• **11:18.** *The ranking priests and the scholars*: the leading members of the Council (14:53), here without "the elders," depicted by Mark as those most responsible for Jesus' arrest (14:1).

• **11:20.** *One morning*: the Greek is ambiguous whether this is the next day or later.

• **11:21.** *Rabbi*: Peter had once before addressed Jesus in this proper Judean way as "my master" (9:5). *Cursed*: the opposite of petitioning for a blessing. The Mosaic covenant attached blessing and life to obedience of the Torah and curse and death to disobedience (Deut 30:19; also associated with the last judgment, Matt 25:34, 41).

• **11:22.** *Have trust*: what the disciples lacked earlier (4:40). Adding *in God* (the Greek genitive *theou*) is a rare instance of Mark providing on object for the "trust" that the disciples are expected to have.

• **11:23.** Having enough trust "to move mountains" became a popular early Christian expression (1 Cor 13:2; Matt 17:20). The Gospel of Thomas (48 and 106) preserves two versions of "Say, 'Mountain, move from here!' and it will move," sayings

*On whose
authority?*

ὑμῖν, πάντα ὅσα προσεύχεσθε καὶ αἰτεῖσθε, πιστεύετε ὅτι ἐλάβετε, καὶ ἔσται ὑμῖν. ²⁵καὶ ὅταν στήκετε προσευχόμενοι, ἀφίετε εἴ τι ἔχετε κατά τινος, ἵνα καὶ ὁ πατὴρ ὑμῶν ὁ ἐν τοῖς οὐρανοῖς ἀφῇ ὑμῖν τὰ παραπτώματα ὑμῶν.[26]

²⁷Καὶ ἔρχονται πάλιν εἰς Ἱεροσόλυμα. καὶ ἐν τῷ ἱερῷ περιπατοῦντος αὐτοῦ ἔρχονται πρὸς αὐτὸν οἱ ἀρχιερεῖς καὶ οἱ γραμματεῖς καὶ οἱ πρεσβύτεροι ²⁸καὶ ἔλεγον αὐτῷ, Ἐν ποίᾳ ἐξουσίᾳ ταῦτα ποιεῖς; ἢ τίς σοι ἔδωκεν τὴν ἐξουσίαν ταύτην ἵνα ταῦτα ποιῇς;

²⁹Ὁ δὲ Ἰησοῦς εἶπεν αὐτοῖς, Ἐπερωτήσω ὑμᾶς ἕνα λόγον, καὶ ἀποκρίθητέ μοι, καὶ ἐρῶ ὑμῖν ἐν ποίᾳ ἐξουσίᾳ ταῦτα ποιῶ· ³⁰τὸ βάπτισμα τὸ Ἰωάννου ἐξ οὐρανοῦ ἦν ἢ ἐξ ἀνθρώπων; ἀποκρίθητέ μοι.

³¹Καὶ διελογίζοντο πρὸς ἑαυτοὺς λέγοντες, Ἐὰν εἴπωμεν, Ἐξ οὐρανοῦ, ἐρεῖ, Διὰ τί οὐκ ἐπιστεύσατε αὐτῷ; ³²ἀλλὰ εἴπωμεν, Ἐξ ἀνθρώπων; ἐφοβοῦντο τὸν ὄχλον, ἅπαντες γὰρ εἶχον τὸν Ἰωάννην ὄντως ὅτι προφήτης ἦν. ³³καὶ ἀποκριθέντες τῷ Ἰησοῦ λέγουσιν, Οὐκ οἴδαμεν.

Καὶ ὁ Ἰησοῦς λέγει αὐτοῖς, Οὐδὲ ἐγὼ λέγω ὑμῖν ἐν ποίᾳ ἐξουσίᾳ ταῦτα ποιῶ.

---

24. *Will receive:* Greek is past tense in the earliest MSS, probably reflecting the language of Old Testament prophets, who talked this way confidently about the future. Some MSS have the future in Greek, most have the present.   **26.** Added by most MSS: *If you do not practice forgiveness, your Father in heaven will not forgive your wrongdoing,* similar to Matt 6:15; but not in the earliest MSS. Its very similar ending to v. 25 could have caused an accidental omission.   **32.** *Considered:* some MSS have *knew.*

I keep telling you, trust that you will receive everything you pray and ask for, and that's the way it will turn out. ²⁵And when you stand up to pray, if you are holding anything against anyone, forgive them, so your father in heaven may forgive your misdeeds."[26]

²⁷Once again they come to Jerusalem. As he walks around in the temple area, the ranking priests and scholars and elders come up to him ²⁸and start questioning him: "By what right are you doing these things?" or, "Who gave you the authority to do these things?"

On whose authority?

²⁹But Jesus said to them: "I have one question for you. If you answer me, then I will tell you by what authority I do these things. ³⁰Tell me, was the baptism of John heaven-sent or was it of human origin? Answer me that."

³¹And they conferred among themselves, saying, "If we say 'heaven-sent,' he'll say, 'Then why didn't you trust him?' ³²But if we say 'Of human origin . . . !'" They were afraid of the crowd. (You see, everybody considered John a genuine prophet.) ³³So they answered Jesus by saying, "We can't tell."

And Jesus says to them: "Neither am I going to tell you by what authority I do these things!"

---

which are not necessarily attached to the theme of "trust."

• **11:25.** This was another popular saying, found by itself (Luke 6:37), in the Lord's Prayer (Luke 11:4), which Mark does not have, or associated with it (Matt 6:14).

• **11:28.** *These things*: must refer to Jesus' attack on the businesses in the temple area (vv. 15–17), since it is the same temple leadership here (v. 27) that immediately after that incident wanted to get rid of Jesus (v. 18).

• **11:29.** *I have one question for you*: a common rejoinder in rabbinic debates.

• **11:30.** *Tell me*: sets up the questions that follow; Greek begins abruptly without any transition. *The baptism of John*: initially endorsed by "all the residents of Jerusalem" (1:5) and the occasion for Jesus' "calling" (1:11), but since then John has been executed (6:17–28), so his reputation is now subject to question.

• **11:33.** *We can't tell*: meaning *we don't know.*

*Leased
vineyard*

12 Καὶ ἤρξατο αὐτοῖς ἐν παραβολαῖς λαλεῖν,

Ἀμπελῶνα ἄνθρωπος ἐφύτευσεν, καὶ περιέθηκεν φραγμὸν καὶ ὤρυξεν ὑπολήνιον καὶ ᾠκοδόμησεν πύργον, καὶ ἐξέδετο αὐτὸν γεωργοῖς, καὶ ἀπεδήμησεν. ²καὶ ἀπέστειλεν πρὸς τοὺς γεωργοὺς τῷ καιρῷ δοῦλον, ἵνα παρὰ τῶν γεωργῶν λάβῃ ἀπὸ τῶν καρπῶν τοῦ ἀμπελῶνος· ³καὶ λαβόντες αὐτὸν ἔδειραν καὶ ἀπέστειλαν κενόν. ⁴καὶ πάλιν ἀπέστειλεν πρὸς αὐτοὺς ἄλλον δοῦλον· κἀκεῖνον ἐκεφαλίωσαν καὶ ἠτίμασαν. ⁵καὶ ἄλλον ἀπέστειλεν, κἀκεῖνον ἀπέκτειναν, καὶ πολλοὺς ἄλλους, οὓς μὲν δέροντες οὓς δὲ ἀποκτέννοντες.

⁶Ἔτι ἕνα εἶχεν, υἱὸν ἀγαπητόν· ἀπέστειλεν αὐτὸν ἔσχατον πρὸς αὐτοὺς λέγων ὅτι Ἐντραπήσονται τὸν υἱόν μου.

⁷Ἐκεῖνοι δὲ οἱ γεωργοὶ πρὸς ἑαυτοὺς εἶπαν ὅτι Οὗτός ἐστιν ὁ κληρονόμος· δεῦτε ἀποκτείνωμεν αὐτόν, καὶ ἡμῶν ἔσται ἡ κληρονομία. ⁸καὶ λαβόντες ἀπέκτειναν αὐτόν, καὶ ἐξέβαλον αὐτὸν ἔξω τοῦ ἀμπελῶνος.

⁹Τί ποιήσει ὁ κύριος τοῦ ἀμπελῶνος; ἐλεύσεται καὶ ἀπολέσει τοὺς γεωργούς, καὶ δώσει τὸν ἀμπελῶνα ἄλλοις.

¹⁰Οὐδὲ τὴν γραφὴν ταύτην ἀνέγνωτε, Λίθον ὃν ἀπεδοκίμασαν οἱ οἰκοδομοῦντες, οὗτος ἐγενήθη εἰς κεφαλὴν γωνίας· ¹¹παρὰ κυρίου ἐγένετο αὕτη, καὶ ἔστιν θαυμαστὴ ἐν ὀφθαλμοῖς ἡμῶν;

¹²Καὶ ἐζήτουν αὐτὸν κρατῆσαι, καὶ ἐφοβήθησαν τὸν ὄχλον, ἔγνωσαν γὰρ ὅτι πρὸς αὐτοὺς τὴν παραβολὴν εἶπεν. καὶ ἀφέντες αὐτὸν ἀπῆλθον.

*The emperor
& God*

¹³Καὶ ἀποστέλλουσιν πρὸς αὐτόν τινας τῶν Φαρισαίων καὶ τῶν Ἡρῳδιανῶν ἵνα αὐτὸν ἀγρεύσωσιν λόγῳ. ¹⁴καὶ ἐλθόντες λέγουσιν αὐτῷ, Διδάσκαλε, οἴδαμεν ὅτι ἀληθὴς εἶ καὶ οὐ μέλει σοι περὶ οὐδενός, οὐ γὰρ βλέπεις εἰς πρόσωπον ἀνθρώπων, ἀλλ᾽ ἐπ᾽ ἀληθείας τὴν ὁδὸν τοῦ θεοῦ διδάσκεις· ἔξεστιν δοῦναι κῆνσον Καίσαρι ἢ οὔ; δῶμεν ἢ μὴ δῶμεν; ¹⁵Ὁ δὲ εἰδὼς αὐτῶν τὴν ὑπόκρισιν εἶπεν αὐτοῖς, Τί με πειράζετε; φέρετέ μοι δηνάριον ἵνα ἴδω.

• **12:1–11.** Jesus only uses two substantial parables in Mark, this one about the leased vineyard and the one about the sower (4:3–8, 14–20). Mark attaches major importance to each as devices for interpreting the larger story.

• **12:1.** The ancient prophets used the vineyard as a metaphor for Israel (Jer 2:21; Ezek 19:10). This parable resembles the allegory developed in Isa 5:1–7, where the Lord lets the vineyard go to waste, because it was not fruitful; the Lord "expected justice, but saw bloodshed."

• **12:6.** *A son who was the apple of his eye:* recalls Jesus as the *favored son* at his baptism (1:11) and at the transfiguration (9:6). The desire to *kill him* fulfills the forecast of what will happen in Jerusalem (10:34).

• **12:9.** *The owner:* Greek *kyrios* can also be *master* or *lord* or *the Lord*, as in v. 11 (§6.4).

• **12:10.** *This scripture:* from Ps 118:22–23,

12 And he began to speak to them in parables: *Leased vineyard*

Someone planted a vineyard, put a hedge around it, dug a winepress, built a tower, leased it out to some farmers, and went abroad. ²In due time he sent a slave to the farmers to collect his share of the vineyard's crop from them. ³But they grabbed him, beat him, and sent him away empty-handed. ⁴So once again he sent another slave to them, but they attacked him and abused him. ⁵Then he sent another, and this one they killed; many others followed, some of whom they beat, others of whom they killed.

⁶He still had one more, a son who was the apple of his eye. This one he finally sent to them, with the thought, "They will show this son of mine some respect."

⁷But those farmers said to one another, "This fellow's the heir! Come on, let's kill him and the inheritance will be ours!" ⁸So they grabbed him, and killed him, and threw him outside the vineyard.

⁹What will the owner of the vineyard do? He will come in person, and do away with those farmers, and give the vineyard to someone else.

¹⁰Haven't you read this scripture, "A stone that the builders rejected has ended up as the keystone. ¹¹ It was the Lord's doing and is something you admire"?

¹²⟨His opponents⟩ kept looking for some opportunity to seize him, but they were still afraid of the crowd, since they realized that he had aimed the parable at them. So they left him there and went on their way.

¹³And they send some of the Pharisees and the Herodians to *The emperor & God* him to trap him with a riddle. ¹⁴They come and say to him, "Teacher, we know that you are honest and impartial, because you pay no attention to appearances, but instead you teach God's way forthrightly. Is it permissible to pay the poll tax to the Roman emperor or not? Should we pay or should we not pay?"

¹⁵But he saw through their trap, and said to them, "Why do you provoke me like this? Let me have a look at a coin."

---

one of the psalms used at Passover (also in 11:9).

• **12:12.** ⟨*His opponents*⟩: Greek has unspecified subjects ever since 11:27, the Council members.

• **12:13.** Unspecified *they* continues. *Pharisees and Herodians*: grouped in 3:6 in a plot against Jesus' life, and since then the Herodian family has done away with John (6:17–29). *Riddle*: a "loaded question," different than Jesus' use of riddle-like stories

(3:23; 7:17).

• **12:14.** *Poll tax*: paid in Roman money to finance the Roman troops stationed in Judea. This would have been a very sensitive issue at the time. Mark implies that Jesus is potentially vulnerable on this matter.

• **12:15.** *Their trap*: or *pretense*, related to calling them *phonies* (7:6). *Provoke*: as earlier he had been *tested*, first by Satan (1:13), then by the Pharisees (8:11; 10:2).

16Οἱ δὲ ἤνεγκαν. καὶ λέγει αὐτοῖς, Τίνος ἡ εἰκὼν αὕτη καὶ ἡ ἐπιγραφή;
Οἱ δὲ εἶπαν αὐτῷ, Καίσαρος.
17 Ὁ δὲ Ἰησοῦς εἶπεν αὐτοῖς, Τὰ Καίσαρος ἀπόδοτε Καίσαρι καὶ τὰ τοῦ θεοῦ τῷ θεῷ. καὶ ἐξεθαύμαζον ἐπ᾽ αὐτῷ.

Wife of seven brothers

18Καὶ ἔρχονται Σαδδουκαῖοι πρὸς αὐτόν, οἵτινες λέγουσιν ἀνάστασιν μὴ εἶναι, καὶ ἐπηρώτων αὐτὸν λέγοντες, 19Διδάσκαλε, Μωϋσῆς ἔγραψεν ἡμῖν ὅτι ἐάν τινος ἀδελφὸς ἀποθάνῃ καὶ καταλίπῃ γυναῖκα καὶ μὴ ἀφῇ τέκνον, ἵνα λάβῃ ὁ ἀδελφὸς αὐτοῦ τὴν γυναῖκα καὶ ἐξαναστήσῃ σπέρμα τῷ ἀδελφῷ αὐτοῦ. 20ἑπτὰ ἀδελφοὶ ἦσαν· καὶ ὁ πρῶτος ἔλαβεν γυναῖκα, καὶ ἀποθνῄσκων οὐκ ἀφῆκεν σπέρμα· 21καὶ ὁ δεύτερος ἔλαβεν αὐτήν, καὶ ἀπέθανεν μὴ καταλιπὼν σπέρμα· καὶ ὁ τρίτος ὡσαύτως· 22καὶ οἱ ἑπτὰ οὐκ ἀφῆκαν σπέρμα. ἔσχατον πάντων καὶ ἡ γυνὴ ἀπέθανεν. 23ἐν τῇ ἀναστάσει, ὅταν ἀναστῶσιν, τίνος αὐτῶν ἔσται γυνή; οἱ γὰρ ἑπτὰ ἔσχον αὐτὴν γυναῖκα.

24 Ἔφη αὐτοῖς ὁ Ἰησοῦς, Οὐ διὰ τοῦτο πλανᾶσθε μὴ εἰδότες τὰς γραφὰς μηδὲ τὴν δύναμιν τοῦ θεοῦ; 25ὅταν γὰρ ἐκ νεκρῶν ἀναστῶσιν, οὔτε γαμοῦσιν οὔτε γαμίζονται, ἀλλ᾽ εἰσὶν ὡς ἄγγελοι ἐν τοῖς οὐρανοῖς. 26περὶ δὲ τῶν νεκρῶν ὅτι ἐγείρονται οὐκ ἀνέγνωτε ἐν τῇ βίβλῳ Μωϋσέως ἐπὶ τοῦ βάτου πῶς εἶπεν αὐτῷ ὁ θεὸς λέγων, Ἐγὼ ὁ θεὸς Ἀβραὰμ καὶ θεὸς Ἰσαὰκ καὶ θεὸς Ἰακώβ; 27οὐκ ἔστιν θεὸς νεκρῶν ἀλλὰ ζώντων· πολὺ πλανᾶσθε.

The greatest commandment

28Καὶ προσελθὼν εἷς τῶν γραμματέων ἀκούσας αὐτῶν συζητούντων, ἰδὼν ὅτι καλῶς ἀπεκρίθη αὐτοῖς, ἐπηρώτησεν αὐτόν, Ποία ἐστὶν ἐντολὴ πρώτη πάντων;

29Ἀπεκρίθη ὁ Ἰησοῦς ὅτι Πρώτη ἐστίν, Ἄκουε, Ἰσραήλ, κύριος ὁ θεὸς ἡμῶν κύριος εἷς ἐστιν, 30καὶ ἀγαπήσεις κύριον τὸν θεόν σου ἐξ ὅλης τῆς καρδίας σου καὶ ἐξ ὅλης τῆς ψυχῆς σου [καὶ

---

23. *After they rise:* omitted in some MSS.   30. *And all your mind:* omitted in some MSS, not part of the Old Testament text.

Let me have a look at a coin: Jesus is never described as carrying Roman money, so *their trap* is exposed when "they" have such a coin.

• **12:16.** *Silver coin:* a Roman coin worth about a day's pay (6:37). *The emperor's name:* such coins said "Tiberius, Caesar Augustus, son of the Divine Augustus."

• **12:17.** *Pay:* or *pay back,* since the coins already "belong" to Caesar. *Dumbfounded:* a word unique to Mark; more intense than the earlier *shock* (6:6).

• **12:18.** *Sadducees:* only here in Mark; a group within ancient Judean religion, more conservative than the Pharisees (2:16),

though apparently willing to cooperate with the Romans; thought to be mostly aristocratic, with strong ties to the temple authorities. The Sadducees did not accept the oral law of the Pharisees regarding how to interpret the scriptures, which led to disagreements with the Pharisees on issues such as resurrection, a belief not found in the Hebrew Bible.

• **12:19.** *Moses wrote:* assumes the traditional Mosaic authorship of the Pentateuch, here combining language from Deut 25:5 and Gen 38:8. The practice of "levirate" (brother-in-law) marriage described in Deuteronomy 25 presupposes a setting in which

¹⁶They handed him a silver coin, and he says to them, "Whose picture is this? Whose name is on it?"

They replied, "The emperor's."

¹⁷Jesus said to them: "Pay the emperor what belongs to the emperor, and God what belongs to God!" And they were dumbfounded at him.

¹⁸And some Sadducees—those who maintain there is no resurrection—come up to him and they start questioning him. ¹⁹"Teacher," they said, "Moses wrote for our benefit, 'If someone's brother dies and leaves his widow childless, his brother is obligated to take the widow as his wife and produce offspring for his brother.' ²⁰There were seven brothers; now the first took a wife but left no children when he died. ²¹So the second married her but died without leaving offspring, and the third likewise. ²²In fact, all seven ⟨married her but⟩ left no offspring. Finally, the wife died too. ²³In the resurrection, after they rise, whose wife will she be?" (Remember, all seven had her as wife.)

Wife of seven brothers

²⁴Jesus said to them: "You've missed the point again, haven't you, all because you underestimate both the scriptures and the power of God. ²⁵After all, when men and women rise from the dead, they do not marry, but resemble heaven's messengers. ²⁶As for whether or not the dead are raised, haven't you read in the book of Moses in the passage about the bush, how God spoke to him: 'I am the God of Abraham and the God of Isaac and the God of Jacob'? ²⁷This is not the God of the dead, only of the living—you're constantly missing the point!"

²⁸And one of the scholars approached when he heard them arguing, and because he saw how skillfully Jesus answered them, he asked him, "Of all the commandments, which is the most important?"

The greatest commandment

²⁹Jesus answered: "The first is,'Hear, Israel, the Lord your God is one Lord, ³⁰and you are to love the Lord your God with all your heart and all your soul [and all your mind] and with all

---

the brothers live together, so there are property rights at stake. The brother-in-law has the right to refuse this obligation, but at the expense of some public embarrassment (Deut 25:7–10).

• **12:22.** *All seven*: quite hypothetical. In actual practice, the brother-in-law obligation probably stopped after no more than two or three.

• **12:25.** *Men and women*: renders an indefinite *they*.

• **12:26.** *Book of Moses*: here Exod 3:6, 15.

• **12:28.** The scholar's question was a debated issue among Judean scholars of that day: how to summarize the essence of the

Torah. The conservative approach insisted all of Torah was equally important. The most famous Judean teacher of Jesus' time, Hillel, is quoted as answering, "What is hateful to you, do not do to your neighbor. That is the whole Torah." Jesus' version of this is in Matt 7:12.

• **12:29.** Jesus quotes the opening prayer of the *Shema*, the traditional Judean statement of faith, from Deut 6:4–5, which pious Judeans recited twice daily as an affirmation of commitment to the Torah.

• **12:30.** *And all your mind*: not part of the Old Testament text, but it was sometimes the LXX translation for "all your heart,"

ἐξ ὅλης τῆς διανοίας σου] καὶ ἐξ ὅλης τῆς ἰσχύος σου. ³¹δευτέρα
αὕτη, Ἀγαπήσεις τὸν πλησίον σου ὡς σεαυτόν. μείζων τούτων
ἄλλη ἐντολὴ οὐκ ἔστιν.

³²Καὶ εἶπεν αὐτῷ ὁ γραμματεύς, Καλῶς, διδάσκαλε, ἐπ'
ἀληθείας εἶπες ὅτι εἷς ἐστιν καὶ οὐκ ἔστιν ἄλλος πλὴν αὐτοῦ·
³³καὶ τὸ ἀγαπᾶν αὐτὸν ἐξ ὅλης τῆς καρδίας καὶ ἐξ ὅλης τῆς
συνέσεως καὶ ἐξ ὅλης τῆς ἰσχύος καὶ τὸ ἀγαπᾶν τὸν πλησίον ὡς
ἑαυτὸν περισσότερόν ἐστιν πάντων τῶν ὁλοκαυτωμάτων καὶ
θυσιῶν.

³⁴Καὶ ὁ Ἰησοῦς ἰδὼν αὐτὸν ὅτι νουνεχῶς ἀπεκρίθη εἶπεν
αὐτῷ, Οὐ μακρὰν εἶ ἀπὸ τῆς βασιλείας τοῦ θεοῦ.

Καὶ οὐδεὶς οὐκέτι ἐτόλμα αὐτὸν ἐπερωτῆσαι.

David's lord & son

³⁵Καὶ ἀποκριθεὶς ὁ Ἰησοῦς ἔλεγεν διδάσκων ἐν τῷ ἱερῷ, Πῶς
λέγουσιν οἱ γραμματεῖς ὅτι ὁ Χριστὸς υἱὸς Δαυίδ ἐστιν; ³⁶αὐτὸς
Δαυὶδ εἶπεν ἐν τῷ πνεύματι τῷ ἁγίῳ, Εἶπεν κύριος τῷ κυρίῳ μου,
Κάθου ἐκ δεξιῶν μου ἕως ἂν θῶ τοὺς ἐχθρούς σου ὑποκάτω τῶν
ποδῶν σου. ³⁷αὐτὸς Δαυὶδ λέγει αὐτὸν κύριον, καὶ πόθεν αὐτοῦ
ἐστιν υἱός;

Καὶ πολὺς ὄχλος ἤκουεν αὐτοῦ ἡδέως.

Scholars' privileges

³⁸Καὶ ἐν τῇ διδαχῇ αὐτοῦ ἔλεγεν, Βλέπετε ἀπὸ τῶν
γραμματέων τῶν θελόντων ἐν στολαῖς περιπατεῖν καὶ
ἀσπασμοὺς ἐν ταῖς ἀγοραῖς ³⁹καὶ πρωτοκαθεδρίας ἐν ταῖς
συναγωγαῖς καὶ πρωτοκλισίας ἐν τοῖς δείπνοις· ⁴⁰οἱ
κατεσθίοντες τὰς οἰκίας τῶν χηρῶν καὶ προφάσει μακρὰ
προσευχόμενοι, οὗτοι λήμψονται περισσότερον κρίμα.

Widow's pittance

⁴¹Καὶ καθίσας κατέναντι τοῦ γαζοφυλακίου ἐθεώρει πῶς ὁ
ὄχλος βάλλει χαλκὸν εἰς τὸ γαζοφυλάκιον· καὶ πολλοὶ πλούσιοι
ἔβαλλον πολλά· ⁴²καὶ ἐλθοῦσα μία χήρα πτωχὴ ἔβαλεν λεπτὰ
δύο, ὅ ἐστιν κοδράντης. ⁴³καὶ προσκαλεσάμενος τοὺς μαθητὰς
αὐτοῦ εἶπεν αὐτοῖς, Ἀμὴν λέγω ὑμῖν ὅτι ἡ χήρα αὕτη ἡ πτωχὴ
πλεῖον πάντων ἔβαλεν τῶν βαλλόντων εἰς τὸ γαζοφυλάκιον·
⁴⁴πάντες γὰρ ἐκ τοῦ περισσεύοντος αὐτοῖς ἔβαλον, αὕτη δὲ ἐκ
τῆς ὑστερήσεως αὐτῆς πάντα ὅσα εἶχεν ἔβαλεν, ὅλον τὸν βίον
αὐτῆς.

---

40. *Widows:* some MSS add *and orphans.*   **41.** *He:* some MSS read *Jesus;*
some of those read *when Jesus stood.*

since "the heart" was often described as the
location of thoughts (§4.5).
- **12:31.** Lev 19:18. The combination of this
with Deut 6:5 (v. 30) was already current in
Judaism ("Love the Lord and your neighbor," Testament of Issachar 5:2, second
century B.C.E.).
- **12:33.** *Mind:* here in the sense of *understanding. Greater than all burnt offerings:*
echoes Hos 6:6, "I desire . . . the knowl-
edge of God, rather than burnt offerings."
- **12:35.** *The Anointed:* a traditional label for

the king of Israel. Mark applied it to Jesus
(1:1), but its use by Peter caused strong
disagreement over its meaning (8:29). *Son
of David:* used by blind Bartimaeus for
Jesus (10:47). Traditionally this was someone from the Davidic family line, who
would be qualified to be the Lord's
"anointed."
- **12:36.** *Under the influence of the holy spirit:*
Judean tradition had David as the author of
the Psalms, even though only about half of
them are attributed to him. This is Ps

your energy.' ³¹The second is this: 'You are to love your neighbor as yourself.' There is no other commandment greater than these."

³²And the scholar said to him, "That's a fine answer, Teacher. You have correctly said that God is one and there is no other beside him. ³³And 'to love him with all one's heart and with all one's mind and with all one's energy' and 'to love one's neighbor as oneself' is greater than all the burnt offerings and sacrifices put together."

³⁴And when Jesus saw that he answered him sensibly, he said to him, "You are not far from God's domain."

And from then on no one dared question him.

³⁵And during the time Jesus was teaching in the temple area, he would pose this question: "How can the scholars claim that the Anointed is the son of David? ³⁶David himself said under the influence of the holy spirit, 'The Lord said to my lord, "Sit here at my right, until I make your enemies grovel at your feet."' ³⁷David himself calls him 'lord,' so how can he be his son?"

And a huge crowd would listen to him with delight.

³⁸During the course of his teaching he would say: "Look out for the scholars who like to parade around in long robes, and insist on being addressed properly in the marketplaces, ³⁹and prefer important seats in the synagogues and the best couches at banquets. ⁴⁰They are the ones who prey on widows and their families, and recite long prayers just to put on airs. These people will get a stiff sentence!"

⁴¹And he would sit across from the treasury and observe the crowd dropping money into the collection box. And many wealthy people would drop large amounts in. ⁴²Then one poor widow came and put in two small coins, which is a pittance. ⁴³And he motioned his disciples over and said to them: "I swear to you, this poor widow has contributed more than all those who dropped something into the collection box! ⁴⁴After all, they were all donating out of their surplus, whereas she, out of her poverty, was contributing all she had, her entire livelihood!"

David's lord & son

Scholars' privileges

Widow's pittance

110:1; *the Lord* = Yahweh; *my lord* = my master (§6.4). If David calls the Anointed his master, the Anointed cannot also be his son, assuming a father does not call his son "master." This logic would challenge the traditional requirement that the Anointed be a Davidic descendant.

• **12:38.** *Long robes*: full-length outer garments usually worn by dignitaries.

• **12:39.** *The best couches*: the equivalent of "the head table."

• **12:41.** *Treasury* and *collection box*: the same

term appears to be used for both the treasury area in the temple courtyard where donors brought their gifts and for the containers where charitable contributions were left. This was also the area for the bankers (11:15).

• **12:42.** *Two small coins*: the Greek refers to the smallest bronze coins in circulation. *Pittance*: translates a word Mark borrowed from Latin for the smallest Roman bronze coin, worth 1/64 of a denarius (12:16).

Monumental buildings destroyed

13 Καὶ ἐκπορευομένου αὐτοῦ ἐκ τοῦ ἱεροῦ λέγει αὐτῷ εἷς τῶν μαθητῶν αὐτοῦ, Διδάσκαλε, ἴδε ποταποὶ λίθοι καὶ ποταπαὶ οἰκοδομαί.

²Καὶ ὁ Ἰησοῦς εἶπεν αὐτῷ, Βλέπεις ταύτας τὰς μεγάλας οἰκοδομάς; οὐ μὴ ἀφεθῇ λίθος ἐπὶ λίθον ὃς οὐ μὴ καταλυθῇ.

Signs of final agonies

³Καὶ καθημένου αὐτοῦ εἰς τὸ Ὄρος τῶν Ἐλαιῶν κατέναντι τοῦ ἱεροῦ ἐπηρώτα αὐτὸν κατ' ἰδίαν Πέτρος καὶ Ἰάκωβος καὶ Ἰωάννης καὶ Ἀνδρέας, ⁴Εἰπὸν ἡμῖν πότε ταῦτα ἔσται, καὶ τί τὸ σημεῖον ὅταν μέλλῃ ταῦτα συντελεῖσθαι πάντα.

⁵Ὁ δὲ Ἰησοῦς ἤρξατο λέγειν αὐτοῖς, Βλέπετε μή τις ὑμᾶς πλανήσῃ· ⁶πολλοὶ ἐλεύσονται ἐπὶ τῷ ὀνόματί μου λέγοντες ὅτι Ἐγώ εἰμι, καὶ πολλοὺς πλανήσουσιν. ⁷ὅταν δὲ ἀκούσητε πολέμους καὶ ἀκοὰς πολέμων, μὴ θροεῖσθε· δεῖ γενέσθαι, ἀλλ' οὔπω τὸ τέλος. ⁸ἐγερθήσεται γὰρ ἔθνος ἐπ' ἔθνος καὶ βασιλεία ἐπὶ βασιλείαν, ἔσονται σεισμοὶ κατὰ τόπους, ἔσονται λιμοί· ἀρχὴ ὠδίνων ταῦτα.

⁹Βλέπετε δὲ ὑμεῖς ἑαυτούς· παραδώσουσιν ὑμᾶς εἰς συνέδρια καὶ εἰς συναγωγὰς δαρήσεσθε καὶ ἐπὶ ἡγεμόνων καὶ βασιλέων σταθήσεσθε ἕνεκεν ἐμοῦ εἰς μαρτύριον αὐτοῖς. ¹⁰καὶ εἰς πάντα τὰ ἔθνη πρῶτον δεῖ κηρυχθῆναι τὸ εὐαγγέλιον. ¹¹καὶ ὅταν ἄγωσιν ὑμᾶς παραδιδόντες, μὴ προμεριμνᾶτε τί λαλήσητε, ἀλλ' ὃ ἐὰν δοθῇ ὑμῖν ἐν ἐκείνῃ τῇ ὥρᾳ τοῦτο λαλεῖτε, οὐ γάρ ἐστε ὑμεῖς οἱ λαλοῦντες ἀλλὰ τὸ πνεῦμα τὸ ἅγιον. ¹²καὶ παραδώσει ἀδελφὸς ἀδελφὸν εἰς θάνατον καὶ πατὴρ τέκνον, καὶ ἐπαναστήσονται τέκνα ἐπὶ γονεῖς καὶ θανατώσουσιν αὐτούς· ¹³καὶ ἔσεσθε μισούμενοι ὑπὸ πάντων διὰ τὸ ὄνομά μου. ὁ δὲ ὑπομείνας εἰς τέλος οὗτος σωθήσεται.

Days of distress

¹⁴Ὅταν δὲ ἴδητε τὸ βδέλυγμα τῆς ἐρημώσεως ἑστηκότα ὅπου οὐ δεῖ, ὁ ἀναγινώσκων νοείτω, τότε οἱ ἐν τῇ Ἰουδαίᾳ φευγέτωσαν εἰς τὰ ὄρη, ¹⁵ὁ ἐπὶ τοῦ δώματος μὴ καταβάτω μηδὲ

---

2. *Left:* some MSS add *here;* Matt 24:2 includes it; MSS vary in Luke 21:6.

- **13:1–37.** Mark presents Jesus' longest speech in this gospel (§2.7); the collection of parables (4:2–32) is the only other extended discourse. This speech combines traditional eschatological ("end time") material, typical of similar Judean writings, with advice for Christian missionaries, which probably reflects the kinds of struggles Christians have already experienced.
- **13:2.** This is the closest any saying comes to the threat Jesus is said to have made against the temple (14:58). After the actual destruction of the temple by the Romans in 70 C.E., many Christians were convinced that Jesus had predicted such destruction, and it was interpreted by them as punishment for the treatment Jesus received in Jerusalem from the temple authorities.
- **13:3.** *Mount of Olives:* a natural lookout spot for viewing the temple area (11:1). The four disciples mentioned are the first four who were called (1:16–20); they are together here for the last time in the story.
- **13:6.** *I'm the one:* the kind of claim made by a "counterfeit messiah" (v. 22).

13 And as he was going out of the temple area, one of his disciples remarks to him, "Teacher, look, what magnificent masonry! What wonderful buildings!"

Monumental buildings destroyed

²And Jesus replied to him, "Take a good look at these monumental buildings! You may be sure not one stone will be left on top of another! Every last one will certainly be knocked down!"

³And as he was sitting on the Mount of Olives across from the temple, Peter would ask him privately, as would James and John and Andrew: ⁴"Tell us, when are these things going to happen, and what will be the sign to indicate when all these things are about to take place?"

Signs of final agonies

⁵And Jesus would say to them, "Stay alert, otherwise someone might just delude you! ⁶You know, many will come using my name and claim, 'I'm the one!' and they will delude many people. ⁷When you hear of wars and rumors of wars, don't be afraid. These are inevitable, but it is not yet the end. ⁸For nation will rise up against nation and empire against empire; there will be earthquakes everywhere; there will be famines. These things mark the beginning of the final agonies.

⁹"But you look out for yourselves! They will turn you over to councils, and beat you in synagogues, and haul you up before governors and kings, on my account, so you can make your case to them. ¹⁰Yet the good news must first be announced to all peoples. ¹¹And when they arrest you to lock you up, don't be worried about what you should say. Instead, whatever occurs to you at the moment, say that. For it is not you who are speaking but the holy spirit. ¹²And one brother will turn in another to be put to death, and a father his child, and children will turn against their parents and kill them. ¹³And you will be universally hated because of me. Those who hold out to the end will be saved!

¹⁴"When you see the 'devastating desecration' standing where it should not (the reader had better figure out what this means), then the people in Judea should head for the hills; ¹⁵no one on

Days of distress

• **13:7.** *Inevitable*: usually means, "according to scripture," especially in the prophetic sense of "in the last days" (Dan 2:28–29).

• **13:8.** *Final agonies*: the labor pains of childbirth, signalling the beginning of the end. Prophets used the image "like a woman in labor" for the suffering that Israel endured in exile before the restoration (Mic 4:9–10; Isa 26:17–19). The image of the agony that accompanies new birth then became one of the "signs" of the last days: "A great portent appeared in heaven: a woman . . . was pregnant and was crying

out in birthpangs, in the agony of giving birth" (Rev 12:1–2).

• **13:9–13.** These horrors of war appear to describe the vivid experiences of those who endured the Roman-Judean War, 66–70 C.E. (§1.3).

• **13:11.** *Lock you up*: what happened to John (1:14) has already been anticipated for Jesus (3:19; 9:31), and is now promised for the followers.

• **13:14.** *Devastating desecration*: a phrase from Dan 9:27 and 12:11, which referred to the use of the temple for pagan sacrifice by

εἰσελθάτω ἆραί τι ἐκ τῆς οἰκίας αὐτοῦ, ¹⁶καὶ ὁ εἰς τὸν ἀγρὸν μὴ ἐπιστρεψάτω εἰς τὰ ὀπίσω ἆραι τὸ ἱμάτιον αὐτοῦ. ¹⁷οὐαὶ δὲ ταῖς ἐν γαστρὶ ἐχούσαις καὶ ταῖς θηλαζούσαις ἐν ἐκείναις ταῖς ἡμέραις. ¹⁸προσεύχεσθε δὲ ἵνα μὴ γένηται χειμῶνος· ¹⁹ἔσονται γὰρ αἱ ἡμέραι ἐκεῖναι θλῖψις οἵα οὐ γέγονεν τοιαύτη ἀπ᾽ ἀρχῆς κτίσεως ἣν ἔκτισεν ὁ θεὸς ἕως τοῦ νῦν καὶ οὐ μὴ γένηται. ²⁰καὶ εἰ μὴ ἐκολόβωσεν κύριος τὰς ἡμέρας, οὐκ ἂν ἐσώθη πᾶσα σάρξ. ἀλλὰ διὰ τοὺς ἐκλεκτοὺς οὓς ἐξελέξατο ἐκολόβωσεν τὰς ἡμέρας. ²¹καὶ τότε ἐάν τις ὑμῖν εἴπῃ, Ἴδε ὧδε ὁ Χριστός, Ἴδε ἐκεῖ, μὴ πιστεύετε· ²²ἐγερθήσονται γὰρ ψευδόχριστοι καὶ ψευδοπροφῆται καὶ δώσουσιν σημεῖα καὶ τέρατα πρὸς τὸ ἀποπλανᾶν, εἰ δυνατόν, τοὺς ἐκλεκτούς. ²³ὑμεῖς δὲ βλέπετε· προείρηκα ὑμῖν πάντα.

Son of Adam
comes on clouds

²⁴Ἀλλὰ ἐν ἐκείναις ταῖς ἡμέραις μετὰ τὴν θλῖψιν ἐκείνην

ὁ ἥλιος σκοτισθήσεται,
καὶ ἡ σελήνη οὐ δώσει τὸ φέγγος αὐτῆς,
²⁵καὶ οἱ ἀστέρες ἔσονται ἐκ τοῦ οὐρανοῦ πίπτοντες,
καὶ αἱ δυνάμεις αἱ ἐν τοῖς οὐρανοῖς σαλευθήσονται.

²⁶καὶ τότε ὄψονται τὸν υἱὸν τοῦ ἀνθρώπου ἐρχόμενον ἐν νεφέλαις μετὰ δυνάμεως πολλῆς καὶ δόξης. ²⁷καὶ τότε ἀποστελεῖ τοὺς ἀγγέλους καὶ ἐπισυνάξει τοὺς ἐκλεκτοὺς ἐκ τῶν τεσσάρων ἀνέμων ἀπ᾽ ἄκρου γῆς ἕως ἄκρου οὐρανοῦ.

²⁸Ἀπὸ δὲ τῆς συκῆς μάθετε τὴν παραβολήν· ὅταν ἤδη ὁ κλάδος αὐτῆς ἁπαλὸς γένηται καὶ ἐκφύῃ τὰ φύλλα, γινώσκετε ὅτι ἐγγὺς τὸ θέρος ἐστίν. ²⁹οὕτως καὶ ὑμεῖς, ὅταν ἴδητε ταῦτα γινόμενα, γινώσκετε ὅτι ἐγγύς ἐστιν ἐπὶ θύραις. ³⁰ἀμὴν λέγω ὑμῖν ὅτι οὐ μὴ παρέλθῃ ἡ γενεὰ αὕτη μέχρις οὗ ταῦτα πάντα

---

27. *Messengers:* some MSS read *his messengers.*

---

the Syrian king Antiochus Epiphanes in 168 B.C.E. (1 Macc 1:54, 59). *It:* could be read in Greek as a veiled reference to a human figure, such as a Roman general—Pompey had entered the temple in 63 B.C.E., and Titus led its destruction in 70 C.E. *The reader had better figure out what this means:* Mark's most explicit comment to the reader (§3.6) suggests veiled language that needs interpreting, possibly a note for the person who reads this to the congregation. *Head for the hills:* begins concrete advice that could be for war-time refugees (§1.3).

- **13:18.** Winter can bring snow and freezing weather. In Josephus' account (§1.3), during the winter of 67–68 C.E., as the Roman

army marched south toward Jerusalem after taking control of Galilee, a coalition of "zealots" from the countryside took over the temple area as its headquarters (see 11:17). In the bloody fighting that followed among local factions, many residents fled, including both Christians and adherents of the Pharisees.

- **13:19.** This description is the same as the last days in Dan 12:1.
- **13:22.** A similar warning is given in Deut 13:1–3 against prophets who provide "portents or miracles." This expression, traditionally translated "signs and wonders," is used mostly in the Old Testament for the plagues performed against Pharaoh by the prophet Moses as divine events signalling

the roof should go downstairs; no one should enter the house to retrieve anything; [16]and no one in the field should turn back to get a coat. [17]It's too bad for pregnant women and for nursing mothers in those days! [18]Pray that none of this happens in winter! [19]For those days will see distress the likes of which has not occurred since God created the world until now, and will never occur again. [20]And if the Lord had not cut short the days, no human being would have survived! But he did shorten the days for the sake of the chosen people whom he selected. [21]And then if someone says to you, 'Look, here is the Anointed,' or 'Look, there he is!' don't count on it! [22]After all, counterfeit messiahs and phony prophets will show up, and they will provide portents and miracles so as to delude, if possible, even the chosen people. [23]But you be on your guard! Notice how I always warn you about these things in advance.

[24]"But in those days, after that tribulation,

Son of Adam comes on clouds

the sun will be darkened,
and the moon will not give off her glow,
[25]and the stars will fall from the sky,
and the heavenly forces will be shaken!

[26]And then they will see the son of Adam coming on the clouds with great power and splendor. [27]And then he will send out messengers and will gather the chosen people from the four winds, from the ends of the earth to the edge of the sky!

[28]"Take a cue from the fig tree. When its branch is already in bud and leaves come out, you know that summer is near. [29]So, when you see these things take place, you ought to realize that he is near, just outside your door. [30]I swear to you, this generation certainly won't pass into oblivion before all these things

---

the exodus. *Portent* suggests not just the visual evidence of a "sign" (8:11–12; 13:4), but a signal for something significant about to happen. *Miracle* here refers to the extraordinary nature of those same events. In contrast, "miracle" used for the deeds of Jesus suggests Jesus' ability (6:2).

• **13:24–25.** The darkening of the heavenly bodies is a common theme of the last days: "the sun and moon shall be darkened" (Joel 2:10 LXX); "the moon shall not give off her light" (Isa 13:10); "all the stars shall fall like leaves" (Isa 34:4 LXX); "I will cover the sun with a cloud, and the moon will not give her light" (Ezek 32:7).

• **13:26.** *The son of Adam coming on the clouds*: a description from Dan 7:13 of a

human figure who represents "the holy ones" and approaches "the Ancient One" to receive "dominion and kingship" (§6:4). Only later does this image get interpreted as someone *returning*, whom Christians identified with Jesus (discussed at 2:10).

• **13:27.** The imagery from Daniel continues: messengers gather *the chosen* from exile, because it is "the holy ones" who receive "the kingdom forever" (Dan 7:18).

• **13:28.** *Take a cue*: the root meaning of Greek *parabole* (§6.5) is to make a comparison.

• **13:29.** *He*: the son of Adam (v. 26).

• **13:30.** *I swear to you*: an oath-like formula used to express strong convictions (§5.2). *This generation*: Mark was convinced that

γένηται. ³¹ὁ οὐρανὸς καὶ ἡ γῆ παρελεύσονται, οἱ δὲ λόγοι μου οὐ μὴ παρελεύσονται.

No one knows the day or minute

³²Περὶ δὲ τῆς ἡμέρας ἐκείνης ἢ τῆς ὥρας οὐδεὶς οἶδεν, οὐδὲ οἱ ἄγγελοι ἐν οὐρανῷ οὐδὲ ὁ υἱός, εἰ μὴ ὁ πατήρ.

³³Βλέπετε ἀγρυπνεῖτε· οὐκ οἴδατε γὰρ πότε ὁ καιρός ἐστιν. ³⁴ὡς ἄνθρωπος ἀπόδημος ἀφεὶς τὴν οἰκίαν αὐτοῦ καὶ δοὺς τοῖς δούλοις αὐτοῦ τὴν ἐξουσίαν, ἑκάστῳ τὸ ἔργον αὐτοῦ, καὶ τῷ θυρωρῷ ἐνετείλατο ἵνα γρηγορῇ. ³⁵γρηγορεῖτε οὖν, οὐκ οἴδατε γὰρ πότε ὁ κύριος τῆς οἰκίας ἔρχεται, ἢ ὀψὲ ἢ μεσονύκτιον ἢ ἀλεκτοροφωνίας ἢ πρωΐ, ³⁶μὴ ἐλθὼν ἐξαίφνης εὕρῃ ὑμᾶς καθεύδοντας. ³⁷ὃ δὲ ὑμῖν λέγω, πᾶσιν λέγω, γρηγορεῖτε.

---

33. *Stay alert:* many MSS add *and pray.*

---

his generation lived to see what Jesus was talking about.

• **13:31.** The Judean rabbis used to say that earth and sky would come to an end, but the Torah has no end.

• **13:32.** *Heaven's messengers:* those who would have to know before anyone on earth would.

• **13:35.** *Landlord:* Greek *kyrios* is also *lord* or *master* (§6.4).

At right. *Arch of Titus,* Rome. Titus' victory in the Roman-Judean War, 66–70 C.E., was celebrated in stone with a grand arch in the Forum in Rome. Inside the arch a triumphal procession is represented carrying the seven member gold lampstand from the Temple of Jerusalem. Photograph: Daryl D. Schmidt.

take place! [31]The earth will pass into oblivion and so will the sky, but my words will never be obliterated!

[32]"As for that exact day or minute: no one knows, not even heaven's messengers, nor even the son, no one, except the Father.

No one knows the day or minute

[33]"Be on guard! Stay alert! For you never know what time it is. [34]It's like a person who takes a trip and puts slaves in charge, each with a task, and enjoins the doorkeeper to be alert. [35]Therefore, stay alert! For you never know when the landlord returns, maybe at dusk, or at midnight, or when the rooster crows, or maybe early in the morning. [36]He may return suddenly and find you asleep. [37]What I'm telling you, I say to everyone: Stay alert!"

Woman
anoints Jesus

14 °Ἦν δὲ τὸ πάσχα καὶ τὰ ἄζυμα μετὰ δύο ἡμέρας. καὶ
ἐζήτουν οἱ ἀρχιερεῖς καὶ οἱ γραμματεῖς πῶς αὐτὸν ἐν δόλῳ
κρατήσαντες ἀποκτείνωσιν· ²ἔλεγον γάρ, Μὴ ἐν τῇ ἑορτῇ,
μήποτε ἔσται θόρυβος τοῦ λαοῦ.

³Καὶ ὄντος αὐτοῦ ἐν Βηθανίᾳ ἐν τῇ οἰκίᾳ Σίμωνος τοῦ λεπροῦ
κατακειμένου αὐτοῦ ἦλθεν γυνὴ ἔχουσα ἀλάβαστρον μύρου
νάρδου πιστικῆς πολυτελοῦς· συντρίψασα τὴν ἀλάβαστρον
κατέχεεν αὐτοῦ τῆς κεφαλῆς.

⁴Ἦσαν δέ τινες ἀγανακτοῦντες πρὸς ἑαυτούς, Εἰς τί ἡ
ἀπώλεια αὕτη τοῦ μύρου γέγονεν; ⁵ἠδύνατο γὰρ τοῦτο τὸ μύρον
πραθῆναι ἐπάνω δηναρίων τριακοσίων καὶ δοθῆναι τοῖς πτωχοῖς·
καὶ ἐνεβριμῶντο αὐτῇ.

⁶Ὁ δὲ Ἰησοῦς εἶπεν, Ἄφετε αὐτήν· τί αὐτῇ κόπους
παρέχετε; καλὸν ἔργον ἠργάσατο ἐν ἐμοί. ⁷πάντοτε γὰρ τοὺς
πτωχοὺς ἔχετε μεθ' ἑαυτῶν, καὶ ὅταν θέλητε δύνασθε αὐτοῖς εὖ
ποιῆσαι, ἐμὲ δὲ οὐ πάντοτε ἔχετε. ⁸ὃ ἔσχεν ἐποίησεν· προέλαβεν
μυρίσαι τὸ σῶμά μου εἰς τὸν ἐνταφιασμόν. ⁹ἀμὴν δὲ λέγω ὑμῖν,
ὅπου ἐὰν κηρυχθῇ τὸ εὐαγγέλιον εἰς ὅλον τὸν κόσμον, καὶ ὃ
ἐποίησεν αὕτη λαληθήσεται εἰς μνημόσυνον αὐτῆς.

Priests promise
to pay

¹⁰Καὶ Ἰούδας Ἰσκαριὼθ ὁ εἷς τῶν δώδεκα ἀπῆλθεν πρὸς τοὺς
ἀρχιερεῖς ἵνα αὐτὸν παραδοῖ αὐτοῖς. ¹¹οἱ δὲ ἀκούσαντες
ἐχάρησαν καὶ ἐπηγγείλαντο αὐτῷ ἀργύριον δοῦναι. καὶ ἐζήτει
πῶς αὐτὸν εὐκαίρως παραδοῖ.

Jesus celebrates
Passover

¹²Καὶ τῇ πρώτῃ ἡμέρᾳ τῶν ἀζύμων, ὅτε τὸ πάσχα ἔθυον,
λέγουσιν αὐτῷ οἱ μαθηταὶ αὐτοῦ, Ποῦ θέλεις ἀπελθόντες
ἑτοιμάσωμεν ἵνα φάγῃς τὸ πάσχα; ¹³Καὶ ἀποστέλλει δύο τῶν μαθητῶν αὐτοῦ καὶ λέγει αὐτοῖς,
Ὑπάγετε εἰς τὴν πόλιν, καὶ ἀπαντήσει ὑμῖν ἄνθρωπος κεράμιον

---

2. *Not during the festival, otherwise:* one important MSS reads *Otherwise
during the festival*, implying they expected a riot to develop if they did
not act.

• **14:1–16:8.** The final sequence of events in
Jesus' life is structured by Mark around the
celebration of Passover. By modern reckon-
ing, this Passover was on a Friday, probably
in 30 C.E.
• **14:1.** *Passover:* begins the week-long *feast of
Unleavened Bread* celebrating the exodus
from slavery (Exod 12:15–20; Deut 16:1–8).
It was the major Israelite/Judean festival,
which each spring attracted many thousands of pilgrims to Jerusalem (estimated as
high as 100,000, in addition to the per-
manent population of about 30,000). *Ranking priests and scholars:* the members of the
Council (v. 53) whom Mark holds most
responsible for the arrest of Jesus.

• **14:2.** *Their slogan:* captures this as Mark's
caricature of the kind of reasoning the
religious authorities must have used in
finally deciding to act.
• **14:3.** This scene seems full of irony (§3.5):
poured on his head finally makes Jesus *the
Anointed* (1:1), but it takes place in the
house of a leper (1:40), who happens to be
named Simon (3:16), and is performed by a
woman (5:34). These circumstances are
especially fitting for the kind of story Mark
is telling, where lepers and women respond
to an anointed one who is destined for
crucifixion. But then in this story, "everything is in parables/riddles" (4:11). *Myrrh:*
fragrant plant derivative used for both per-

14 Now it was two days until Passover and the feast of Unleavened Bread. And the ranking priests and the scholars were looking for some way to arrest him by trickery and kill him. ²For their slogan was: "Not during the festival, otherwise the people will riot."

³When he was in Bethany at the house of Simon the leper, he was just reclining there, and a woman came in carrying an alabaster jar of myrrh, of pure and expensive nard. She broke the jar and poured ⟨the myrrh⟩ on his head.

⁴Now some were annoyed ⟨and thought⟩ to themselves: "What good purpose is served by this waste of myrrh? ⁵For she could have sold the myrrh for more than three hundred silver coins and given ⟨the money⟩ to the poor." And they were angry with her.

⁶Then Jesus said, "Let her alone! Why are you bothering her? She has done me a courtesy. ⁷Remember, there will always be poor around, and whenever you want you can do good for them, but I won't always be around. ⁸She did what she could—she anticipates in anointing my body for burial. ⁹So help me, wherever the good news is announced in all the world, what she has done will also be told in memory of her!"

¹⁰And Judas Iscariot, one of the twelve, went off to the ranking priests to turn him over to them. ¹¹When they heard, they were delighted, and promised to pay him in silver. And he started looking for some way to turn him in at the right moment.

¹²On the first day of Unleavened Bread, when they would sacrifice the Passover lamb, his disciples say to him, "Where do you want us to go and get things ready for you to celebrate Passover?"

¹³He sends two of his disciples and says to them, "Go into the city, and someone carrying a waterpot will meet you. Follow

Woman anoints Jesus

Priests promise to pay

Jesus celebrates Passover

---

fume and embalming, which may add to Mark's irony that this is anointing for burial (v. 8). *Nard*: made from parts of the spikenard herb grown in Asia.

- **14:5.** *More than three hundred silver coins*: about a year's wages (6:30).
- **14:7.** *There will always be poor around*: echoes Deut 15:11, "the poor will not cease from the land."
- **14:8.** *Anointing*: not from the same Greek as "the Anointed," but it captures well the irony. The ritual just performed (v. 3), imitative of a royal coronation, is now reinterpreted as preparation for death.
- **14:9.** *So help me*: introduces a solemn declaration (§5.2).

- **14:10.** Judas fulfills his prescribed role (3:19).
- **14:12.** *The first day of Unleavened Bread*: properly began with Passover, at sundown, according to the Judean calendar. However, Mark appears to mean "on the day when Passover would begin," which views it from the perspective of the Roman calendar. *When they would sacrifice the Passover lamb*: the Judean "day of preparation," when all arrangements are made for the evening Passover meal, including the proper slaughter of the Passover lambs by the temple priests.

ὕδατος βαστάζων· ἀκολουθήσατε αὐτῷ, ¹⁴καὶ ὅπου ἐὰν εἰσέλθῃ
εἴπατε τῷ οἰκοδεσπότῃ ὅτι ʽΟ διδάσκαλος λέγει, Ποῦ ἐστιν τὸ
κατάλυμά μου ὅπου τὸ πάσχα μετὰ τῶν μαθητῶν μου φάγω;
¹⁵καὶ αὐτὸς ὑμῖν δείξει ἀνάγαιον μέγα ἐστρωμένον ἕτοιμον· καὶ
ἐκεῖ ἑτοιμάσατε ἡμῖν.
¹⁶Καὶ ἐξῆλθον οἱ μαθηταὶ καὶ ἦλθον εἰς τὴν πόλιν καὶ εὗρον
καθὼς εἶπεν αὐτοῖς, καὶ ἡτοίμασαν τὸ πάσχα.
¹⁷Καὶ ὀψίας γενομένης ἔρχεται μετὰ τῶν δώδεκα. ¹⁸καὶ
ἀνακειμένων αὐτῶν καὶ ἐσθιόντων ὁ ᾽Ιησοῦς εἶπεν, ᾽Αμὴν λέγω
ὑμῖν ὅτι εἷς ἐξ ὑμῶν παραδώσει με, ὁ ἐσθίων μετ᾽ ἐμοῦ.
¹⁹῏Ηρξαντο λυπεῖσθαι καὶ λέγειν αὐτῷ εἷς κατὰ εἷς, Μήτι
ἐγώ;
²⁰ʽΟ δὲ εἶπεν αὐτοῖς, Εἷς ἐκ τῶν δώδεκα, ὁ ἐμβαπτόμενος μετ᾽
ἐμοῦ εἰς τὸ τρύβλιον. ²¹ὅτι ὁ μὲν υἱὸς τοῦ ἀνθρώπου ὑπάγει
καθὼς γέγραπται περὶ αὐτοῦ, οὐαὶ δὲ τῷ ἀνθρώπῳ ἐκείνῳ δι᾽ οὗ ὁ
υἱὸς τοῦ ἀνθρώπου παραδίδοται· καλὸν αὐτῷ εἰ οὐκ ἐγεννήθη ὁ
ἄνθρωπος ἐκεῖνος.
²²Καὶ ἐσθιόντων αὐτῶν λαβὼν ἄρτον εὐλογήσας ἔκλασεν καὶ
ἔδωκεν αὐτοῖς καὶ εἶπεν, Λάβετε, τοῦτό ἐστιν τὸ σῶμά μου. ²³καὶ
λαβὼν ποτήριον εὐχαριστήσας ἔδωκεν αὐτοῖς, καὶ ἔπιον ἐξ
αὐτοῦ πάντες. ²⁴καὶ εἶπεν αὐτοῖς, Τοῦτό ἐστιν τὸ αἷμά μου τῆς
διαθήκης τὸ ἐκχυννόμενον ὑπὲρ πολλῶν· ²⁵ἀμὴν λέγω ὑμῖν ὅτι
οὐκέτι οὐ μὴ πίω ἐκ τοῦ γενήματος τῆς ἀμπέλου ἕως τῆς ἡμέρας
ἐκείνης ὅταν αὐτὸ πίνω καινὸν ἐν τῇ βασιλείᾳ τοῦ θεοῦ.
²⁶Καὶ ὑμνήσαντες ἐξῆλθον εἰς τὸ ῎Ορος τῶν ᾽Ελαιῶν.

*Peter takes
an oath*

²⁷Καὶ λέγει αὐτοῖς ὁ ᾽Ιησοῦς ὅτι Πάντες σκανδαλισθήσεσθε,
ὅτι γέγραπται, Πατάξω τὸν ποιμένα, καὶ τὰ πρόβατα

---

20. *Into the bowl:* some MSS read *into the one bowl*, emphasizing the
intimacy of the group.   24. *Covenant:* some MSS read *new covenant* as in
Luke 22:20; 1 Cor 11:25.   25. *Again:* omitted in some MSS.

• **14:14.** *My guest room:* implies prior arrangement has been made, a necessity given the
large crowds (v. 1).
• **14:15.** *Upstairs room:* the "guest room" of a
large house, where guests are entertained,
or a room on the roof with outside access
(2:4). *Arranged:* probably means *furnished*,
with rugs and cushions.
• **14:17.** *When evening comes:* Passover, like
all days for Judeans, begins at sundown.
• **14:18.** *As they reclined at table:* the common
custom (2:15), especially for Passover. *One
of you. . .is going to turn me in:* as had been
forecast for "the son of Adam" (10:33; §4.11)
• **14:20.** *The one who is:* or *One who is.* The

Greek construction is the same as v. 18,
"One of you eating with me," implying
anyone of the group. It is unclear whether
v. 20 should be read as parallel to that,
"One of the twelve dipping into the bowl
with me," or as specifying which of the
twelve, namely, "the one who is. . . ." The
usual Passover custom was for a separate
bowl for each person, with a mixture of
dried fruit, spices and vinegar for dipping
the bitter herbs.
• **14:21.** *As the scriptures predict:* not explicitly, but in the same sense as at 9:12, that
Christians had scriptural explanations for
what happened to Jesus.

him, ¹⁴and whatever place he enters say to the head of the
house, 'The teacher asks, "Where is my guest room where I can
celebrate Passover with my disciples?"' ¹⁵And he'll show you a
large upstairs room that has been arranged. That's the place
you're to get ready for us."

¹⁶And the disciples left, went into the city, and found it
exactly as he had told them; and they got things ready for
Passover.

¹⁷When evening comes, he arrives with the twelve. ¹⁸And as
they reclined at table and were eating, Jesus said, "So help me,
one of you eating with me is going to turn me in!"

¹⁹They began to fret and to say to him one after another, "I'm
not the one, am I?"

²⁰But he said to them, "It's one of the twelve, the one who is
dipping into the bowl with me. ²¹The son of Adam departs just
as the scriptures predict, but damn the one responsible for
turning the son of Adam in! It would be better for that man had
he never been born!"

²²And as they were eating, he took a loaf, gave a blessing,
broke it into pieces and offered it to them. And he said, "Have
some, this is my body!" ²³And he took a cup, gave thanks and
gave it to them, and they all drank from it. ²⁴And he said to
them: "This is my blood of the covenant, which has been
poured out for many! ²⁵So help me, I certainly won't drink any
of the fruit of the vine again until that day when I drink it for the
first time in God's domain!"

²⁶And they sang a hymn and left for the Mount of Olives.

²⁷And Jesus says to them, "You will all lose faith. Remember,
scripture says, 'I will strike the shepherd and the sheep will be

*Peter takes
an oath*

- **14:22.** The sequence of actions is exactly
the same as at the feeding stories (6:41,
where the traditional blessing is noted; 8:6).
- **14:23.** A proper Passover meal includes two
cups of wine, one both before (as in Luke
22:17) and after the meal. The traditional
thanksgiving offered each time is, "Blessed
are you, O Lord our God, Ruler of the
universe, who creates the fruit of the vine."
- **14:24.** *Blood of the covenant*: language from
the ceremony in Exod 24:8, which Moses
performed as a binding commitment between Yahweh and the people. Moses and
his inner circle then went up the mountain,
"saw God" and "ate and drank" (Exod
24:9-11). *Poured out for many*: may reflect
Isa 53:12, "he bore the sins of many," an
important text in early Christian interpretation of the crucifixion (see Mark 10:45, "a
ransom for many").

- **14:25.** This solemn declaration (v. 9), after
the last cup of wine (v. 23), is in the form
of an oath of abstinence: Jesus vows that his
next cup of wine will be in *God's domain*.
Jesus elsewhere associates "God's imperial
rule" with a banquet (2:19), an image the
prophets used for celebrating the messianic
age in Zion: "On this mountain the Lord of
hosts will make for all peoples. . .a feast of
well-aged wines" (Isa 25:6).
- **14:26.** *Sang a hymn*: the Passover meal
concludes with Psalms 115-118 (already
used in Mark 11:9).
- **14:27.** *Lose faith*: recalls "easily shaken"
when distress comes, the description of
those "sown on rocky ground" (4:17).
Ironically, it is Peter, "the Rock," who
quickly protests that it won't happen to him
(v. 29), but indeed, "they *all* deserted" Jesus
(v. 50). *Scripture says*: Zech 13:7, "Strike

διασκορπισθήσονται· ²⁸ ἀλλὰ μετὰ τὸ ἐγερθῆναί με προάξω ὑμᾶς εἰς τὴν Γαλιλαίαν.

²⁹ Ὁ δὲ Πέτρος ἔφη αὐτῷ, Εἰ καὶ πάντες σκανδαλισθήσονται, ἀλλ᾽ οὐκ ἐγώ.

³⁰ Καὶ λέγει αὐτῷ ὁ Ἰησοῦς, Ἀμὴν λέγω σοι ὅτι σὺ σήμερον ταύτῃ τῇ νυκτὶ πρὶν ἢ δὶς ἀλέκτορα φωνῆσαι τρίς με ἀπαρνήσῃ. ³¹ Ὁ δὲ ἐκπερισσῶς ἐλάλει, Ἐὰν δέῃ με συναποθανεῖν σοι, οὐ μή σε ἀπαρνήσομαι. ὡσαύτως δὲ καὶ πάντες ἔλεγον.

Jesus in Gethsemane

³² Καὶ ἔρχονται εἰς χωρίον οὗ τὸ ὄνομα Γεθσημανί, καὶ λέγει τοῖς μαθηταῖς αὐτοῦ, Καθίσατε ὧδε ἕως προσεύξωμαι.

³³ Καὶ παραλαμβάνει τὸν Πέτρον καὶ Ἰάκωβον καὶ Ἰωάννην μετ᾽ αὐτοῦ, καὶ ἤρξατο ἐκθαμβεῖσθαι καὶ ἀδημονεῖν, ³⁴ καὶ λέγει αὐτοῖς, Περίλυπός ἐστιν ἡ ψυχή μου ἕως θανάτου· μείνατε ὧδε καὶ γρηγορεῖτε.

³⁵ Καὶ προελθὼν μικρὸν ἔπιπτεν ἐπὶ τῆς γῆς, καὶ προσηύχετο ἵνα εἰ δυνατόν ἐστιν παρέλθῃ ἀπ᾽ αὐτοῦ ἡ ὥρα, ³⁶ καὶ ἔλεγεν, Ἀββα ὁ πατήρ, πάντα δυνατά σοι· παρένεγκε τὸ ποτήριον τοῦτο ἀπ᾽ ἐμοῦ· ἀλλ᾽ οὐ τί ἐγὼ θέλω ἀλλὰ τί σύ.

³⁷ Καὶ ἔρχεται καὶ εὑρίσκει αὐτοὺς καθεύδοντας, καὶ λέγει τῷ Πέτρῳ, Σίμων, καθεύδεις; οὐκ ἴσχυσας μίαν ὥραν γρηγορῆσαι; ³⁸ γρηγορεῖτε καὶ προσεύχεσθε, ἵνα μὴ ἔλθητε εἰς πειρασμόν· τὸ μὲν πνεῦμα πρόθυμον ἡ δὲ σὰρξ ἀσθενής.

³⁹ Καὶ πάλιν ἀπελθὼν προσηύξατο τὸν αὐτὸν λόγον εἰπών. ⁴⁰ καὶ πάλιν ἐλθὼν εὗρεν αὐτοὺς καθεύδοντας, ἦσαν γὰρ αὐτῶν οἱ ὀφθαλμοὶ καταβαρυνόμενοι, καὶ οὐκ ᾔδεισαν τί ἀποκριθῶσιν αὐτῷ.

⁴¹ Καὶ ἔρχεται τὸ τρίτον καὶ λέγει αὐτοῖς, Καθεύδετε τὸ λοιπὸν καὶ ἀναπαύεσθε· ἀπέχει· ἦλθεν ἡ ὥρα, ἰδοὺ παραδίδοται ὁ υἱὸς τοῦ ἀνθρώπου εἰς τὰς χεῖρας τῶν ἁμαρτωλῶν. ⁴² ἐγείρεσθε ἄγωμεν· ἰδοὺ ὁ παραδιδούς με ἤγγικεν.

---

30. *Twice:* omitted in some MSS; not in Matthew or Luke.   **31.** *I will never:* some MSS, *I would never* or *I certainly won't* (§5.2).   **41.** *It's all over:* some MSS add *the end,* maybe in the sense, "Can the end be far away?" or "The end is pressing!"

---

the shepherd, and the sheep will be scattered," which makes them *sheep without a shepherd* (6:34). This Old Testament theme is used here to forecast the disciples' desertion.

• **14:28.** *I'll go ahead of you:* means either (or both) *I'll lead you* or *I'll precede you.*

• **14:30.** *Disown me:* the opposite of *deny themselves. . .and follow me,* the definition of disciples (8:34).

• **14:31.** *With more bluster:* translates a word,

apparently rarely used in ancient Greek literature, that suggests "excessively." It is related to another rare word in Mark, translated "completely" (7:37). *The same oath:* calls attention to the oath-like language Peter just used.

• **14:32.** *Gethsemane:* meaning "oil press" in Hebrew, an uncertain location somewhere on or near the Mount of Olives.

• **14:34.** *I'm so sad I could die:* echoes the lament of someone facing death in Ps 42:5,

scattered!' [28]But after I'm raised I'll go ahead of you to Galilee."

[29]Peter said to him, "Even if everyone else loses faith, I won't!"

[30]And Jesus says to him, "So help me, tonight before the rooster crows twice you will disown me three times!"

[31]But he repeated it with more bluster: "If they condemn me to die with you, I will never disown you!" And they took the same oath, all of them.

[32]And they go to a place the name of which was Gethsemane, and he says to his disciples, "Sit down here while I pray."

Jesus in Gethsemane

[33]And he takes Peter and James and John along with him, and he grew apprehensive and full of anguish. [34]He says to them, "I'm so sad I could die. You stay here and be alert!"

[35]And he would move on a little, fall on the ground, and pray that he might avoid the crisis, if possible. [36]And he would say, "**Abba** (Father), all things are possible for you! Take this cup away from me! But it's not what I want ⟨that matters⟩, but what you want."

[37]And he returns and finds them sleeping, and says to Peter, "Simon, are you sleeping? Couldn't you stay awake for one hour? [38]Be alert and pray that you won't be put to the test! Though the spirit is willing, the flesh is weak."

[39]And once again he went away and prayed, saying the same thing. [40]And once again he came and found them sleeping, since their eyes had grown very heavy, and they didn't know what to say to him.

[41]And he comes a third time and says to them, "You may as well sleep on now and get your rest. It's all over! The time has come! Look, the son of Adam is being turned over to foreigners. [42]Get up, let's go! See for yourselves! Here comes the one who is going to turn me in."

"Why am I so sad?" and Jonah 4:9 LXX, "I am so very saddened, I could die."

- **14:36.** *Abba*: Aramaic, Jesus' native language (see 5:41), for *father*; elsewhere preserved only by Paul (Rom 8:15; Gal 4:6). Judean family members used this term in the sense of "Dad," but there is very little evidence that they may have used it this way in prayers. The Greek equivalent *pater* is used in prayers in the Apocrypha (Wis 14:3; Sir 23:1, 4, "O Lord, Father and God of my life;" 3 Macc 6:3, 8). Also, the relationship between the anointed king and God was officially explained as, "I will be a father to him and he shall be a son to me" (2 Sam 7:14). *This cup*: symbolic of anticipated suffering, which Jesus had already

promised the disciples (10:38–39).
- **14:38.** *You*: Greek shifts to plural from the singular *you* in v. 37. *Put to the test*: typically part of the scenario of the last days, "Many must be tested" (Dan 12:10), and also part of the Lord's Prayer tradition (Matt 6:13; Luke 11:4). *The spirit is willing*: in the sense of "eager."
- **14:41.** *You may as well sleep on and get your rest*: interprets this scene as Jesus expressing resignation. The possibility of reading this as a question, *Still sleeping and taking a rest?*, is less well suited to the context. *It's all over*: a one-word Greek sentence whose precise meaning is uncertain. In the business world it meant "(It's) paid in full;" another metaphor might be

⁴³Καὶ εὐθὺς ἔτι αὐτοῦ λαλοῦντος παραγίνεται Ἰούδας εἷς τῶν δώδεκα καὶ μετ' αὐτοῦ ὄχλος μετὰ μαχαιρῶν καὶ ξύλων παρὰ τῶν ἀρχιερέων καὶ τῶν γραμματέων καὶ τῶν πρεσβυτέρων. ⁴⁴δεδώκει δὲ ὁ παραδιδοὺς αὐτὸν σύσσημον αὐτοῖς λέγων, Ὃν ἂν φιλήσω αὐτός ἐστιν· κρατήσατε αὐτὸν καὶ ἀπάγετε ἀσφαλῶς. ⁴⁵καὶ ἐλθὼν εὐθὺς προσελθὼν αὐτῷ λέγει, Ραββί, καὶ κατεφίλησεν αὐτόν.

⁴⁶Οἱ δὲ ἐπέβαλον τὰς χεῖρας αὐτῷ καὶ ἐκράτησαν αὐτόν. ⁴⁷εἷς δέ τις τῶν παρεστηκότων σπασάμενος τὴν μάχαιραν ἔπαισεν τὸν δοῦλον τοῦ ἀρχιερέως καὶ ἀφεῖλεν αὐτοῦ τὸ ὠτάριον. ⁴⁸καὶ ἀποκριθεὶς ὁ Ἰησοῦς εἶπεν αὐτοῖς, Ὡς ἐπὶ λῃστὴν ἐξήλθατε μετὰ μαχαιρῶν καὶ ξύλων συλλαβεῖν με; ⁴⁹καθ' ἡμέραν ἤμην πρὸς ὑμᾶς ἐν τῷ ἱερῷ διδάσκων καὶ οὐκ ἐκρατήσατέ με· ἀλλ' ἵνα πληρωθῶσιν αἱ γραφαί.

⁵⁰Καὶ ἀφέντες αὐτὸν ἔφυγον πάντες. ⁵¹καὶ νεανίσκος τις συνηκολούθει αὐτῷ περιβεβλημένος σινδόνα ἐπὶ γυμνοῦ, καὶ κρατοῦσιν αὐτόν· ⁵²ὁ δὲ καταλιπὼν τὴν σινδόνα γυμνὸς ἔφυγεν.

⁵³Καὶ ἀπήγαγον τὸν Ἰησοῦν πρὸς τὸν ἀρχιερέα, καὶ συνέρχονται πάντες οἱ ἀρχιερεῖς καὶ οἱ πρεσβύτεροι καὶ οἱ γραμματεῖς.

⁵⁴Καὶ ὁ Πέτρος ἀπὸ μακρόθεν ἠκολούθησεν αὐτῷ ἕως ἔσω εἰς τὴν αὐλὴν τοῦ ἀρχιερέως, καὶ ἦν συγκαθήμενος μετὰ τῶν ὑπηρετῶν καὶ θερμαινόμενος πρὸς τὸ φῶς.

⁵⁵Οἱ δὲ ἀρχιερεῖς καὶ ὅλον τὸ συνέδριον ἐζήτουν κατὰ τοῦ Ἰησοῦ μαρτυρίαν εἰς τὸ θανατῶσαι αὐτόν, καὶ οὐχ ηὕρισκον· ⁵⁶πολλοὶ γὰρ ἐψευδομαρτύρουν κατ' αὐτοῦ, καὶ ἴσαι αἱ μαρτυρίαι οὐκ ἦσαν. ⁵⁷καί τινες ἀναστάντες ἐψευδομαρτύρουν κατ' αὐτοῦ λέγοντες ⁵⁸ὅτι Ἡμεῖς ἠκούσαμεν αὐτοῦ λέγοντος ὅτι Ἐγὼ καταλύσω τὸν ναὸν τοῦτον τὸν χειροποίητον καὶ διὰ

"This chapter is closed;" another suggestion has been, "Enough of this!" *Son of Adam is being turned over to foreigners*: summarizes the prediction in 10:33. The language here is similar to the judgment announced in Ezek 11:9, "I will turn you over to the hands of strangers" (§4.11).

• **14:43.** *Ranking priests, scholars, elders*: the authorities who make up the Sanhedrin, the high council in Jerusalem (v. 53).

• **14:45.** *Rabbi*: Hebrew for "my master," used especially for teachers; elsewhere only Peter addresses Jesus this way (9:5; 11:21).

• **14:48.** *A common rebel*: the type of "crook" who misuses the temple area (11:17). It was also used as a politically derogatory label (15:27), later given to the revolutionaries of the Roman-Judean War.

• **14:49.** *But the scriptures must come true*: an awkward construction in Greek that is grammatically not a complete sentence. The initial "but" is similar to 13:24, although here it is followed by a conjunction that usually means, "so that," which functions as a dependent clause, the way it is in Matt 26:56, *All of this happened so the writings of the prophets would come true.* The statement in Mark seems meant as a general claim about the whole passion story (§2.8; §4.11), without any particular text in mind, as elsewhere in Mark (9:12–13; 14:21). It is also possible to read this not as something Jesus says but as an editorial comment, the way Matthew interpreted it. However, it is fitting for Mark's Jesus, who just said, "It's all over" (v. 41).

• **14:51–52.** *Shroud*: linen cloth used especially for wrapping dead bodies, including Jesus' (15:46). *They grab him*, the same way they had earlier "seized" Jesus (v. 46). The

⁴³And right away, while he was still speaking, Judas, one of the twelve, shows up, and with him a crowd, dispatched by the ranking priests and the scholars and the elders, wielding swords and clubs. ⁴⁴Now the one who was to turn him in had arranged a signal with them, saying, "The one I'm going to kiss is the one you want. Arrest him and escort him safely away!" ⁴⁵And right away he arrives, comes up to him, and says, "Rabbi," and kissed him.

*Judas turns
Jesus in*

⁴⁶And they seized him and held him fast. ⁴⁷One of those standing around drew his sword and struck the high priest's slave and cut off his ear. ⁴⁸In response Jesus said to them, "Have you come out to take me with swords and clubs as though you were apprehending a rebel? ⁴⁹I was with you in the temple area day after day teaching and you didn't lift a hand against me. But the scriptures must come true!"

⁵⁰And they all deserted him and ran away. ⁵¹And a youth was following him, wearing a shroud over his nude body, and they grab him. ⁵²But he dropped the shroud and ran away naked.

⁵³And they brought Jesus before the high priest, and all the ranking priests and elders and scholars assemble.

*Trial before
the Council*

⁵⁴Peter followed him at a distance until he was inside the courtyard of the high priest, and was sitting with the attendants and keeping warm by the fire.

⁵⁵The ranking priests and the whole Council were looking for evidence against Jesus in order to issue a death sentence, but they couldn't find any. ⁵⁶Although many gave false evidence against him, their stories didn't agree. ⁵⁷And some people stood up and testified falsely against him: ⁵⁸"We have heard him saying, 'I'll destroy this temple made with hands and in three

---

youth escaping the death shroud seems to anticipate symbolically Jesus' escape from a similar shroud at the end of the story. It also echoes Amos 2:16, "The naked shall flee on that day."

• **14:53.** *The high priest*: chief official over all temple activities, and president of the Council (v. 55), the highest administrative office in Judean religion. During the Roman occupation of Judea, the Roman governor selected the high priest from among a few aristocratic priestly families. Caiaphas (Matt 26:3, 57; John 18:13, 24) was high priest from 18–37 c.e. *The ranking priests*: from the same aristocratic families, the other members, probably about 10, of the executive committee of the Council, the high priest's administrative cabinet for all temple affairs.

• **14:54.** *Attendants*: probably the high priest's

servants, which could include temple guards.

• **14:55.** *Issue a death sentence*: the Council's authority over capital offenses would have been restricted to internal Judean affairs. The only death sentence they could give was for blasphemy (v. 64).

• **14:58.** *We have heard him saying*: not reported anywhere in Mark, but repeated by the taunters (15:29). *Temple made with hands/not made with hands*: probably derived from the way Christians outside Judea contrasted themselves with Judeans as "the temple of the living God" (2 Cor 6:16), "a more perfect tabernacle not made with hands, that is, not of this creation" (Heb 9:11). *In three days*: a reference to the resurrection, the beginning of the Christian community. Mark's Christian readers would then hear this as another irony; the "false"

τριῶν ἡμερῶν ἄλλον ἀχειροποίητον οἰκοδομήσω· 59καὶ οὐδὲ οὕτως ἴση ἦν ἡ μαρτυρία αὐτῶν.

60Καὶ ἀναστὰς ὁ ἀρχιερεὺς εἰς μέσον ἐπηρώτησεν τὸν Ἰησοῦν λέγων, Οὐκ ἀποκρίνῃ οὐδέν; τί οὗτοί σου καταμαρτυροῦσιν; 61Ὁ δὲ ἐσιώπα καὶ οὐκ ἀπεκρίνατο οὐδέν.

Πάλιν ὁ ἀρχιερεὺς ἐπηρώτα αὐτὸν καὶ λέγει αὐτῷ, Σὺ εἶ ὁ Χριστὸς ὁ υἱὸς τοῦ εὐλογητοῦ; 62Ὁ δὲ Ἰησοῦς εἶπεν, Ἐγώ εἰμι, καὶ ὄψεσθε τὸν υἱὸν τοῦ ἀνθρώπου ἐκ δεξιῶν καθήμενον τῆς δυνάμεως καὶ ἐρχόμενον μετὰ τῶν νεφελῶν τοῦ οὐρανοῦ.

63Ὁ δὲ ἀρχιερεὺς διαρρήξας τοὺς χιτῶνας αὐτοῦ λέγει, Τί ἔτι χρείαν ἔχομεν μαρτύρων; 64ἠκούσατε τῆς βλασφημίας· τί ὑμῖν φαίνεται; οἱ δὲ πάντες κατέκριναν αὐτὸν ἔνοχον εἶναι θανάτου.

65Καὶ ἤρξαντό τινες ἐμπτύειν αὐτῷ καὶ περικαλύπτειν αὐτοῦ τὸ πρόσωπον καὶ κολαφίζειν αὐτὸν καὶ λέγειν αὐτῷ, Προφήτευσον, καὶ οἱ ὑπηρέται ῥαπίσμασιν αὐτὸν ἔλαβον.

A rooster crows　66Καὶ ὄντος τοῦ Πέτρου κάτω ἐν τῇ αὐλῇ ἔρχεται μία τῶν παιδισκῶν τοῦ ἀρχιερέως, 67καὶ ἰδοῦσα τὸν Πέτρον θερμαινόμενον ἐμβλέψασα αὐτῷ λέγει, Καὶ σὺ μετὰ τοῦ Ναζαρηνοῦ ἦσθα τοῦ Ἰησοῦ.

68Ὁ δὲ ἠρνήσατο λέγων, Οὔτε οἶδα οὔτε ἐπίσταμαι σὺ τί λέγεις. καὶ ἐξῆλθεν ἔξω εἰς τὸ προαύλιον.

69Καὶ ἡ παιδίσκη ἰδοῦσα αὐτὸν ἤρξατο πάλιν λέγειν τοῖς παρεστῶσιν ὅτι Οὗτος ἐξ αὐτῶν ἐστιν.

70Ὁ δὲ πάλιν ἠρνεῖτο.

Καὶ μετὰ μικρὸν πάλιν οἱ παρεστῶτες ἔλεγον τῷ Πέτρῳ, Ἀληθῶς ἐξ αὐτῶν εἶ, καὶ γὰρ Γαλιλαῖος εἶ. 71Ὁ δὲ ἤρξατο ἀναθεματίζειν καὶ ὀμνύναι ὅτι Οὐκ οἶδα τὸν ἄνθρωπον τοῦτον ὃν λέγετε. 72καὶ εὐθὺς ἐκ δευτέρου ἀλέκτωρ ἐφώνησεν. καὶ ἀνεμνήσθη ὁ Πέτρος τὸ ῥῆμα ὡς εἶπεν αὐτῷ ὁ Ἰησοῦς ὅτι Πρὶν ἀλέκτορα δὶς φωνῆσαι τρίς με ἀπαρνήσῃ· καὶ ἐπιβαλὼν ἔκλαιεν.

---

67. *Forecourt:* some MSS add *and a rooster crowed.*　　**72.** *A second time:* omitted in some MSS (14:30).

---

accusation against Jesus was true at a level the accusers could not have intended.

• **14:61.** *Refused to answer:* captures the sense of an imperfect tense verb (§6.2), possibly influenced by the description of the one who suffers in Isa 53:7, "He does not open his mouth," even though he had the right to defend himself. *Are you the Anointed:* makes a question out of Peter's earlier statement (8:29). *Son of the Blessed One:* for

Judeans, a pious way to say, "Son of God."

• **14:62.** *I am:* a startling admission after all the secrecy (§4.4), unless the reader remembers an actual anointing has since taken place (14:3). As when Peter initially introduces *the Anointed* (8:29, 31), it is immediately reinterpreted in terms of *the son of Adam* (a term first used at 2:10; §6.4). This time the imagery combines the future messianic figure of Dan 7:13 (13:26) with

days I'll build another, not made with hands!'" ⁵⁹Yet even then their stories did not agree.

⁶⁰And the high priest got up and questioned Jesus: "Don't you have some answer to give? Why do these people testify against you?"

⁶¹But he was silent and refused to answer.

Once again the high priest questioned him and says to him, "Are you the Anointed, the son of the Blessed One?"

⁶²Jesus replied, "I am! And you will see the son of Adam sitting at the right hand of Power and coming with the clouds of the sky!"

⁶³Then the high priest tore his vestments and says, "Why do we still need witnesses? ⁶⁴You have heard the blasphemy! What do you think?" And they all concurred in the death penalty.

⁶⁵And some began to spit on him, and to put a blindfold on him, and punch him, and say to him, "Prophesy!" And the guards abused him as they took him into custody.

⁶⁶And while Peter was below in the courtyard, one of the high priest's slave women comes over, ⁶⁷and sees Peter warming himself; she looks at him closely, then speaks up: "You too were with that Nazarene, Jesus!"

⁶⁸But he denied it, saying, "I haven't the slightest idea what you're talking about!" And he went outside into the forecourt.

⁶⁹And when the slave woman saw him, she once again began to say to those standing nearby, "This fellow is one of them!"

⁷⁰But once again he denied it.

And a little later, those standing nearby would again say to Peter, "You really are one of them, since you also are a Galilean!"

⁷¹But he began to curse and swear, "I don't know the fellow you're talking about!" ⁷²And just then a rooster crowed a second time, and Peter remembered what Jesus had told him: "Before a rooster crows twice you will disown me three times!" And he broke down and started to cry.

A rooster crows

---

the enthronement language of Ps 110:1 (12:36).

• **14:63.** *Tore his vestments*: a prescribed gesture when blasphemy has been heard (Num 14:6; 2 Kgs 18:37).

• **14:64.** *Blasphemy*: the first accusation made against Jesus (2:7) and the only capital offense in Israelite religion (v. 55).

• **14:65.** *Abused him*: physically beat him up.

• **14:67.** *That Nazarene*: the demonstrative *that* captures the very emphatic position this expression has, compared with its earlier use as a modifier (1:24; 10:47).

• **14:68.** *Forecourt*: towards the gate.

• **14:70.** *Galilean*: only here in Mark, interpreted in Matt 26:73 to mean a distinctive accent.

• **14:71.** *Began to curse*: to invoke *anathema*, God's wrath, on someone, "May God do such and such, if. . . ." Traditional translations assume Peter invoked "a curse on himself," but Mark does not so indicate. *And to swear*: generally to the effect, "By God, I'm telling the truth!"

• **14:72.** *Broke down and started to cry*: the first verb in Greek is in an unusual context here, apparently giving the combined sense, "burst into tears."

15 Καὶ εὐθὺς πρωῒ συμβούλιον ποιήσαντες οἱ ἀρχιερεῖς μετὰ τῶν πρεσβυτέρων καὶ γραμματέων καὶ ὅλον τὸ συνέδριον δήσαντες τὸν Ἰησοῦν ἀπήνεγκαν καὶ παρέδωκαν Πιλάτῳ. ²καὶ ἐπηρώτα αὐτὸν ὁ Πιλᾶτος, Σὺ εἶ ὁ βασιλεὺς τῶν Ἰουδαίων; Ὁ δὲ ἀποκριθεὶς αὐτῷ λέγει, Σὺ λέγεις.

³Καὶ κατηγόρουν αὐτοῦ οἱ ἀρχιερεῖς πολλά. ⁴ὁ δὲ Πιλᾶτος πάλιν ἐπηρώτα αὐτὸν λέγων, Οὐκ ἀποκρίνῃ οὐδέν; ἴδε πόσα σου κατηγοροῦσιν.

⁵Ὁ δὲ Ἰησοῦς οὐκέτι οὐδὲν ἀπεκρίθη, ὥστε θαυμάζειν τὸν Πιλᾶτον.

⁶Κατὰ δὲ ἑορτὴν ἀπέλυεν αὐτοῖς ἕνα δέσμιον ὃν παρῃτοῦντο. ⁷ἦν δὲ ὁ λεγόμενος Βαραββᾶς μετὰ τῶν στασιαστῶν δεδεμένος οἵτινες ἐν τῇ στάσει φόνον πεποιήκεισαν. ⁸καὶ ἀναβὰς ὁ ὄχλος ἤρξατο αἰτεῖσθαι καθὼς ἐποίει αὐτοῖς.

⁹Ὁ δὲ Πιλᾶτος ἀπεκρίθη αὐτοῖς λέγων, Θέλετε ἀπολύσω ὑμῖν τὸν βασιλέα τῶν Ἰουδαίων; ¹⁰ἐγίνωσκεν γὰρ ὅτι διὰ φθόνον παραδεδώκεισαν αὐτὸν οἱ ἀρχιερεῖς.

¹¹Οἱ δὲ ἀρχιερεῖς ἀνέσεισαν τὸν ὄχλον ἵνα μᾶλλον τὸν Βαραββᾶν ἀπολύσῃ αὐτοῖς.

¹²Ὁ δὲ Πιλᾶτος πάλιν ἀποκριθεὶς ἔλεγεν αὐτοῖς, Τί οὖν θέλετε ποιήσω ὃν λέγετε τὸν βασιλέα τῶν Ἰουδαίων; ¹³Οἱ δὲ πάλιν ἔκραξαν, Σταύρωσον αὐτόν.

¹⁴Ὁ δὲ Πιλᾶτος ἔλεγεν αὐτοῖς, Τί γὰρ ἐποίησεν κακόν; Οἱ δὲ περισσῶς ἔκραξαν, Σταύρωσον αὐτόν. ¹⁵ὁ δὲ Πιλᾶτος βουλόμενος τῷ ὄχλῳ τὸ ἱκανὸν ποιῆσαι ἀπέλυσεν αὐτοῖς τὸν Βαραββᾶν, καὶ παρέδωκεν τὸν Ἰησοῦν φραγελλώσας ἵνα σταυρωθῇ.

---

12. *What do you want me to do* (v. 9): some MSS read *What should I do?*
The fellow you call: omitted in some MSS.

• **15:1.** *The ranking priests:* the dominant group in the *Council* (14:55), here singled out as the ones most directly responsible (vv. 3, 11) for the fate of Jesus. *Pilate:* procurator (governor) of Judea, 26–36 C.E., appointed by emperor Tiberius. *Turned him over to Pilate:* begins the final process of *being turned over to foreigners* (14:41).

• **15:2.** *You* (emphasized): the emphatic pronoun makes this a mock question, not an innocent inquiry. *The King of the Judeans:* a title Herod used for himself (6:14), so a sensitive political charge. *If you say so:* an in-kind reply back to Pilate, "*You* say so."

• **15:6.** This *custom* cannot be verified historically, and it does seem unlikely, given Pilate's reputation (noted at v. 7). Nonetheless, since Passover was a celebration of freedom, Mark's suggested symbolic gesture is not entirely far-fetched.

• **15:7.** *Barabbas:* Aramaic *bar-abba*, already explained in Mark, *bar* = "son of" (10:46) and *abba* = "father" (14:36). This sets up an ironical contrast between two *bar-abba* types, each a very different kind of threat to the religious establishment. *The insurgents*

15 And right away, at daybreak, the ranking priests, after consulting with the elders and scholars and the whole Council, bound Jesus and led him away and turned him over to Pilate. ²And Pilate questioned him: "*You* are 'the King of the Judeans'?"

And in response he says to him, "If you say so."

³And the ranking priests started a long list of accusations against him. ⁴Again Pilate tried questioning him: "Don't you have some answer to give? You see what a long list of charges they bring against you!"

⁵But Jesus still did not respond, so Pilate was baffled.

⁶At each festival it was the custom for him to set one prisoner free for them, whichever one they requested. ⁷And one called Barabbas was being held with the insurgents who had committed murder during the uprising. ⁸And when the crowd arrived, they began to demand that he do what he usually did for them.

⁹And in response Pilate said to them, "Do you want me to set 'the King of the Judeans' free for you?" ¹⁰After all, he realized that the ranking priests had turned him over out of envy.

¹¹But the ranking priests incited the crowd to get Barabbas set free for them instead.

¹²But in response ⟨to their request⟩ Pilate would again say to them, "What do you want me to do with the fellow you call 'the King of the Judeans'?"

¹³And they in turn shouted, "Crucify him!"

¹⁴Pilate kept saying to them, "Why? What has he done wrong?"

But they shouted all the louder, "Crucify him!" ¹⁵And because Pilate was always looking to satisfy the crowd, he set Barabbas free for them, had Jesus flogged, and then turned him over to be crucified.

Trial before Pilate

---

and *the uprising* both suggest a recent, well-known armed revolt, about which there is no additional specific information. However, Josephus does describe Pilate as imposing policies on Judea that led to riotous massacres and numerous crucifixions.

• **15:9.** *The King of the Judeans*: again used mockingly as in v. 2.

• **15:10.** *After all*: an indication of a Markan explanatory comment (§3.6).

• **15:12.** *The fellow you call*: only ironically, as an insult (v. 18).

• **15:15.** Pilate's reputation (noted at v. 7) was not one of satisfying Judean crowds. *Flogged*: beaten with metal-tipped leather whips as part of the procedure leading to crucifixion, the form of capital punishment used by the Roman government for non-citizens who posed a public threat. *Turned him over to be crucified*: the process reaches its completion; the "foreigners" can now get rid of him (v. 1; §4.11).

Soldiers make fun of Jesus

¹⁶Οἱ δὲ στρατιῶται ἀπήγαγον αὐτὸν ἔσω τῆς αὐλῆς, ὅ ἐστιν πραιτώριον, καὶ συγκαλοῦσιν ὅλην τὴν σπεῖραν. ¹⁷καὶ ἐνδιδύσκουσιν αὐτὸν πορφύραν καὶ περιτιθέασιν αὐτῷ πλέξαντες ἀκάνθινον στέφανον· ¹⁸καὶ ἤρξαντο ἀσπάζεσθαι αὐτόν, Χαῖρε, βασιλεῦ τῶν Ἰουδαίων· ¹⁹καὶ ἔτυπτον αὐτοῦ τὴν κεφαλὴν καλάμῳ καὶ ἐνέπτυον αὐτῷ, καὶ τιθέντες τὰ γόνατα προσεκύνουν αὐτῷ. ²⁰καὶ ὅτε ἐνέπαιξαν αὐτῷ, ἐξέδυσαν αὐτὸν τὴν πορφύραν καὶ ἐνέδυσαν αὐτὸν τὰ ἱμάτια τὰ ἴδια. καὶ ἐξάγουσιν αὐτὸν ἵνα σταυρώσουσιν αὐτόν.

Soldiers crucify Jesus

²¹Καὶ ἀγγαρεύουσιν παράγοντά τινα Σίμωνα Κυρηναῖον ἐρχόμενον ἀπ᾽ ἀγροῦ, τὸν πατέρα Ἀλεξάνδρου καὶ Ῥούφου, ἵνα ἄρῃ τὸν σταυρὸν αὐτοῦ.

²²Καὶ φέρουσιν αὐτὸν ἐπὶ τὸν Γολγοθᾶν τόπον, ὅ ἐστιν μεθερμηνευόμενον Κρανίου Τόπος. ²³καὶ ἐδίδουν αὐτῷ ἐσμυρνισμένον οἶνον, ὃς δὲ οὐκ ἔλαβεν. ²⁴καὶ σταυροῦσιν αὐτὸν καὶ διαμερίζονται τὰ ἱμάτια αὐτοῦ, βάλλοντες κλῆρον ἐπ᾽ αὐτὰ τίς τί ἄρῃ. ²⁵ἦν δὲ ὥρα τρίτη καὶ ἐσταύρωσαν αὐτόν. ²⁶καὶ ἦν ἡ ἐπιγραφὴ τῆς αἰτίας αὐτοῦ ἐπιγεγραμμένη, Ὁ βασιλεὺς τῶν Ἰουδαίων. ²⁷καὶ σὺν αὐτῷ σταυροῦσιν δύο λῃστάς, ἕνα ἐκ δεξιῶν καὶ ἕνα ἐξ εὐωνύμων αὐτοῦ.[28]

²⁹Καὶ οἱ παραπορευόμενοι ἐβλασφήμουν αὐτὸν κινοῦντες τὰς κεφαλὰς αὐτῶν καὶ λέγοντες, Οὐὰ ὁ καταλύων τὸν ναὸν καὶ οἰκοδομῶν ἐν τρισὶν ἡμέραις, ³⁰σῶσον σεαυτὸν καταβὰς ἀπὸ τοῦ σταυροῦ.

---

28. Some MSS add: *And the scripture was fulfilled which says, 'He was counted with the criminals'* (Isa 53:12; also in Luke 22:37).

• **15:16.** *The governor's residence*: Latin *praetorium*. Pilate (v. 1) stayed mostly in the coastal city of Caesarea, where the Roman troops were stationed. For the tumultuous holiday festivals, however, he brought additional troops to Jerusalem and stayed either at the Palace of Herod in the western part of the city or at the Fortress of Antonia next to the temple area. Mark's use of *courtyard* may suggest that the Palace is meant, though the Fortress would seem more likely. *The whole company* of Roman soldiers: at full strength 600, but could be as few as 200.

• **15:17.** *Purple*: designated the emperor; here done in jest, possibly with a soldier's scarlet uniform. *Garland*: wreath often seen on the heads of emperors on Roman coins. *Thorns*: from thorny vines on thistles and bushes that were very common in Judea.

• **15:18.** *Greetings*: mimics the Latin address

to the emperor, *Ave, Caesar*, which repeats Pilate's original accusation (v. 2).

• **15:19.** *Get down on their knees and bow down*: postures that were common in the ancient world to show reverence to royalty or humility before someone of higher social class. Such action also expressed religious reverence, so the mocking here is surely part of Mark's irony (§3.5).

• **15:21.** *Conscript*: the Roman army could force someone to render public service. *Cyrene*: city in North Africa, so a foreigner, but still might be a Judean on pilgrimage. *Alexander and Rufus*: otherwise unknown to us; both were common Greek names. *Carry his cross*: by Mark's definition this is what disciples do (8:34), but they had deserted him (14:50). The one to be executed had his arms attached to a cross-beam before he was led to the crucifixion site. The crossbeam was then placed on top

¹⁶And the soldiers led him away to the courtyard of the governor's residence, and they called the whole company together. ¹⁷And they dressed him in purple and crowned him with a garland woven of thorns. ¹⁸And they began to salute him: "Greetings, 'King of the Judeans'!" ¹⁹And they kept striking him on the head with a staff, and spitting on him; and they would get down on their knees and bow down to him. ²⁰And when they had made fun of him, they stripped off the purple and put his own clothes back on him. And they lead him out to crucify him.

Soldiers make fun of Jesus

²¹And they conscript someone named Simon of Cyrene, who was coming in from the country, the father of Alexander and Rufus, to carry his cross.

Soldiers crucify Jesus

²²And they bring him to the place Golgotha (which means "Place of the Skull"). ²³And they tried to give him wine mixed with myrrh, but he didn't take it. ²⁴And they crucify him, and they divide up his garments, casting lots to see who would get what. ²⁵It was 9 o'clock in the morning when they crucified him. ²⁶And the inscription, which identified his crime, read, 'The King of the Judeans.' ²⁷And with him they crucify two rebels, one on his right and one on his left.[28]

²⁹Those passing by kept taunting him, wagging their heads, and saying, "Ha! You who would destroy the temple and rebuild it in three days, ³⁰save yourself and come down from the cross!"

---

of a post fixed in the ground and a nail was driven through his ankles.

- **15:22.** *Golgotha:* Aramaic for "skull," translated into Latin as *calvaria*, probably a common execution site, but exact location is unknown. Judean and Roman regulations required that executions take place outside the city walls.
- **15:23.** *Myrrh:* already used for the anointing (14:3). This version of it could refer to a pungent tree resin used as a drug, here in a narcotic drink. Jesus' refusal to drink the wine mixture recalls his oath not to drink wine again until in "God's domain" (14:25).
- **15:24.** No crucifixion description is ever given (vv. 15, 21). The Roman historian Tacitus, in his account of Nero's treatment of Christians, says "Christus, the founder of the name, had undergone the death penalty in the reign of Tiberius, by sentence of the procurator Pontius Pilate." *Divide up his garments casting lots:* language from Ps 22:19 that describes the mistreatment of someone who suffers innocently.
- **15:25.** Only Mark provides time references

throughout the day of the crucifixion, using Roman three-hour divisions: *daybreak* (v. 1), *9:00* (here), *noon* (v. 33), *3:00* (v. 34), at *dark* (v. 42).
- **15:26.** It was Roman custom to give the official cause for the execution. The title used in jest (v. 18) becomes the official public record, another ironical part of Mark's story.
- **15:27.** *Rebels:* used by Josephus to describe the "zealots" of the Roman-Judean war. The term's basic meaning is *crooks*, as used earlier by Jesus for those who misuse the temple area (11:17). When he is arrested, the use of it as "rebel" (14:48) is quite ironic in contrast to these rebels. *On his right, on his left:* the positions of privilege sought by the disciples (10:37, 40), who were promised suffering instead.
- **15:29.** *Wagging their heads:* the taunters description from Ps 22:7 (the same psalm used in vv. 24, 34). *Ha!* an exclamation used by tormentors (Ps 35:21).
- **15:30.** *Save yourself:* which Jesus has already explained is not possible (8:35).

³¹ ῾Ομοίως καὶ οἱ ἀρχιερεῖς ἐμπαίζοντες πρὸς ἀλλήλους μετὰ τῶν γραμματέων ἔλεγον, "Ἄλλους ἔσωσεν, ἑαυτὸν οὐ δύναται σῶσαι· ³² ὁ Χριστὸς ὁ βασιλεὺς Ἰσραὴλ καταβάτω νῦν ἀπὸ τοῦ σταυροῦ, ἵνα ἴδωμεν καὶ πιστεύσωμεν.
Καὶ οἱ συνεσταυρωμένοι σὺν αὐτῷ ὠνείδιζον αὐτόν.

Jesus breathes
his last

³³ Καὶ γενομένης ὥρας ἕκτης σκότος ἐγένετο ἐφ᾽ ὅλην τὴν γῆν ἕως ὥρας ἐνάτης. ³⁴ καὶ τῇ ἐνάτῃ ὥρᾳ ἐβόησεν ὁ Ἰησοῦς φωνῇ μεγάλῃ, Ελωι ελωι λεμα σαβαχθανι; ὅ ἐστιν μεθερμηνευόμενον ῾Ο θεός μου ὁ θεός μου, εἰς τί ἐγκατέλιπές με;
³⁵ Καί τινες τῶν παρεστώτων ἀκούσαντες ἔλεγον, "Ἴδε Ἠλίαν φωνεῖ. ³⁶ δραμὼν δέ τις καὶ γεμίσας σπόγγον ὄξους περιθεὶς καλάμῳ ἐπότιζεν αὐτόν, λέγων, "Ἄφετε ἴδωμεν εἰ ἔρχεται Ἠλίας καθελεῖν αὐτόν.
³⁷ ῾Ο δὲ Ἰησοῦς ἀφεὶς φωνὴν μεγάλην ἐξέπνευσεν.
³⁸ Καὶ τὸ καταπέτασμα τοῦ ναοῦ ἐσχίσθη εἰς δύο ἀπ᾽ ἄνωθεν ἕως κάτω. ³⁹ ἰδὼν δὲ ὁ κεντυρίων ὁ παρεστηκὼς ἐξ ἐναντίας αὐτοῦ ὅτι οὕ- τως ἐξέπνευσεν εἶπεν, Ἀληθῶς οὗτος ὁ ἄνθρωπος υἱὸς θεοῦ ἦν.
⁴⁰ Ἦσαν δὲ καὶ γυναῖκες ἀπὸ μακρόθεν θεωροῦσαι, ἐν αἷς καὶ Μαρία ἡ Μαγδαληνὴ καὶ Μαρία ἡ Ἰακώβου τοῦ μικροῦ καὶ Ἰωσῆτος μήτηρ καὶ Σαλώμη, ⁴¹ αἳ ὅτε ἦν ἐν τῇ Γαλιλαίᾳ ἠκολούθουν αὐτῷ καὶ διηκόνουν αὐτῷ, καὶ ἄλλαι πολλαὶ αἱ συναναβᾶσαι αὐτῷ εἰς Ἱεροσόλυμα.

---

34. Some MSS have the Hebrew equivalent, *Eli, Eli,* as in Matt 27:46, which fits better with v. 35.

• **15:31.** *He saved others*: when he *cured* them, because of their *trust* (5:34; 10:52). This adds more ironic testimony about Jesus (§3.5).

• **15:32.** *The Anointed*: final, ironic confirmation of Mark's preferred title for Jesus (1:1); *the King of Israel*: the Judean leaders give the more correct version of the Roman designation, "King of the Judeans" (v. 26). *See and trust for ourselves*: expresses extreme irony, since people have eyes, but don't see (4:12; 8:18), while the blind get their sight back (8:25; 10:52).

• **15:33.** *Darkness* at noon: anticipates the prophetic day of judgment (Amos 8:9, "the sun shall go down at noon").

• **15:34.** *Eloi, Eloi, lema sabachthani*: the Aramaic opening line of Psalm 22, which begins as a lament on the suffering of the righteous and then turns to trust in God's faithful response. This psalm clearly influenced early Christian interpretation of Jesus' suffering (vv. 24, 29).

• **15:35.** *Elijah*: Elia in Hebrew. This could be meant as a simple misunderstanding of *Eloi* (v. 34), or an allusion to the tradition of appealing to Elijah in hopeless situations, or as an appeal to the one who prepares for the end time.

• **15:36.** *Sour wine*: echoes Ps 69:22, "They gave me sour wine for my thirst," possibly to revive someone for more torture. *Let's see if Elijah comes*: a taunt; Elijah (v. 35) would not rescue a fake.

• **15:37.** *Great shout*: as in v. 34, maybe like a fallen hero.

³¹Likewise the ranking priests had made fun of him to each other, along with the scholars; they would say, "He saved others, but he can't save himself! ³²'The Anointed,' 'the King of Israel,' should come down from the cross here and now, so that we can see and trust for ourselves!"

Even those being crucified along with him would abuse him.

³³And when noon came, darkness blanketed the whole land until mid-afternoon. ³⁴And at 3 o'clock in the afternoon Jesus shouted at the top of his voice, *"Eloi, Eloi, lema sabachthani"* (which means "My God, my God, why did you abandon me?").

Jesus breathes his last

³⁵And when some of those standing nearby heard, they would say, "Listen, he's calling Elijah!" ³⁶And someone ran and filled a sponge with sour wine, fixed it on a pole, and offered him a drink, saying, "Let's see if Elijah comes to rescue him!"

³⁷But Jesus let out a great shout and breathed his last.

³⁸And the curtain of the temple was torn in two from top to bottom! ³⁹When the Roman officer standing opposite him saw that he had died like this, he said, "This man really was God's son!"

⁴⁰Now some women were observing this from a distance, among whom were Mary of Magdala, and Mary the mother of James the younger and Joses, and Salome. ⁴¹⟨These women⟩ had regularly followed and assisted him when he was in Galilee, along with many other women who had come up to Jerusalem in his company.

• **15:38.** *The curtain of the temple*: likely the outer curtain to the temple building, rather than the inner one to the altar, where only the high priest went. *Torn*: the way the skies were at baptism (1:10). Is this how Jesus (ironically) "destroys" the temple (14:58)?

• **15:39.** *Roman officer*: commander of a hundred troops. His "confession" unites several important Markan themes: it is based on what he *saw*, which is what the taunters said they wanted (v. 32), and what he saw was something no one else had seen before, how Jesus *had died*. Jesus was an innocent one publicly tortured for all to see and hear, but Mark had already explained to the reader Jesus' real significance, *to give his life as a ransom for many* (10:45). *God's son*: commonly used for the emperor and great heroes, in the sense, *son of a god*. The

translation here captures the ambiguity of the Greek, which can be heard as *a son of God* or *the son of God*. The context can be interpreted as a statement of amazement by an "unbeliever," maybe likening Jesus to great heroes of the past (v. 37), or as a statement of Mark's kind of faith, ironically given first by a Roman.

• **15:40.** *Magdala*: town on the west shore of the Sea of Galilee (8:10). This Mary is always mentioned first among Jesus' women disciples (Matt 27:55; Luke 8:2). Later tradition, especially in religious art, identifies her as the unnamed "sinner" woman at Jesus' feet in Luke 7:37. *James the younger*: elsewhere simply "James" (16:1), traditionally identified with James the son of Alphaeus (3:18). *Salome*: not mentioned outside Mark (also 16:1).

Joseph buries Jesus

⁴²Καὶ ἤδη ὀψίας γενομένης, ἐπεὶ ἦν παρασκευή, ὅ ἐστιν προσάββατον, ⁴³ἐλθὼν Ἰωσὴφ ὁ ἀπὸ Ἀριμαθαίας εὐσχήμων βουλευτής, ὃς καὶ αὐτὸς ἦν προσδεχόμενος τὴν βασιλείαν τοῦ θεοῦ, τολμήσας εἰσῆλθεν πρὸς τὸν Πιλᾶτον καὶ ᾐτήσατο τὸ σῶμα τοῦ Ἰησοῦ. ⁴⁴ὁ δὲ Πιλᾶτος ἐθαύμασεν εἰ ἤδη τέθνηκεν, καὶ προσκαλεσάμενος τὸν κεντυρίωνα ἐπηρώτησεν αὐτὸν εἰ πάλαι ἀπέθανεν· ⁴⁵καὶ γνοὺς ἀπὸ τοῦ κεντυρίωνος ἐδωρήσατο τὸ πτῶμα τῷ Ἰωσήφ. ⁴⁶καὶ ἀγοράσας σινδόνα καθελὼν αὐτὸν ἐνείλησεν τῇ σινδόνι καὶ ἔθηκεν αὐτὸν ἐν μνημείῳ ὃ ἦν λελατομημένον ἐκ πέτρας, καὶ προσεκύλισεν λίθον ἐπὶ τὴν θύραν τοῦ μνημείου. ⁴⁷ἡ δὲ Μαρία ἡ Μαγδαληνὴ καὶ Μαρία ἡ Ἰωσῆτος ἐθεώρουν ποῦ τέθειται.

• **15:42.** Mark's double time reference is confusing. He continues his sequence of three-hour time blocks (v. 25) with his typical expression for "evening" (1:32; 4:35; 6:47; 14:17). However, he then qualifies it as still *the day before the sabbath*, which implies late Friday afternoon, not quite sundown. Burial was expected to be done

the same day someone died, and it could not be done on a sabbath day.
• **15:43.** *Arimathea*: a town in western Judea. *Council member*: the general Greek term for *councilor* is used, which suggests he was apparently not a member of the Jerusalem Council, and therefore had not participated in the hearing against Jesus (15:1). *God's*

⁴²And when it had already grown dark, since it was prepa-   *Joseph buries*
ration day (the day before the sabbath), ⁴³Joseph of Arimathea, a   *Jesus*
respected council member, who himself was anticipating God's
imperial rule, appeared on the scene, and dared to go to Pilate to
request the body of Jesus. ⁴⁴And Pilate was surprised that he had
died so soon. He summoned the Roman officer and asked him
whether he had been dead for long. ⁴⁵And when he had been
briefed by the Roman officer, he granted the body to Joseph.
⁴⁶And he bought a shroud and took him down and wrapped him
in the shroud, and placed him in a tomb that had been hewn out
of rock, and rolled a stone up against the opening of the tomb.
⁴⁷And Mary of Magdala and Mary the mother of Joses noted
where he had been laid to rest.

---

imperial rule: the final mention of this theme seems to bridge the expectations of a "mainstream" Judean, such as Joseph, with the meaning given it by Jesus, who introduced it in this story (1:15; §6.3).

• **15:44.** Crucifixion could be a slow agonizing death.

• **15:45.** *Body*: dead body, *corpse*, as distinct from "body" in v. 43, the term used for the anointed body (14:8), and for interpreting the bread at the last supper (14:22).

• **15:46.** *Shroud*: like the death cloth the naked youth had been wearing (14:51). *Tomb*: typically cave-like in a rock formation (5:2).

Silver Shekel of the Judean War, of the Year 5 (70 c.e.). Obverse (facing page): Chalice; inscription: *shekel of Israel, year 5*, in ancient Hebraic script. Reverse (above): Branch with three pomegranates; inscription: *Jerusalem the Holy*, in ancient Hebraic script. The Judeans demonstrated their rejection of Roman control by coining their own money. Courtesy Nelson Bunker Hunt Collection. Photographs: Andrew Daneman.

16 Καὶ διαγενομένου τοῦ σαββάτου Μαρία ἡ Μαγδαληνὴ καὶ Μαρία ἡ Ἰακώβου καὶ Σαλώμη ἠγόρασαν ἀρώματα ἵνα ἐλθοῦσαι ἀλείψωσιν αὐτόν. ²καὶ λίαν πρωῒ τῇ μιᾷ τῶν σαββάτων ἔρχονται ἐπὶ τὸ μνημεῖον ἀνατείλαντος τοῦ ἡλίου. ³καὶ ἔλεγον πρὸς ἑαυτάς, Τίς ἀποκυλίσει ἡμῖν τὸν λίθον ἐκ τῆς θύρας τοῦ μνημείου; ⁴καὶ ἀναβλέψασαι θεωροῦσιν ὅτι ἀποκεκύλισται ὁ λίθος, ἦν γὰρ μέγας σφόδρα.

⁵Καὶ εἰσελθοῦσαι εἰς τὸ μνημεῖον εἶδον νεανίσκον καθήμενον ἐν τοῖς δεξιοῖς περιβεβλημένον στολὴν λευκήν, καὶ ἐξεθαμβήθησαν.

⁶Ὁ δὲ λέγει αὐταῖς, Μὴ ἐκθαμβεῖσθε· Ἰησοῦν ζητεῖτε τὸν Ναζαρηνὸν τὸν ἐσταυρωμένον· ἠγέρθη, οὐκ ἔστιν ὧδε· ἴδε ὁ τόπος ὅπου ἔθηκαν αὐτόν. ⁷ἀλλὰ ὑπάγετε εἴπατε τοῖς μαθηταῖς αὐτοῦ καὶ τῷ Πέτρῳ ὅτι Προάγει ὑμᾶς εἰς τὴν Γαλιλαίαν· ἐκεῖ αὐτὸν ὄψεσθε, καθὼς εἶπεν ὑμῖν.

⁸Καὶ ἐξελθοῦσαι ἔφυγον ἀπὸ τοῦ μνημείου, εἶχεν γὰρ αὐτὰς τρόμος καὶ ἔκστασις· καὶ οὐδενὶ οὐδὲν εἶπαν, ἐφοβοῦντο γάρ.

• **16:1.** *Spices*: probably spiced oils, such as myrrh (14:3). *Embalm*: anoint a corpse with such spices to retard decay. These women are unaware of the earlier anointing that Jesus had interpreted as "preparation for burial" (14:8).

• **16:4.** *For in fact*: introduces an editorial explanation (§6.1).

• **16:5.** *A youth*: the only other one in Mark fled naked from his shroud (14:51). The focus is again on what he is wearing. *A white robe*: for Christian readers, symbolic of purity and victory, the appropriate garment for the resurrected (Rev 6:11; 7:9, 13). *Sitting on the right*: echoes the language of exaltation from Ps 110:1, which has already

been used to interpret the future role of the Anointed (14:62).

• **16:6.** *Jesus the Nazarene*: the label used for Jesus the first time he is addressed (1:24) is now used the last time he is referred to. *He was raised*: not the verb "rise" that was used in the resurrection predictions (8:31; 9:31; 10:34), which is more typical for the final resurrection.

• **16:7.** *Including 'Rock'*: singles out Peter in such a way as to suggest the irony of his name (§3.5; §5.1). After putting his life on the line (14:31), he had denied all (14:71), acting indeed like "rocky soil," where distress causes a person to fall (4:17). Using "Rock" to translate *Petros* the last time also

16 And when the sabbath day was over, Mary of Magdala and Mary the mother of James and Salome bought spices so they could go and embalm him. ²And very early on the first day of the week they got to the tomb just as the sun was coming up. ³And they had been asking themselves, "Who will help us roll the stone away from the opening of the tomb?" ⁴Then they look up and discover that the stone has been rolled away! (For in fact the stone was very large.)

Three Women at the tomb

⁵And when they went into the tomb, they saw a youth sitting on the right, wearing a white robe, and they grew apprehensive.

⁶He says to them, "Don't be alarmed! You are looking for Jesus the Nazarene who was crucified. He was raised, he is not here! Look at the spot where they put him! ⁷But go and tell his disciples, including 'Rock,' he is going ahead of you to Galilee! There you will see him, just as he told you."

⁸And once they got outside, they ran away from the tomb, because great fear and excitement got the better of them. And they didn't breathe a word of it to anyone: talk about terrified . . .

---

recalls the introduction of the name (3:16). It seems especially appropriate here for Mark's open-ended narrative, which does not resolve Peter's status. *He is going ahead of you to Galilee:* fulfills Jesus' promise, *After I'm raised I'll go ahead of you to Galilee* (14:28).

• **16:8.** *They didn't breathe a word of it to anyone:* captures the very emphatic Greek sentence that begins with two forms of the same negated word, "no one, nothing." *Talk about terrified . . .* renders Mark's very striking two-word ending. The last word is the conjunction *gar* (*for*), always the second word in its sentence, but usually with something following it. Mark uses it often

to introduce an explanatory note (such as in v. 4; §3.6). Its use here is similar to two stories in Genesis. When Sarah denies that she laughed to herself at the promise of a son in her old age, the author explains, "for she was afraid" (Gen 18:15). In the Greek translation (LXX) it is the same as Mark's ending. When Joseph discloses himself to his brothers, they are unable to answer, "for they were dismayed" (Gen 45:3). Mark's use is even more startling because he ends the whole story with it. As the last word of the text, it suggests a sudden ending, rather than a resolution.

*Longer ending
to Mark*

[[⁹ Ἀναστὰς δὲ πρωῒ πρώτῃ σαββάτου ἐφάνη πρῶτον Μαρίᾳ τῇ Μαγδαληνῇ, παρ' ἧς ἐκβεβλήκει ἑπτὰ δαιμόνια. ¹⁰ἐκείνη πορευθεῖσα ἀπήγγειλεν τοῖς μετ' αὐτοῦ γενομένοις πενθοῦσι καὶ κλαίουσιν· ¹¹κἀκεῖνοι ἀκούσαντες ὅτι ζῇ καὶ ἐθεάθη ὑπ' αὐτῆς ἠπίστησαν.

¹²Μετὰ δὲ ταῦτα δυσὶν ἐξ αὐτῶν περιπατοῦσιν ἐφανερώθη ἐν ἑτέρᾳ μορφῇ πορευομένοις εἰς ἀγρόν· ¹³κἀκεῖνοι ἀπελθόντες ἀπήγγειλαν τοῖς λοιποῖς· οὐδὲ ἐκείνοις ἐπίστευσαν.

¹⁴Ὕστερον δὲ ἀνακειμένοις αὐτοῖς τοῖς ἕνδεκα ἐφανερώθη, καὶ ὠνείδισεν τὴν ἀπιστίαν αὐτῶν καὶ σκληροκαρδίαν ὅτι τοῖς θεασαμένοις αὐτὸν ἐγηγερμένον οὐκ ἐπίστευσαν. ¹⁵καὶ εἶπεν αὐτοῖς, Πορευθέντες εἰς τὸν κόσμον ἅπαντα κηρύξατε τὸ εὐαγγέλιον πάσῃ τῇ κτίσει. ¹⁶ὁ πιστεύσας καὶ βαπτισθεὶς σωθήσεται, ὁ δὲ ἀπιστήσας κατακριθήσεται. ¹⁷σημεῖα δὲ τοῖς πιστεύσασιν ταῦτα παρακολουθήσει· ἐν τῷ ὀνόματί μου δαιμόνια ἐκβαλοῦσιν, γλώσσαις λαλήσουσιν καιναῖς, ¹⁸ὄφεις ἀροῦσιν, κἂν θανάσιμόν τι πίωσιν οὐ μὴ αὐτοὺς βλάψῃ, ἐπὶ ἀρρώστους χεῖρας ἐπιθήσουσιν καὶ καλῶς ἕξουσιν.

¹⁹Ὁ μὲν οὖν κύριος μετὰ τὸ λαλῆσαι αὐτοῖς ἀνελήμφθη εἰς τὸν οὐρανὸν καὶ ἐκάθισεν ἐκ δεξιῶν τοῦ θεοῦ. ²⁰ἐκεῖνοι δὲ ἐξελθόντες ἐκήρυξαν πανταχοῦ, τοῦ κυρίου συνεργοῦντος καὶ τὸν λόγον βεβαιοῦντος διὰ τῶν ἐπακολουθούντων σημείων.]]

*Shorter ending
to Mark*

[[Πάντα δὲ τὰ παρηγγελμένα τοῖς περὶ τὸν Πέτρον συντόμως ἐξήγγειλαν. μετὰ δὲ ταῦτα καὶ αὐτὸς ὁ Ἰησοῦς ἀπὸ ἀνατολῆς καὶ ἄχρι δύσεως ἐξαπέστειλεν δι' αὐτῶν τὸ ἱερὸν καὶ ἄφθαρτον κήρυγμα τῆς αἰωνίου σωτηρίας. ἀμήν.]]

9–20. The two oldest Greek MSS, and some early versions in Latin, Syriac, Armenian and Georgian, end Mark at 16:8 (§8.2). The "longer ending" exhibits a style and vocabulary very different from the rest of the gospel of Mark. Possible sources for this material are indicated in the translations notes.   **Shorter ending:** occurs in a few MSS, mostly with vv. 9–20.

• **16:9–20.** This ending does not appear in the earliest copies of Mark that have survived (see also the textual note). The abruptness of Mark's ending was apparently unacceptable after other "gospels" were circulating that ended with stories about Jesus' appearance after his resurrection. The material for this ending seems to have been based on the endings of the gospels of Luke and John, along with Christian legends from the second century C.E. A version of this ending may have circulated separately before it was used for this purpose.

• **16:9.** Mary of Magdala is alone at the tomb only in John (20:1), and she is described this way only in Luke (8:2).

• **16:11.** *They didn't believe it:* the response the women received in Luke (20:11).

• **16:12–13.** The appearance to two people on their way out of town, who return to tell the others, corresponds to Luke's Emmaus story (24:13, 35).

• **16:14.** Jesus himself appears to the gathered disciples in both Luke (24:36; specifically "the eleven" in 24:33) and John (20:19). The disciples' *obstinacy:* a rare distinctive Markan feature (6:52; 8:17) in this ending. *They did not believe:* the theme of their continuing unbelief after the resurrection

[[⁹Now after he arose at daybreak on the first day of the week, he appeared first to Mary of Magdala, from whom he had driven out seven demons. ¹⁰She went and told those who were close to him, who were mourning and weeping. ¹¹But when those folks heard that he was alive and had been seen by her, they didn't believe it.

¹²A little later he appeared to two of them in a different guise as they were walking along, on their way to the country. ¹³And these two returned and told the others. They did not believe them either.

¹⁴Later he appeared to the eleven as they were reclining ⟨at a meal⟩. He reproached them for their lack of trust and obstinacy, because they did not believe those who had seen him after he had been raised. ¹⁵And he said to them: "Go out into the whole world and announce the good news to every creature. ¹⁶Whoever trusts and is baptized will be saved. The one who lacks trust will be condemned. ¹⁷These are the signs that will accompany those who have trust: they will drive out demons in my name; they will speak in new tongues; ¹⁸they will pick up snakes with their hands; and even if they swallow poison, it certainly won't harm them; they will lay their hands on those who are sick, and they will get well."

¹⁹The Lord Jesus, after he said these things, was taken up into the sky and sat down at the right hand of God. ²⁰Those ⟨to whom he had spoken⟩ went out and made their announcement everywhere, and the Lord worked with them and certified what they said by means of accompanying signs.]]

Longer ending to Mark

[[All the instructions they had been given they promptly reported to Peter and his companions. Afterwards Jesus himself, using them as agents, broadcast the sacred and imperishable message of eternal salvation from one end of the earth to the other.]]

Shorter ending to Mark

---

apparently was an embarrassment for Christians sufficient for one later copyist (second or third century) to insert here an explanation preserved in one fifth-century Greek MS (See the Freer Logion below).

- **16:15.** Similar to Matthew's ending (28:19).
- **16:16.** The promise of salvation to believers is a Pauline theme (Rom 10:9).
- **16:17–18.** The evidence of *signs* was rejected by Jesus in Mark (8:12), but they became part of Christian faith in an ever more spectacular way into the second century. Jesus' disciples already could "drive out demons" (Mark 3:15; 6:13); early Christians could "speak in tongues" (Acts 10:46;

19:6; 1 Cor 14); and Paul is said to have survived snake bite (Acts 28:3, 5) and to cure someone by laying hands on him (Acts 28:8). Jesus is presented in Luke 10:19 as promising those sent out to preach that not even stepping on snakes or scorpions would hurt them. However, the drinking of poison is not mentioned elsewhere is early Christian writings.

- **16:19.** The ascension is a feature of the Lukan writings (Luke 24:51; Acts 1:9).
- **16:20.** A generalized summary derived from this longer ending itself.
- **Shorter ending.** This is another ending, apparently written explicitly to provide a

Freer Logion

[[Κἀκεῖνοι ἀπελογοῦντο λέγοντες ὅτι ὁ αἰὼν οὗτος τῆς ἀνομίας καὶ τῆς ἀπιστίας ὑπὸ τὸν Σατανᾶν ἐστιν, ὁ μὴ ἐῶν τὰ ὑπὸ τῶν πνευμάτων ἀκάθαρτα τὴν ἀλήθειαν τοῦ θεοῦ καταλαβέσθαι δύναμιν· διὰ τοῦτο ἀποκάλυψον σοῦ τὴν δικαιοσύνην ἤδη, ἐκεῖνοι ἔλεγον τῷ Χριστῷ.

Καὶ ὁ Χριστὸς ἐκείνοις προσέλεγεν ὅτι πεπλήρωται ὁ ὅρος τῶν ἐτῶν τῆς ἐξουσίας τοῦ Σατανᾶ, ἀλλὰ ἐγγίζει ἄλλα δεινὰ· καὶ ὑπὲρ ὧν ἐγὼ ἁμαρτησάντων παρεδόθην εἰς θάνατον, ἵνα ὑποστρέψωσιν εἰς τὴν ἀλήθειαν καὶ μηκέτι ἁμαρτήσωσιν, ἵνα τὴν ἐν τῷ οὐρανῷ πνευματικὴν καὶ ἄφθαρτον τῆς δικαιοσύνης δόξαν κληρονομήσωσιν.]]

---

more adequate ending for Mark. It "undoes" Mark's original ending, using words unfamiliar elsewhere in Mark. The few copies of Mark that have this ending, with the exception of one Latin copy, also have the longer ending (vv. 9–20). The majority of copies have only the longer ending; the earliest surviving copies have neither of these endings.

• **Freer Logion.** This insert appears in the "Freer Gospels," now located at the Smithsonian Institution, named after the person who, in 1906, purchased the fifth-century MS of the four gospels in which this peculiar ending of Mark appears. It was apparently designed to explain the statement that the eleven disciples failed to believe the first reports of the resurrection (see note at v. 14).

At right. *Freer Logion.* Greek manuscript, fifth century C.E. Dark brown ink on parchment. Box shows the location of the logion in the manuscript. Courtesy of the Freer Gallery of Art, Smithsonian Institution, Washington, D.C.

[[And they would apologize and say, "This lawless and faithless age is under the control of Satan, who by using filthy spirits doesn't allow the real power of God to be appreciated. So," they would say to the Anointed, "let your justice become evident now."

And the Anointed would respond to them, "The time when Satan is in power has run its course, but other terrible things are just around the corner. I was put to death for the sake of those who sinned, so they might return to the truth and stop sinning, and thus inherit the spiritual and indestructible righteous glory that is in heaven."]]

Bookshelf of Basic Works

1 Basic Study Tools

Achtemeier, Paul J., ed. *Harper's Bible Dictionary*. San Francisco, Harper & Row, 1985.

Funk, Robert W., ed. *New Gospel Parallels*. Vol I,2: *Mark*. Rev. ed. Sonoma, CA: Polebridge Press, 1990.

Funk, Robert W., et al. *The Gospel of Mark: Red Letter Edition*. Sonoma, Polebridge Press, 1991.

Funk, Robert W., and Roy W. Hoover. *Five Gospels, One Jesus: What did Jesus really say?* Sonoma: Polebridge Press, 1992.

Schmidt, Daryl D. *New Gospel Parallels: Original Language Version*. Vol I,2: *Mark*. Sonoma, CA: Polebridge Press, 1992.

2 General Studies on Mark

Best, Ernest. *Mark: The Gospel as Story*. Edinburgh: T. & T. Clark, 1983.

Collins, Adela Yarbro. *Is Mark's Gospel a Life of Jesus? A Question of Genre*. Milwaukee: Marquette University, 1990.

France, R. T. *Divine Government: God's Kingship in the Gospel of Mark*. London: SPCK, 1990.

van Iersel, Bas. *Reading Mark*. Trs. W. H. Bisscheroux. Edinburgh: T. & T. Clark, 1989.

Kelber, Werner H. *Mark's Story of Jesus*. Philadelphia: Fortress Press, 1979.

Kingsbury, Jack Dean. *The Christology of Mark's Gospel*. Philadelphia: Fortress Press, 1983.

———. *Conflict in Mark: Jesus, Authorities, Disciples*. Minneapolis: Fortress Press, 1989.

Mack, Burton L. *A Myth of Innocence: Mark and Christian Origins*. Philadelphia: Fortress Press, 1988.

Matera, Frank J. *What Are They Saying About Mark?* New York: Paulist Press, 1987.

Myers, Ched. *Binding the Strong Man: A Political Reading of Mark's Story of Jesus*. Maryknoll, NY: Orbis, 1988.

Rhoads, David & Donald Michie. *Mark as Story: An Introduction to the Narrative of a Gospel*. Philadelphia: Fortress Press, 1982.

Robbins, Vernon K. *Jesus the Teacher: A Socio-Rhetorical Interpretation of Mark*. Philadelphia: Fortress Press, 1984.

Senior, Donald. *The Passion of Jesus in the Gospel of Mark*. Wilmington, DE: Michael Glazier, 1984.

Sergeant, John. *Lion Let Loose: The Structure and Meaning of St. Mark's Gospel*. Exeter, Great Britain, 1988.

Tolbert, Mary Ann. *Sowing the Gospel: Mark's World in Literary-Historical Perspective*. Minneapolis: Fortress Press, 1989.

Thompson, Mary R. *The Role of Disbelief in Mark: A New Approach to the Second Gospel*. New York: Paulist Press, 1989.

Waetjen, Herman C. *A Reordering of Power: A Socio-Political Reading of Mark's Gospel*. Minneapolis: Fortress Press, 1989.

3 Studies Within Mark

Beavis, Mary Ann. *Mark's Audience: The Literary and Social Setting of Mark 4.11–12*. JSNTSS 33. Sheffield: JSOT Press, 1989.

Booth, Roger P. *Jesus and the Laws of Purity: Tradition History and Legal History in Mark 7*. JSNTSS 13. Sheffield: JSOT Press, 1986.

Chilton, Bruce and J. I. H. McDonald. *Jesus and the Ethics of the Kingdom*. Biblical Foundations in Theology. London: SPCK, 1987.

Cook, Michael J. *Mark's Treatment of the Jewish Leaders*. Supplements to Novum Testamentum 51. Leiden: Brill, 1978.

Fowler, Robert M. *Loaves and Fishes: The Function of the Feeding Stories in the Gospel of Mark*, SBLDS 54. Chico: CA: Scholars Press, 1981.

Geddert, Timothy J. *Watchwords: Mark 13 in Markan Eschatology*. JSNTSS 26. Sheffield: JSOT Press, 1989.

Hengel, Martin. *Studies in the Gospel of Mark*. Philadelphia: Fortress Press, 1985.

Malbon, Elizabeth Struthers. *Narrative Space and Mythic Meaning in Mark*. San Francisco: Harper & Row, 1986.

Marcus, Joel. *The Mystery of the Kingdom of God*. SBLDS 90. Atlanta: Scholars Press, 1986.

Marshall, Christopher D. *Faith as a Theme in Mark's Narrative*. Society for New Testament Studies Monograph Series 64. Cambridge: Cambridge University Press, 1989.

Peabody, David B. *Mark as Composer*. Macon, GA: Mercer University Press, 1987.

Raisanen, Heikki. *The 'Messianic Secret' in Mark's Gospel*. Trs. Christopher Tuckett. Studies of the New Testament and its World; Edinburgh: T. & T. Clark, 1990.

Telford, William R. *The Barren Temple and the Withered Tree*. JSNTSS 1. Sheffield: JSOT Press, 1980.

Via, Dan O. *The Ethics of Mark's Gospel: In the Middle of Time*. Philadelphia: Fortress Press, 1985.

Williams, James K. *Gospel Against Parable: Mark's Language of Mystery*. Bible and Literature Series 12. Sheffield: Almond Press, 1985.

4 Studies Related to Mark

Borg, Marcus. *Jesus: A New Vision—Spirit, Culture and the Life of Discipleship*. San Francisco, Harper & Row, 1987.

Horsley, Richard A. *Jesus and the Spiral of Violence: Popular Jewish Resistance in Roman Palestine*. San Francisco: Harper & Row, 1987.

Koester, Helmut. *Ancient Christian Gospels*. Philadelphia: Trinity Press International, 1990.

Lachs, Samuel T. *A Rabbinic Commentary on the New Testament: The Gospels of Matthew, Mark, and Luke*. Hoboken, NJ: KTAV, 1987.

Mack, Burton L. & Vernon K. Robbins. *Patterns of Persuasion in the Gospels*. Sonoma, CA: Polebridge Press, 1989.

Rhoads, David. *Israel in Revolution 6–74CE: A Political History Based on the Writings of Josephus*. Philadelphia: Fortress Press, 1976.

Rivkin, Ellis. *What Crucified Jesus? The Political Execution of a Charismatic*. Nashville: Abingdon Press, 1984.

Glossary

Anecdote: See Chreia.

Aphorism: Aphorisms are pithy one-liners that challenge the accepted view of things: "It's not what goes into a person that can defile, but what comes out of the person" (Mark 7:15). In contrast, proverbs are one-liners expressing the common sense view: "Nobody pours young wine into old wineskins" (Mark 2:22).

Apologetic: An apologetic perspective defends a point of view. For example, the description of the circumstances of Jesus' death are made to prove that scripture was coming true.

C.E., B.C.E: C.E. stands for Common Era, B.C.E. for Before the Common Era. These designations, rather than A.D. and B.C., are used out of deference to those from other religious traditions, as a more neutral way of marking the transition associated with the birth of Jesus.

Chreia (plural: chreiai): Chreia is a Greek term for a kind of anecdote, a short story that ends with a noteworthy aphorism or action by a wise or prominent person.

Council: The Council ("Sanhedrin") in Jerusalem controlled all legal and religious affairs in Judean life during the time of Jesus. The 70-member Council consisted of ranking priests, "elders" (prominent aristocrats), and "scholars," trained legal authorities.

Didache: The Didache (the title means "teaching") is a "catechism" of early Christian instruction attributed to the twelve apostles. It was compiled in the early second century C.E.

Eschatology: Eschatology is talk about the "last things," such as resurrection, final judgment, and the coming of the son of Adam.

Hasmonean: See Maccabees.

Herodians: Herodians probably refers to government officials, or supporters, of Herod Antipas, the tetrarch of Galilee and Perea (4 B.C.E.–39 C.E.) in Jesus' lifetime. He was son of "King" Herod the Great (40–4 B.C.E.).

Irony: Dramatic irony is a literary device used in a story where the characters speak or act at one level of meaning, but the reader is aware of a very different meaning or outcome. Peter speaks ironically when he claims, "If they condemn me to die with you, I will never disown you!" (Mark 14:31), but the reader knows otherwise.

Josephus: Flavius Josephus was a Judean writer who died shortly after 100 C.E. He wrote two massive histories: *The Jewish War*, his account of the events leading up to the destruction of Jerusalem by the Romans in 70 C.E., and *The Jewish*

159

Antiquities, a complete retelling of the history of the Israelites, who were later known as Jews.

Judean: Judeans are the residents of Judea and their descendants. Judea was the Roman name for Judah, the southern portion of ancient Israel. The Israelites who returned from exile in Babylonia in the sixth century B.C.E. resettled this area and rebuilt the temple. The religion of the Judeans centered around the sacrificial cult controlled by the priests at the temple. After the destruction of this second temple in 70 C.E., the surviving Judeans continued the religious practices that had been shaped in the synagogues by the Pharisees. They became known as "Jews," and their religion is now called Judaism.

Maccabees: Maccabees is the nickname for a Judean family, properly the Hasmoneans, who rededicated the temple in 164 B.C.E. after successfully leading a revolt against Syrian control that eventually brought full independence. Hasmoneans provided both political and religious leadership in Jerusalem until the Romans ended it in 63 B.C.E. The writings in the Apocrypha (1, 2, 3 Maccabees) related to these events are named after the Maccabees.

Pagan: A pagan, or heathen, is someone who is not Jewish or Christian (or later, Moslem), that is, does not follow "biblical" religious practices. In biblical times it means all non-Israelites, or non-Judeans, or non-Jews.

Papyrus: Papyrus is an early form of paper made in ancient Egypt from reeds cut in strips, dried, and glued together to form sheets. Thousands of papyrus documents, including the earliest copies of any New Testament writings, have been found in the sands of Egypt during the past one hundred years.

Parable: A parable is a simile ("You resemble sheep without a shepherd," Mark 6:34) or metaphor ("you're a bunch of sheep"), which draws an analogy with nature or everday life, extended into a brief story ("God's imperial rule is like this: suppose someone sows seed on the ground," Mark 4:26). "Riddle" is another sense of the Greek *parabole*. A riddle is a kind of proverb with hidden meaning that has to be explained. Parables can become riddles for those who do not understand them.

Parchment: Parchment is a more expensive kind of writing material made from animal skin, usually sheep or goat, prepared for use as writing material.

Pentateuch: See Torah.

Pharisees: The Pharisees were apparently a small, but influential group of Judeans committed to full practice of the food and sabbath day regulations that were required only of priests. They developed an oral law for how to interpret the Mosaic law, the written Torah. Their influence was mainly in the synagogues. They were the early rabbis who gave shape to the religion of Judaism after 70 C.E.

Proverb: See Aphorism.

Rabbi: Rabbi, Hebrew for "my master," was the title used for the leading teachers of Judaism after 70 C.E.

Riddle: See Parable.

Saducees: The Sadducees were a conservative group of Judeans, mostly aristocratic and influential around the temple. They rejected the Pharisees oral law.

Sanhedrin: See Council.

Scholars: The scholars in ancient Judea were trained in the practices of interpreting and preserving the Mosaic law (Torah). They were important members of the Jerusalem Council.

Scholars Version: The Scholars Version is a new translation of the gospels prepared by members of the Jesus Seminar.

Son of Adam: The term "son of Adam" appears to be used in three different ways in the gospels: (1) a figure coming in the future on clouds of glory to judge the world, derived from Daniel 7 (Mark 8:38; 13:26; 14:62); (2) a way to refer to human beings, descendants of Adam and Eve, in contrast to God (Mark 2:10, 28); (3) a roundabout way of saying "I" (for example, Mark 8:31; 9:31; 10:33, 45; 14:21).

Titus: Titus was the Roman army General who led the assult on Jerusalem in the 66–70 C.E. war, followed by a triumphal march to Rome, where the feat was later commemorated by a huge stone arch with scenes depicting the procession.

Torah: Torah means instruction. In the Hebrew Bible it designated the first major section, the Pentateuch, the first five books, which are traditionally attributed to Moses, but were actually a compilation of materials, mostly legal, gathered over several centuries. Torah is often translated as "law," and its contents called the "Mosaic law."

Zealot: A zealot ("zealous" for God) is someone who opposed the Roman occupation of Judea that ended Hasmonean rule in 63 B.C.E. After the time of Jesus the zealots emerged as a political party actively fighting against Rome. They provided the armed resistance within Jerusalem that Rome crushed by destroying the temple area in 70 C.E.

Indexes

Index of Scriptures

Index of Subjects

ABOUT THE
AUTHOR

Daryl D. Schmidt was John F. Weatherly Professor of New
Testament at Texas Christian University in Fort Worth. A New
Testament scholar and specialist in Hellenistic Greek grammar,
he was an active Fellow of the Jesus Seminar, serving as the
general editor of the Scholars Version translation of the gospels,
as coordinator for the translation of the Pauline letters, and as
editor for Westar's academic journal, Forum. Schmidt was a
contributor to *The Authentic Letters of Paul* (2010, with Arthur J.
Dewey, Roy W. Hoover, and Lane C. McGaughy) and author of
Hellenistic Greek Grammar and Noam Chomsky (1981).

CPSIA information can be obtained
at www.ICGtesting.com
Printed in the USA
FFOW02n1844110715
14877FF

9 780944 344149